DEDICATED TO MY CHILDREN DANIEL, DIANA, KAREN, AND MICHAEL; AND MY GRANDCHILDREN ANDREA, JAMES, JUSTIN, AND ASHLEY

THE LORD AND THE WEEDPATCHER

Samuel D. G. Heath, Ph. D.

iUniverse, Inc.
New York Bloomington

The Lord and The Weedpatcher

iUniverse books may be ordered through booksellers or by contacting:

iUniverse
1663 Liberty Drive
Bloomington, IN 47403
www.iuniverse.com
1-800-Authors (1-800-288-4677)

ISBN: 978-1-4401-6317-3 (sc)
ISBN: 978-1-4401-6318-0 (ebook)

Printed in the United States of America

iUniverse rev. date: 07/22/2009

THE LORD AND THE WEEDPATCHER

I often wish my grandparents had written the stories of their past that my brother and I were told as children. Since they didn't, I made the decision I wouldn't make this mistake and wrote this book in order that my children would have the stories of my wilderness adventures in hand.

For example, my years spent on a mining claim without any conveniences like electricity, gas or indoor plumbing. The thousands of acres of the Sequoia National Forest, the wild and untamed Kern River that ran through the valley in those days, these were my personal playground and made for many an interesting incident and adventure.

The collection of stories grew into this book in the hope that they will not only be entertaining to others, but will inspire some of that pioneer spirit in people who are too easily caught up in a concrete and plastic world. I also include stories of my experiences in the Camelot of the fifties California South Bay area of Redondo, Hermosa and Manhattan Beach when the air and water were pure and the beaches clean and uncrowded. In this environment, we were the Lotus Eaters of our generation.

In such places, I lived a life the great majority of people have only known through the vicarious titillation of films. Sadly, it was a life the present generation will never have a chance to know apart from books like this. But it makes such books important for the sake of keeping the pioneer spirit of our heritage in this nation alive, a spirit that reaches out to the stars as our heritage and our destiny.

I was born 1935 in Weedpatch, California. That was the year Billy Sunday and T. E. Lawrence died, Hoover Dam was completed, Huey Long was shot and President Franklin D. Roosevelt signed the Social Security Act. It was also a year of great films. Hopalong Cassidy made his first appearance in a movie, Nelson Eddy and Jeanette MacDonald in Naughty Marietta and Roberta, Fred Astaire and Ginger Rogers in Top Hat, Clark Gable in Mutiny on the Bounty and Call of the Wild, Errol Flynn in Captain Blood, and a real thriller The Bride of Frankenstein- and Bruno Hauptmann was found guilty of kidnapping the Lindbergh's baby.

Apparently my mother, who was only sixteen at the time, didn't like seeing doctors and the hospital in Bakersfield was out of the question. So I was born on a kitchen table in the little farmhouse surrounded by cotton fields. That might have been just as well. At least I escaped circumcision.

However, the lack of prenatal care led to complications that caused some doubt of my surviving birth. But having survived, when I was older, my grandparents told me they had dedicated me to God if he allowed me to live. My name was to be Samuel in honor of the prophet because of a somewhat similar situation in the Old Testament. Since the day of my birth I believe there have been angels attending me else I would not have survived many things throughout my life. But for some reason, perhaps our mother's resentment of her parent's religious beliefs, I was called Donnie, my full name being Samuel Donald Glenn Heath, rather than Samuel. I would never be called Sammy.

My brother, Ronnie, was born a little over 11 months after I was. My birthday was December 4th, his November 16th. But for some reason I never learned, probably because of my difficult birth at the farm, he got to be born at the hospital in Bakersfield. As a consequence, his birth certificate read Bakersfield. Mine read Weedpatch (in small, crabbed lettering a doctor who was called in at the last minute, Talbert E. Scherb, M.D., had noted: Near Bakersfield).

Weedpatch had a few ramshackle shacks, an irrigation canal, dirt roads and its cotton. That was all; hotter than Hades in summer and freezing in winter. Like most of the San Joaquin Valley. The fine, alkali dust was all-pervasive.

Our grandparents named our mother India Joyce. The India came from our grandad's Indian heritage. He wasn't ashamed of this and wanted to remind his only child he wasn't ashamed of it. But I don't think mom agreed because everyone called her Joyce. I never heard anyone call her India.

I remember my father being a tall, lean Texan. My birth certificate gives his birthplace as Big Springs, Texas, and his occupation as farmer. It further states that my mother was born in Carlyle, Arkansas.

I also remember the farmhouse had a big, ancient cottonwood in the front yard. I vaguely recall my baby brother and me playing under it. A rope hung down from one large branch. Maybe I swung on it. I don't remember.

But I remember my father making me a toy airplane. It looked like it was made of a rough lathing slat. Or it might have been made of a strip of wood from an orange crate. It had a propeller and the wing was fastened to the top of the fuselage by wire wound around it. Maybe my love of airplanes started with this crude toy.

We also had a metal top; one of those multi-colored ones that had a spiral piece of metal coming out of it with a wooden ball at the end. You placed the top on the floor, pulled the metal spiral up by the wood knob and as you pushed it down, the top would begin to spin.

I'll never know how I did it but I got my lip caught between the spiral and the opening in the top. I remember crawling onto the bed with that top drooping from my lip. Mercifully, I don't remember how my parents got it loose.

I was standing in the front of the house one day. I couldn't have been but about two years old. The road was built up at the front of the house to around ten feet above the end of our yard to accommodate a large culvert. I watched as a car came off the road and rolled over twice before coming to rest on its wheels. It was a brown sedan.

The driver got out and shook his head. I don't remember any blood.

Ronnie and I got on that road once. I was calling him Dee Dee by then. I don't remember when I started calling him Ronnie.

There were small holes in the road about one-inch in diameter and spaced at about one-foot intervals. They continued up the road and we began to follow them.

Eventually they stopped and we climbed down from the road into the cotton field below. But we didn't know where the house was. We couldn't see it over the high cotton.

Our mother spotted me jumping up trying to see the house and came and got us.

I don't remember this but my mother told me I got my father's straight razor one time and came downstairs with a bloody face and was saying: I bin shabin'.

Our grandparents would visit often. Grandad always brought his bolt action .410 single-shot shotgun.

He would lay the gun on the ground and sit. As a flock of blackbirds would fly over, he would pick up the gun and shoot at them. I loved the smell of the burnt powder.

When he had enough, our mother would clean the birds and fry them.

Sometimes, when the weather had been just right, the folks would pick mushrooms. Some of these would be over six-inches in diameter. Mom would butterfly and sauté them in butter. Marvelous. Grandad was especially fond of these and so was I.

Our grandmother, Lorene Caldwell, was very fat. Maybe this is why Ronnie and I called her Tody. She would never be grandma, always Tody. We loved her dearly.

But we had a great-grandmother, Mary Hammond Smith, Tody's mother, who lived with our grandparents. And we called her grandma. We loved her best of all.

She bought two New Testaments with Psalms from the Jewel Tea salesman for Ronnie and Me. She underlined passages in each of them that she hoped we would pay special attention to as we grew up.

There was a dance once. I remember our mother and father in the front seat of the car outside the dance hall, Ronnie and I in the back seat. They were drinking beer and drunkenly singing You Are My Sunshine over and over. Our father was wearing a gun. It looked like a cowboy pistol. I wanted to touch it but somehow knew I shouldn't.

Our father left us when I was three years old. We never heard from him again.

After our father had gone, we left Weedpatch and moved to the grandparent's place in Little Oklahoma in Southeast Bakersfield on the corner of Cottonwood and Padre.

It was 1938.

I don't recall much more of Weedpatch. I don't remember any birthday, Easter or Christmas there.

I remember very little of Weedpatch apart from the things mentioned.

Contents

CHAPTER ONE

It was winter and my grandparents and I had just moved into one of the two, tarpaper shacks on the mining claim in Boulder Gulch. There was snow on the ground and that night was very cold.

Not yet being supplied with firewood and there being plenty of pine cones available, grandad filled the iron wood stove with them and we went to bed.

Shortly after falling asleep we were awakened in a profusely sweating condition. It must have been 130 degrees in the little cabin and the reason was immediately apparent; the little wood stove was glowing bright cherry red all over, nearing meltdown.

Grandad ran and opened the door and we all followed him out into the blessed coolness of the snow. The cabin cooled quickly in the winter night with the door open. The pinecones burned rapidly down, the stove returned to its natural state and we went back inside.

Thus it was that we intrepid pioneers of Boulder Gulch early established the combustibility and intense heating properties of pitch-laden pinecones. You sure couldn't beat them for instant heat but one had to be judicious in their use.

It was while standing with my grandparents outside the cabin, the moon gleaming off the fresh snow, giving a brilliant and surreal cast to the whole enterprise, that I came to the conclusion that things would not be dull in our move to the wilderness. I somehow sensed my grandad, as he always had, would continue to bring a certain liveliness to the whole business.

***

I had an old hound, Tippy, a mongrel Collie, that we inherited with the mining claim. When I would get one of the guns and take off, Tippy would traipse along. He wasn't worth anything for hunting but sometimes we just wanted each other's company.

I had taken the old .410 single-shot hoping for a rabbit, some quail or, if I was really lucky, a nice young tree squirrel (just an aside: the gray tree squirrels that used to be plentiful around our area of Sequoia National Forest were a real delicacy. But over the years they have, like so many other animals, declined dramatically. I could never bring myself to shoot one now. It is sad that these marvelous, humorous, beautiful creatures are losing their habitat. I so enjoy just watching them now).

It was a nice summer afternoon and things felt great out there in the forest among the critters. Sneaking up a hill behind the cabin, I noticed Tippy had disappeared. Suddenly, not more than fifteen feet away from me, slowly trotting around a large boulder up the hill, was a mountain lion headed straight toward me!

The lion saw me at the same time I saw it, his big, baleful, yellow eyes staring right at me. He had his ears laid flat back against his huge head and his tail, all fluffed out and looking about four inches in diameter and six feet long was hung low to the ground.

Now anyone who knows anything about pussycats knows when they are irritated. And this was one large and irritated pussycat. And here I was, equipped with a .410 single-shot loaded with number eight birdshot. Talk about being prepared. I knew how David must have felt about that slingshot against Goliath. But at least David had the advantage of knowing God was with him. And, I'm sure; David didn't have to worry about becoming a Philistine Hors d'oeuvre.

Much to my intense relief and surprise, the lion made an abrupt 90-degree turn to my left and continued on his way tail dragging the ground. And there came Tippy right behind him.

Several thoughts passed through my mind at the time, abject terror, anger at the fact that I didn't have my .270 instead of the .410, anger with Tippy for chasing up the lion and sending him my way, relief that I had sense enough to know that had I shot the lion with a load of .410 number eight birdshot I would only have succeeded in arousing his interest in me and so forth. I settled for grabbing Tippy by the scruff of the neck and running pell-mell back to the cabin.

I regaled my grandparents and school chums with the story of my close encounter with the angel of death and the lion grew with the telling. He probably was only your average, run of the mill mountain lion, but he was an African giant up that close.

***

Ghost stories are fun. There is a man (Larry) out there somewhere still telling, no doubt, about the night a huge beast almost got him in the Piute Mountains. I am ashamed to admit that I am responsible for this lurid, dread tale that may have falsely captured the imaginations of countless folks. Thanks to me, the Piute Bigfoot began his legendary career.

Back in the late forties, my grandad managed to acquire a mineral light. Tungsten is a very valuable mineral, essential to making steel. Tungsten (and uranium) prospecting was popular in our hills and the light would allow us to look for tungsten traces at night. This material fluoresces a strikingly beautiful blue under ultraviolet. My first experience using the light was startling. I discovered scorpions are fluorescent. I was also amazed at how many of the varmints were out and about our place of a summer's eve. In further nocturnal forays, I was more careful about being barefoot.

One night I came across a large, rose quartz boulder one side of which lit up like the starry heavens. Nearby, I found a nugget about two inches long. I knew I had struck it rich! Unhappily, try as I might, I could find no other traces of these magnificent specimens. For those of you that are interested in treasure maps, I'm open to offers. Time, and sore, old joints permitting, I may even take up the search myself someday. At least I know where to start.

But back to the serious matter at hand. Harold and Ruby along with her boy, Larry, invited me to go tungsten prospecting in the Piutes. We camped at Saddle Springs and began our search. The days were beautiful in these high mountains and we scarcely ever saw another soul. The nights were glorious. We spent part of our days looking for promising spots to check out at night. We thought we had really found a strike once but the material turned out to be something used in manufacturing fireworks. We also discovered that while it had some value, it was cheaper to ship the stuff from China than to mine it here— an early lesson in foreign trade economics.

One day while in camp trying to amuse myself, a couple of tin can lids caught my attention (I still think kids are better off using cans and boxes than most of the trash that passes as toys today). Harold, Ruby and Larry had gone to town to get supplies and the idle mind is the devil's playground. A plan, unbidden mind you, to destroy Larry began to invade my dark side. It was a sheer stroke of genius worthy of deSade, an inspiration to a future Stephen King.

Now I want to make it clear at the outset that I have never been a particularly mean or malicious person, not even as a child. But some opportunities present themselves that one, in all responsibility, cannot avoid. This was one such. I am also constrained to point out, in my defense, that Harold did not care much for Larry and children are quick to recognize good professional victim material when they see it. I was really fond of old Harold and he and I had a good relationship.

Unfortunately, this mitigated against the victim. Grownups should be more cautious in making their likes and dislikes clear to children, particularly about other children. I knew, as a result, that I would have a willing ally in my diabolical plot against the hapless victim, Larry. It was sheer genius in its simplicity. Taking two can lids, I folded them in half. Next, I found a suitable length of firewood about two feet long and nailed the lids to it about a foot apart and slanted them slightly. I placed my "eyes" up the side of the mountain from our campsite where I knew they would easily be caught in the beam of a flashlight. As Wylie Coyote would say: Sheer Genius!

That evening when the folks returned, I took Harold aside and unfolded my sadistic plot. He was genuinely proud to take part in such an imaginative undertaking whose end, we hoped, would not only strike total terror in Larry, reducing him to blathering idiocy, but might also have the fringe benefit of making Ruby soil herself as well: Two for one.

As usual, that evening we stoked up the campfire and once it was blazing nicely, according to our plan, Harold suggested we tell ghost stories for the fun of it. I had primed the pump by telling how I had discovered strange tracks of some large animal around the camp that day. The night was pitch black, no moon, and the heavily forested mountains in the firelight provided a shadowy backdrop that a Vincent Price or Bela Lugosi might well envy.

In the middle of an especially lurid tale of a little boy entering a haunted house on a dare (Harold doing the telling at this point), I suddenly whispered: "What was that?" indicating by my manner that I had heard something on the mountainside. Now everyone was listening, Harold and I pretending, for the suspicious sound. Harold: "Yes, I hear it now." Me: "I'll get the flashlight."

Of course there are natural, night sounds in the forest but Larry and Ruby were sure they also heard something strange now. Switching on the light, I began to play it around the side of the mountain until, suddenly, my eyes lit up in its beam. The reaction was most gratifying. Larry and Ruby's eyes suddenly plumbed new dimensions of growth and the stifled screech of Ruby was accompanied by a satisfactory burrowing of Larry's whimpering head into her lap. I used the light in such a way as to make it appear that the creature had moved out of the way into the trees. Grabbing my rifle, I said to Harold, "Let's go see if we can spot it," bravery to the nth degree.

Harold and I proceeded up the mountain where I then picked up the eyes and, under cover of the darkness, moved them to another spot. Coming back down to the camp and finding Ruby and Larry clutching each other in abject terror was most gratifying. We explained that while we were unable to see the creature, we had found very large tracks that looked like a cross between human, Grizzly bear and mountain lion. Hunkering down to the fire, Harold and I repeated the scene of hearing something and, using the flashlight, I was able to pick up the eyes in their new location. Three times this experiment in terrorism was repeated. By now our victims were reduced to the satisfactory level of hysteria and, crawling into our sleeping bags, Harold and I could sleep the sleep of self-righteous terrorists. Ruby and Larry kept a large fire stoked all night.

It has occurred to me over the years that the great, Tehachapi earthquake that took place a couple of days later might be, in some measure, due to God's attitude toward my little joke. It literally pounded us out of our sleeping bags. You could actually see the ground heaving up and down, throwing gravel into the air. At any rate, while I repented of my wickedness, neither Harold nor I ever disabused Ruby or Larry of the notion that somewhere in the Piutes there lurked a phenomenal beast of terrifying proportions and features. Between the beast and the ensuing earthquake, our prospecting was soon halted and we returned to civilization. Larry and Ruby did acquire some little renown in describing their close encounter with the creature and Harold and I enjoyed the status of brave and intrepid men who fearlessly faced certain death at its jaws and claws. Hence, the Piute Bigfoot still lurks in the forest and only now is the truth, ashamedly, told. Confession is good for the soul and perhaps I am seeking absolution by laying bare, to all, this sordid act.

But, if there is a moral to be derived from this story it has successfully eluded me. I enjoyed frightening the wits out of Ruby and Larry; and apart from the earthquake, which may not have been directed at me at all, I got away with it. My grandad gave it four stars. But, then, he didn't particularly care for Larry either. No morality there. And you might guess who contributed the quirky gene for my own sense of humor. Children can, of course, be unwittingly cruel; but adults should learn to distinguish what is done in fun and judge carefully in raising their own children.

Some of the other stories which belong in the category of eating the owl, gigging frogs, putting the mouse down the back of the dress of one of my mother's (ex) friends, my pet porcupine, nearly catching the cabin on fire and mundane, workaday trivia, of which I'm sure the average reader has similar experiences enough, are covered in the following pages.

***

It was a great day for fishing. Charlie and I were at the old bridge just South of Kernville. Trout and catfish liked to laze in the shadows of the bridge over the deep canal sluggishly flowing beneath, and if you didn't spook them you had a chance at some good ones. J.L. had gotten a five-pound trout just the other day not far from where the aqueduct went south of Erskine creek.

Fishing season had just officially opened for the tourists and flat-landers. They came, primarily, from the Big City: Bakersfield. Occasionally, we got some real foreigners from Los Angeles.

We arrived at the bridge too late to try any serious fishing and, being bored tried to think of something to do while drowning our worms to no effect. Once in a while a car full of out-landers would disturb our reverie.

Charlie was twelve and I had just turned thirteen, a teenager at last. Big time! So I suppose it naturally fell to me as the mature member of the duo to find something to do.

I had noticed an old can on the bank and in desperation thought it might be fun to hang it on my hook and let it drift downstream. Then, I thought, I could play it like a fish. At least I could enjoy the tug of something on the end of my line.

The scheme worked well. As the can filled with water and sank, drifting downstream, there was a very satisfactory, weighty pull on the end of the line, just as if I had hooked a big cat. I would let it drift out a distance and begin to horse the giant in, rod arched in a good, honest, bamboo bow.

Charlie and I were having our innocent fun when a car full of tourists stopped at the end of the bridge. There were four men in the car, obvious fishermen, who, upon seeing me holding nicely arched rod in hand, naturally assumed they had come upon a real Norman Rockwell bit of Americana in progress; a country boy hooked onto a real lunker.

Immediately the men started shouting encouragement and advice: "Don't lose him boy! Play him! Atta boy! Be careful, he's a big one! Give him line! Don't horse him so much!"

Now gentle readers, you must not think that cruelty to innocent people was a part of the early childhood training of the youth in the old Kern River Valley. We children were civilized and took off our caps indoors and always said "Thank you, Yes mam" or "sir," etc., but an angel from heaven could not be blamed if he succumbed to the ensuing lapse of morality that followed this golden opportunity.

It occurred to Charlie and me that we might have a good thing going here. With an audience of out-land adults shouting encouragement, Charlie naturally joining in now, I redoubled my efforts not to allow this leviathan of the deep (the can) to outwit me and escape. And then another car pulled up behind the first.

No actors on any stage could have been our equals in the life and death struggle unfolding before our most noisy and appreciative audience. And a third car stopped at the other end of the bridge.

A niggling twinge of doubt began to entrude itself on me as to the wisdom of our little joke. Then a fourth car stopped. We now had about fourteen, enthusiastically screaming adults cutting us off at both ends of the bridge. It occurred to Charlie and me that there might be some expression of disappointment on the part of all these people once the game was up and I hauled in the can. Besides, my arms were getting tired.

Fortunately, I don't to this day know why, no one had left their car to come onto the bridge to personally inspect the action. I attribute this to a profound belief in children's guardian angels.

I told Charlie to get ready to make a run for it. Our only chance was to jump the bridge and run along the bank until we were where no one could follow. Why, in our childish innocence, we thought anyone would take offense at our little prank, I don't know. It just seemed like a wise precaution to assume the worst.

On the signal, I hauled in the can. As it came into view, there was a hush over our audience. This, of course, was momentary. As Charlie and I cleared the railing of the bridge, we were hastened on our way by some of the most colorful and imaginative language we had ever been privileged to hear. Some of the words and phrases were decidedly new to us and threatened most unusual acts on our various anatomical parts. It gave us new insights and made us popular among our peers in the retelling. I won't bore the reader with the many examples of our newly learned vocabulary.

Charlie and I decided it wouldn't serve any useful purpose to share this incident with his parents or my grandparents or ask them to define or interpret this newly learned vocabulary for us; thus we kept the whole affair from them. Given our own childhood adventures, parents can only wonder at times what their children withhold from them.

I hope this provides some insight into my own concerns for the education our young people are decidedly not getting. No, I don't worry that their slang, vulgar and profane vocabulary is lacking; would that it were. But it does lack imagination. The Arabs have it all over us in imaginative cursing. This is not to say that our victims were entirely lacking in their knowledge of invective, expletives and epithets that, hurled in our direction, hastened Charlie's and my departure; but American cursing just does not compare with: "May the fleas of a thousand camels nest in your nose!"

There are many moral lessons to be derived from my little joke on the fishermen. But the truth is that in today's society the threats might just be actually carried out. Today, someone might pull a gun and shoot you. Of course they don't need the excuse of being made fools of today. They might shoot just for the fun of it. Such is the world our young people face today.

***

Obviously, if this world is the proving ground and we are supposed to learn and apply that learning for eternity, someone has really fallen down on the job of equipping us. God is supposed to use men to teach and train others for the task. But what are we getting? Idiots!

In education, religion and politics, the "leadership" is appalling and little better in sight. The thoroughgoing incompetence and sheer laziness of these "leaders" reminds me of a couple of incidents that occurred while I was living in Boulder Gulch.

It had rained all night. The sound was marvelous in the old cabin and the flames from the fireplace were making dancing shadows on the walls. Times like these are magic. Snug in bed, I fell asleep to the wonder of it all.

It was not quite dawn when I was awakened by the sound of running water close by. There was a streambed behind the cabin and it was a wonderful and rare treat when it rained enough to cause it to flow.

Anxious to get up and get outside, I threw my legs out of bed into a slowly moving current of water about a foot deep. I became instantly alert. One: water was not supposed to be running through the cabin. Two: it was. Talk about quick -witted!

The old cabin we had originally moved into had a wood floor. When the room with the fireplace had been added by grandad we moved several wheelbarrows of decomposed granite, plentiful all around us, in to make the floor. We then laid miscellaneous pieces of carpet over the DG. Voila! Instant (and cheap) floor.

It seems that the construction company responsible for the new highway (the dam in Isabella was nearing completion at this time) had caused the stream behind us to divert right through the middle of our cabin. The water had simply pushed in one wall and pushed out the other end. The walls were made of thin veneer shipping crates grandad had scrounged somewhere, covered over with the ubiquitous tarpaper so they offered little resistance.

Now I'm sure the construction company never intended to flood us out. The government would take care of that later. But they had neglected to notice where all that water would go in the event of rain. As with so many other things in life, one thing leads to another, often quite unexpected.

It was quite a task to clean out the mud once the river retreated. I have always, consequently, been able to sympathize with flood victims.

Now leaving out a bridge on the new highway was really another matter entirely, particularly if there are no warning signs.

It was late on a summer's evening and we were preparing to put out the kerosene lamps and go to bed. Suddenly there was a pounding on the cabin door. Opening the door, we were confronted by a man and boy, clothes torn and bloody.

They explained that they had gotten onto the new highway and, rounding the curve at French Gulch, in the pitch dark of night has sailed off the road into the boulder-strewn chasm below. Scratch one brand new 1950 Ford.

It turned out that while they had been able to extricate themselves, another man was still trapped in the car and was badly injured. They had seen our light in the cabin when they had driven by earlier and these two had walked back for help.

Grandad took the man to the crash site in his old Ford pickup while the boy stayed with me at the cabin. He and the man were not too badly hurt and a few bandages and iodine were sufficient for their injuries.

Since we had no phone it was necessary to get the other man out of the wreckage and transport all three to Bakersfield. It seems that grandad knew the badly injured man. His name was Kirk Ragland, the owner of a large dairy in Bakersfield.

It was obvious that the construction company either failed to put caution signs on the new road under construction or someone had removed them. But it does not take much imagination to know what it feels like to be on a beautiful, new stretch of highway at night and suddenly be flying off the end of it into an abyss. Terrifying! I suppose my point is obvious. Teachers and politicians have become notorious for building roads that lead people sailing off into nowhere. But Mr. Ragland sued the construction company. Who do we sue when teachers and politicians do us in?

***

I am grateful that God must have a sense of humor. He has, of course, the finest sense of humor of all. In spite of the fact that He must be the best parent, thereby seeming to spoil all the fun while we are growing up, He does bear with a lot. My grandparents' church in Little Oklahoma was a happy place. I am an Honorary Okie myself by virtue of my birth in Weedpatch and early raisin' in Southeast Bakersfield. The little tarpaper and dirt floor temple had an actual steeple and bell. One of life's little pleasures was ringing that bell on Sunday mornings.

Cottonwood and Padre: Dirt roads, dirt floors and dirt poor living, but proud people. No one stole from friends or relatives. *Tookin'* wasn't stealing and considerable tookin' took place from the local railyard and packing plant. The aroma of the plant together with the oil fields gave Bakersfield an early start on air pollution. But, as with the outhouses, there is a perverted kind of nostalgia I associate with these fumes.

Blue and Austin Hall were my closest, childhood friends. Their mother was the literal spitting image (thanks to the ubiquitous snuff and chewing tobacco) of Mammy Yokum. Being honest pagans, Blue and Austin's parents didn't often attend church but sent the kids.

The war was on and here and there you saw the small flags in the windows with blue, and, tragically, occasionally, gold stars. We children bought war stamps at school (Mt. Vernon) and turned in toys for metal drives. I helped grandad flatten tin cans with a hammer on an anvil for this purpose. My mother dutifully painted stockings on her legs and my brother and I helped her peel the foil from cigarette packages and roll it in a ball for the war effort.

Meat was rationed and we raised rabbits. My grandparents had the largest rabbitry in Kern County at this time. We saved things like grease and lard for the war effort and listened to Gabriel Heatter and the Lone Ranger. We watched from the schoolyard as planes from Minter Field engaged in mock combat overhead. Teachers warned about finding any strange items on the school grounds, as they might be explosive devices cleverly left by saboteurs. Israeli and Arabian children know this drill too well.

The war was made very real to us as children and we were thoroughly propagandized. The media from comic books to movies taught us to hate the *rotten Japs and stinkin' Knocksies*. I can imagine how children in other countries are taught to hate us. But we were simple folks, believing in the righteousness of our cause and our leaders, even, I'm sure, as do the simple folks in other lands now. There were few social services and we didn't think of ourselves as poor or underprivileged because there was no TV or bureaucrats coming around telling us we were poor and underprivileged.

The uniform deguere for children was bare feet and bib overalls for summer (sans shirts) and, if you had them, shoes and overalls for winter (with shirts). Socks and underwear were sometime things. While Bakersfield winters could be cruel, the summers were glorious. We could swim in the weir or the irrigation canals, shoot marbles, catch frogs and catfish, pick cotton (my brother and I were forbidden this noble occupation, I suspect from the exalted position my grandparents held in the community) catch lizards and other local reptiles and, in sum, enjoy being children. Shoes, if you had them, were the first things to go in summer. And not just among the children. Most of the womenfolk went barefoot as well. The warm, alkali dust felt marvelous to our feet, particularly if you had spent the winter shod. At night, if you chanced around an electric light (they were scarce in Little Oklahoma) you could find June bugs and mammoth moths; worlds of fun with these critters.

I wonder how many of you real Kern Countyians recall a song of the time that went: "Dear Okie if you see Arkie tell him Tex has got a job for him in California; picking up prunes, they're all out of oranges"

You shouldn't get the impression that we children were perfectly innocent of worldly things just because we lacked the preeminent teacher, TV, in that area. There were certain ones that exhibited a certain savoir-faire and knowledge of things illegitimate and carnal beyond their tender years (many of that old gang of mine went to the 'pen' or got a permanent crease cooked into their trousers from some state's special seating arrangement).

Fortunately, any trouble my brother and I got into in this regard was easily attributable to wicked companions, not our own proclivity for evil. Or so our grandparents believed to our good fortune. When memory turns back to that simple church and time, the old songs of Zion (from the very popular

Latter Rain Revival hymnbook) come to mind. What memories does recalling the sylvan cacophony of mingled guitars, tambourines, triangles and piano evoke. Perhaps you too remember some of those old favorites: If I Could Hear My Mother Pray Again, God's Radio, Oh Why Tonight? Over The Top For Jesus, You'll Wish You Were One Of Us By and By (there's a real message in that one), When I Can Read My Title Clear, 'Twas Rum That Spoiled My Boy, but we really swung into high gear on When The Roll Is Called Up Yonder and Beulah Land. A problem of course with a dirt floor is that if a lot of people really get into the spirit, all that toe-tapping and hand slapping music can raise a good deal of dust (one of the mysteries of childhood was how you could go to bed when grandma or great-grandma didn't remember to tell you to wash your feet and they would be so clean in the morning?).

But the sensitive reader might be offended by elaboration on this theme so I will relegate it to the chapter on spit-washing young faces and other less tidy subjects of Dust Bowl memorabilia. In a more serious vein I will tell you of the little queer.

Now my brother Ronnie and I didn't know about queers when we were children. Of course, we didn't know about sex of any kind. The delicacy of the subject prevented our grandparents from ever talking about it (I suspect our mother could have given us a few hints).

But, on the whole, sex was simply a taboo of our youth. The intriguing mystery was before us in the conversation and actions of our more knowledgeable playmates, especially since several of them seemed to derive some special pleasure in playing with themselves before an audience. I will never forget the look on an Aunt's face when I showed her a cute trick I learned from an older kid. This simple maneuver merely required you to stick your hand in your pants and push one finger through the fly. It seemed like a good idea at the time. As I say, I'll never forget her expression on my aunt's face, and though having not the slightest idea of all the Freudian implications, I never did it again. I may not have understood it, but from my aunt's reaction I knew it was somehow wrong.

It is very much to our grandparent's credit that we boys were definitely taught right from wrong, that we never used profanity and that we had a strict, moral code worthy of a conqueror knight seeking the Holy Grail (This did cause some slight adjustment as we grew older, particularly in regard to the fairer sex). But about the little queer. This kid definitely had bubbles in his think-tank. As Good Samaritans, our grandparents occasionally did take in some of the walking wounded of this world system. Two such were this kid and his mother.

Other than a clubfoot, which required the strangest shoe we had ever seen and a right hand that went 90 degrees from the normal, the boy seemed quite average (there was also some facial disfigurement from small pox). Anyhow, they were both shouting fundies, raging warm on the need to live good Christian lives. This kid held my brother and I spellbound on such lively topics as sodomy and descriptive female anatomy. While utterly lacking any experiential frame of reference, we did not wish to appear unappreciative in the presence of such a learned and enlightened one, and one that was so obviously willing to tell anyone who would listen of his exploits into that forbidden world of "It!" On more than one occasion Ronnie and I felt we were listening to an episode of Inner Sanctum.

Such was the tender delicacy of our minds compared to this august personage. But Ronnie (also called Dee Dee by me, and Fuzz by grandad because of Ronnie's curly hair. Dee Dee hated that name, Fuzz) and I were well acquainted with hell-fire and damnation and did not want to intrude too far into that dark and enticing, evil world no matter how good its practitioner made it sound. Homosexuality was a term and a fact neither of us boys had ever heard or had any knowledge.

But one night during the evening Sunday service it was Testimony Time and the saints were popping up like fleas shouting that they were glad they were saved and had the Holy Ghost! While this inspiring display of religious fervor was going on, this kid was putting his arm around me and trying to kiss me. Somehow this didn't strike me as the work of God, especially as his hand was feeling my leg. I moved away from him and suddenly he leaped up with an "I'm glad I'm saved and got the Holy Ghost and God's called me to be a preacher!" I was certainly surprised by this revelation under the circumstances, but the kid sat down amid shouted Hallelujahs! Amens! and the proud, beaming look of his mother. Then he said to me: "Now it's your turn; you gotta testify!"

A rather peculiar thing then occurred. No one had ever asked me if I was "saved;" I guess my grandparents just took it for granted that no boy could be loved and preached at with such fervor as I had been and not be a sure-fire contender for salvation. "Well," I thought, "whatever 'saved' means, I'm not and I sure don't have that 'Holy Ghost' that knocks old lady Walker off her hinges." Nor was I at all sure I wanted that dreadful power pushing me all over the place making me cluck, spit, and moan in strange ways. And, so, I remained nailed to my bench, refusing to be this kid's first convert to holy-rollerism (not that many of them really rolled much, but they sure twitched a lot). I knew I was a sinner but I also knew that being saved must be a different thing than what this kid was.

Later, as a teenager, a kindly, old man was to ask me directly, for the first time, if I was saved. I will never forget, since my grandad was present, saying I was just to satisfy him. I felt intense guilt for this deception. I still didn't know what Saved was then. It wasn't that the Bible and Jesus weren't made prominent in the little church or that I lacked examples of real Christians. But the Gospel was so distorted by ignorance and, sometimes, terrible hypocrisy, that it was never really explained in its pure simplicity. It was not until I read the Bible for myself that I discovered this.

One of the greater things I found by reading the Bible for myself was that so much of what others had told me was Scriptural was nowhere contained in the Bible. The world our children will inherit will be filled with ignorance. Not the ignorance of being able to use a VCR or flip hamburgers, but the hurtful ignorance of prejudice and bigotry, ignorance of science and real art and literature, ignorance of what a clear, mountain stream and a starry sky represent.

***

Grandad used to work with an old fellow that claimed to be Indian. The Indian and I used to go hunting together in the mountains around the mining claim. At that time, the hills were full of quail, deer and other game. I'll never forget the time he got his car stuck in Erskine Creek and we had to spend the night. It was very cold and we built a fire, but you may know how hard it is to try to keep warm when it is so cold that one side of you is frying and the other side is freezing. Then, to top it off, the first snow of winter began to fall. I have no romantic illusions of roughing it in such circumstances. It was a thoroughly miserable night. Anyhow, this old fellow had many tales and I never contradicted him or acted as though I disbelieved him. I was raised never to do this with adults. But I will recount one story to make the point.

The fellow was visiting one evening at our cabin and he told us of a pistol he once owned. It seems that this gun was used to commit a murder. He slept with it under his pillow, and in the morning it would be covered with blood. He said he would clean it thoroughly, but every morning it would, once more, be bloody. He said he finally had to get rid of it.

Now he would have been grievously wounded in his soul if my grandad or I had expressed disbelief over what he obviously expected us to accept as gospel truth. Like the old lady in Little Oklahoma that stuffed rags into empty light sockets to keep electricity from leaking out and the old man that would never eat anything from a can that had been opened from the bottom because this "pizened" the contents, such ignorance and fanciful imagination was not really hurtful or intended to do harm. But the ignorance of prejudice and bigotry, the ignorance of basic skills in a technological society and the selfish ignorance of Me! Me! Me! that is entirely something else.

This together with the ignorance of real values that makes other people worth caring about and leads to self-discipline and self-sacrifice, the ignorance of these is dooming our children. We were poor in material things in Weedpatch, Little Oklahoma, and Boulder Gulch; but thank God we did not lack in the things that make life worth living. Family, community, patriotism, faith in God and our country, these were real to us simple folk. Would that today's children were equally "poor!"

***

In order to give the reader a fuller appreciation of the function of our little church, Faith Tabernacle, in Dust Bowl Era Little Oklahoma, I will describe a typical service.

Call to worship was accomplished by ringing the bell Sunday morning. This was the only sound to be heard at this time and day in our little community. No lawns so no mowers. No loud radios (and no TV's of course). No cars so no traffic. Only, in summer the noise of flitting insects and birds and the occasional yap of some hound.

The congregation filtered in, women in flour or grain sack dresses and straw hats, children in the conventional overalls, and mostly shoeless. The men tried to dress in Sunday-go-to-meeting attire of miscellaneous items, some with uncomfortable bow ties and, here and there, a white shirt might be seen. Folks tried to dress up the little girls but the boys, while reasonably clean, escaped such nonsense. We would begin with a few rousers like Come and Dine to warm up the audience. The cardboard fans donated by a mortuary in Bakersfield that grandad did business with would begin to flutter by now.

Bakersfield summers were hot and it didn't take much to work up a sweat among the faithful. Prayer requests were taken and testimonies given of what God had done for (or to) various people in the neighborhood. At prayer time, The Lord's favor was implored for all our boys overseas and His righteous judgment against the enemies of Democracy. After the people had prayed (we had no Amen corner, everybody had the liberty to interject Amen and Hallelujah as the spirit moved them) it was Show time! I do not mean to interject irreverence. We all took the service seriously. But, to us children, it was definitely show time.

While we enjoyed the singing and Sunday school lessons very much, it was the grown-ups that could be counted on to gay-up the time something fierce. How we looked forward to the fun as people began to warm to grandad's preaching. My grandfather's face would contort with rage against the iniquitous Philistines and Pharisees. His voice boomed out like thunder as his fist pounded again and again on the old, wood pulpit. His whole body lurched in cadence with the words and seemed to help hurl them out like bullets at the helpless spectators in the pews (actually the pews were ramshackle benches more or less nailed together and sitting on the dirt floor).

Old lady Walker suddenly jumped to her feet, flang her arms toward heaven, threw her head back and with eyes closed began shouting in tongues. To my childish ears she seemed to be spouting a kind of sound like our make-believe Indian talk. "O lalla lalla keba o notchaway, O lalla lalla keba o notchaway" she repeated over and over, her voice growing softer until she was finally slain by the spirit and slipped to the ground. Another old saint, Mrs. Hall, taking her cue, jumped to her feet and took off on "Helagumba, hellagumba, hellagumba, hellagumba" until she also was mowed down by this terrible force of heaven. I thought again for the umpteenth time that old lady Walker sure had it all over Mrs. Hall. After all, an entire sentence must be a greater accomplishment than one word. Also, old lady Walker had a certain way of falling which left her in a more decorous position than Mrs. Hall. We children took great notice of how each dear old saint fell and writhed and twitched not just their facility with grunts, yelling, jumping, tongue clicking and enthusiasm in general.

My grandfather would halt his thunderous barrage against all sorts of wickedness from bob-hair to hug dancing each time the spirit moved on one of the saints. I always admired my grandfather's great sense of delicate timing. When the spirit moved he had sense enough not to interfere with such a terrifying power. No sooner had this dread force accomplished its work and felled its victim but grandad would pick up as though nothing had interrupted his discourse.

Up jumped Mrs. Young as though goosed forcefully and indiscreetly. "Geeda geeda lamasabathany, geeda geeda lamasabathany, geeda geeda lamasabathany" until the ambushing spirit polled her like an ox. This was one part we children really liked because Mrs. Young had the heft of a cord of wood. We often wondered how Mr. Young, who could have posed as the 90-pound weakling for Charles Atlas advertisements, controlled this pulchritudinous behemoth. And Mrs. Young had class. No twitching, groaning or moaning. After the performance, she just lay quiet with flecks of spittle on her hairy, upper lip. At the end of the service (performance), there was the altar call. This was the opportunity for each member of the congregation to come to the front of the church and kneel and pray. If the spirit really moved, a real catharsis of sins, real and imagined, would be poured out with much crying and shouting. This was a treat for the children as we heard many things our parents would never say in front of us otherwise.

Lest the reader misunderstand, the altar call was real in many cases. People often needed the gathering together to confess and pray for one another. Many wounds were healed in this fashion and fellowship restored.

On rare occasions, we would have a baptism. This was accomplished only during the summer because we had to make a day of it at the Jordan (otherwise known as the Kern River). Real baptism must be done by completely submerging the penitent in a real river. None of that sissy bathtub or Sprinkled Dandy stuff for Little Oklahoma believers. And, you wore your Sunday best, not baptismal robes. Grandad would remove his shoes and roll up his pants, but it was still Black suit, black bow tie and white shirt.

A picnic atmosphere was always a part of the ceremony and a great time would be had by all. If the congregation was not so small, I'm sure many a sinner would have gone back for seconds just for the fun of it. Fried chicken, rabbit, catfish and frog legs were plentiful. Pies and cakes. In all, with so much deep-fried, there was enough cholesterol to make a mortician smile.

We children would be occupied catching crawdads for the feast. The summer Mrs. Young was baptized was especially entertaining. She kept bobbing up like an elephantine cork and grandad had to have two of the deacons help him to get her under. At that, she proceeded to float downstream and it took half the congregation to beach her.

My grandfather always dressed the part. Black suit with white shirt and black bow tie. He was a large, raw-boned man, over six foot and about 200 pounds. He had a commanding presence and a thunderous voice. He had actually played a gambler in a silent movie made locally and he and my grandmother had done a stint in a circus, he as a Barker and my grandmother as the Fat Lady. Grandma played the piano marvelously and grandad loved to sing; and keeping time with a tambourine, his deep, loud and resonant voice overpowered us. Faith Tabernacle could always be counted on to make a truly joyous noise unto The Lord.

My grandma's piano playing and the spirited singing meant a lot to culturally starved Okies and Arkies and the success of the church. The church was truly a great social need-fulfilling thing as well as meeting the spiritual needs of the poor white trash, as they were known to the greater Bakersfield City dwellers. While it was true that the community was dirt poor and many were on the lam and had criminal records, there was no shame attached. We were all aware of the frailty of the law in understanding some of the injustices of extremity. Many were criminals for things like stealing food or material to put a makeshift roof on a shack.

But no deputy sheriff ever intruded into Little Oklahoma in those days. My grandad was sworn in as a Special Deputy, complete with uniform, Sam Brown, a Smith and Wesson .32-20 (peculiar caliber), clamshell breakaway holster, handcuffs and a copy of the California Penal Code. He, like Judge Roy Bean, became The Law and arbiter of justice in the community. His primary function was that of liaison with the powers in Bakersfield.

Grandad's preaching was dynamic. The format was to have my grandmother read from The Scriptures and when she came to a spot that hit my grandad right, he would take off. This was the "lining" format of our colonial ancestors and picked up by Negroes, primarily for the singing of hymns.

Grandad, as with so many others of similar background, had no formal training for his calling. But, like many that heeded the call, knew The Lord would give him the message. Now my grandfather tolerated exaggerated behavior on the part of the saints and expected them to have a good time in church and a certain flexibility was needed amid the shouts of hallelujah and amen in order for them to enjoy their religion. When one of the sisters would feel the moving of the spirit and jump up to speak in tongues, my grandfather would halt his thunderous barrage and wait for the fit to pass. He did not hold with most of this nonsense but had enough insight to understand the need of his constituents. When the spirit finally fled, grandad would resume his discourse as though nothing had happened.

While he looked askance at women speaking in the church (believing Paul's admonition that this was a shameful thing) he also knew that human nature and culture required outlets of expression. I suspect he also realized that it was a lot of fun for us children. Curiously, it was always the women that spoke in tongues, never the men. Years later I would read: "If the women in the church stopped speaking in tongues, the movement would soon cease to move!"

But this was before the formal churches like the Roman Catholic and Anglicans got into the act and legitimized the gibberish, even giving it a good, solid Greek name; *Glossolalia*. Too bad Amy Simple wasn't around to cash in on that. But, Swaggart, Baker, et al. would make up for her and then some.

My grandfather's own conversion experience needs a little elaboration. It was supposed to have occurred during a tent meeting somewhere in the South.

Being a real heller as a young man, he obviously presented one of those challenges that so inspire the fervent, holy pursuit of the godly. As he told the story, he went to the meeting with some other young bloods to heckle and enjoy the show. But one dear, old saint who recognized him decided the time was ripe for his call to repentance. So enthusiastic did she become under the influence of the spirit that she literally began to chase my grandfather around the meeting place shouting the imprecations of his lost condition and his need to call on the mercy of God for salvation. No fire-breathing dragon could have so consumed its prey as effectively.

The woman, aided by several who had joined in the chase, finally brought grandad to ground. Turning to face his tormenters, grandad said: "The Spirit suddenly took hold of me and rattled me good!" To the holy delight of his hounds of heaven, he cried out to God and began to speak in tongues (grandad never did this as long as I knew him. This was the only occasion of which he gave any credence to this hysteria). There was no doubt to any that such a Saul-like experience could betoken anything but a divine call to preach.

And it was thus that my grandfather was impelled on his colorful career in the Lord's army. Buying himself a Pharisee Bible (these are large Bibles, usually with thumb indexing, color plates, glossary, index, concordance, doctrinal notes, maps, short histories, biographies and pebble grained leather bindings weighing enough to tire any but the most energetic thumper and providing a not inconsiderable weapon should need arise) a Cruden's Concordance and equipping himself further with a few well-selected hell-fire and damnation verses, he, like so many others of similar background, was in the preaching business.

While my grandfather did not have any training in Theology and might not even have heard the word, or use any commentaries, he had a pretty fair grasp of what was reasonable in religion and what was not and preached accordingly. A curious aberration was his refusing to take up a collection or to ever ask for money from the pulpit. His curious response when pressed on the issue was to reply: "God never made a beggar out of any man or His church."

Grandad had built the little church on his own lot at the corner of Cottonwood and Padre. It was built, like our house, of material he had scrounged from various places. The bulk of the wood was from a wrecked boxcar at the rail yard, and he lined most of the inside with thin veneer coffin shipping crates as well as heavy cardboard and what was called "Beaverboard," a cellulose insulation product painted white on one side.

The last couple of years we lived in Bakersfield, grandad acquired a PA system for the church. By attaching two large speakers outside, the entire neighborhood received the benefit of hearing sin denounced in the booming thunder of grandad's preaching. I'm sure the local sinners thought the terror of the heavens had descended upon them when they were first bombarded with this wrath and vengeance unleashed upon the ungodly.

No doubt the local sink of iniquity (a combination cuttin, shootin, liquor and grocery store where you could steal Bull Durham by holding the bell with your hand as you opened the door) profited mightily. They must have, as they were the only ones to complain of this counter-point to their customers' lively language and cultural pursuits.

At one time, he and grandma also had a little mom and pop grocery store (Faith Grocery) next door to the church. It fell victim to a fire, a not uncommon occurrence in our neighborhood. Our home, an architectural curiosity fronting Padre was as I said built of box car lumber, rail ties, coffin shipping crates and anything else substantial enough to use as building material. Like our neighbors, we made do with whatever came to hand. Along with the traditional tarpaper, you would find tin signs used as roofing material and cardboard for interior finish.

We were considered rich by our poorer neighbors because grandad had a steady job at the time with the post office, had a car and such a magnificent home. The beautiful chandelier in what we called the dining room helped support this accusation. There was always something incongruous about the crystal chandelier hanging from our cardboard and veneer coffin shipping crate covered ceiling. Other incongruities included the lovely French doors in our grandparent's bedroom and living room and the marvelous tapestries hung on various walls. I understand tapestries were used in castles to ward off the chill. They undoubtedly served a like purpose in our home.

In the beginning, we had no electricity and had an outhouse. We boys discovered an interesting phenomenon once electricity came to Little Oklahoma. When you turned on the light in the kitchen, large roaches would be running like crazy all over the floor and disappear. If you waited a little while and turned the light back on, the loathsome bugs were back like magic. Indoor plumbing, like electricity, was slow in coming to the community. One of our more odoriferous chores as children was emptying the thundermugs of the accumulation of "night soil." No job for the weak and would today be, doubtless, called "child abuse."

Being a preacher, special deputy, and having a Federal job gave my grandad somewhat unusual status in the neighborhood. His California Penal Code book was always lying with his Bible and Cruden's Concordance. His Smith and Wesson with its breakaway, clamshell holster accounted for a hole in the ceiling of our cabin when we moved to the mining claim in Kernville.

I was practicing my "fast-draw" when I touched the trigger a might too much pressure (it never occurred to me that doing this with live ammo might result in an embarrassing situation). There is something unique about the sound of a powerful handgun going off in a room. It certainly gets the attention of the occupants.

I wouldn't want you to get the impression that we did not live in a fine house in Little Oklahoma. Though it was built of salvaged boxcar lumber, coffin-shipping crates and the inside was finished with cardboard, it was, nonetheless, a great house compared with the neighbors'. Some simply dug a hole in the ground on arrival and covered it with whatever they could find. If it rained, they would just move the roof of tin or canvas and sit under it as a kind of lean-to until the storm passed and the hole was dry. Eventually some of them acquired tents or built tarpaper shacks with material gleaned from the rail yard or the local dump.

It was a unique time in history. WWII was our constant absorption in play as children. Superman, Batman, Captain Marvel and Captain America were doing their part to win the war and we children applauded their efforts against the rotten Japs and stinkin' Knocksies. The toys of those years were fashioned as guns, bayonets, savings banks that were shaped like pigs with Hitler or Tojo's faces, which squealed when you deposited a coin for the war effort. If you want to forecast the future of a culture, take a look at the toys of the children. Stores were filled with cute, diminutive uniforms; our mother often decked out my brother and me as sailors, marines or soldiers according to the present stepfather's occupation. Our mother, patriot that she was, tried to marry into each branch of the service during this era.

It seems incredible in looking back that children were so involved in the war that people should actually think it "cute" to dress them in such a fashion. But we children loved it. Hitler knew what he was doing in this regard in brainwashing the youth of Germany. We too were ready to repel, with our lives, any enemy that should come to our shores. While a war raged, we children played at war, contributed our metal toys to scrap drives, bought war stamps at school and dreamed dreams of honorable and heroic conquest. As I said, it was a unique time in history. In no other decade has the country seemed as united as in the war against the Axis powers. We had a national purpose and the enemy was clear. The bad guys still wore black and the good guys, white. Tom Mix, Hopalong Cassidy (an aberration of the white/black theme but an unmistakable good guy), Gene Autry, The Lone Ranger, Red Ryder and Roy Rogers could be counted on to always do the right thing (kiss the horse, not the girl).

***

Since playing cowboys and Indians involved a lot of gunplay, the transition to killing Japs and Germans was natural. I have often wondered whether our government continued to make caps so readily available to children during this period of time, when you would have thought gunpowder so necessary to the war effort, wasn't a shrewd way to keep us practicing for our eventually becoming cannon fodder.

Guns were a natural part of our culture. Unhappily, instruction in the safe use of them was not. A kid was simply given a gun, usually a BB gun, to start.

I earned my Daisy Red Ryder carbine by selling garden seed and Cloverine Salve door to door. But the real thing was all too readily available. Grandad had, in addition to the Smith, a .25 caliber Browning, a .22 rifle and a .410 shotgun. There were no large bores until we moved to the mining claim and deer, quail, pheasants and ducks were available. Children and guns are, of course, a deadly combination even with adults trying to make them aware of the danger. The fascination is too much. If they are within reach, kids will try to get them. Only adult supervision is acceptable with such weapons. But, with guns treated with such familiarity, it was perfectly understandable that I would have my close calls with the things.

The Browning was especially captivating since it was so small and toy-like in appearance. Unfortunately, the safety catch on this gun was very easily disengaged when removing it from its small holster. Grandad may have thought he had it safely hidden but children are quite expert at ferreting out grownups' hiding places. I had found the Browning and often played with it. The familiarity breeds contempt concept came into full bloom in this instance leading to the nearly untimely demise of one of my playmates. This occurred after we had moved to the claim and this boy and I were in the woods.

I was old enough by then to have a modicum of sense about weapons, but crazy enough to still play with them. The boy's dad had driven us out to cut wood. While he was down the canyon from us, we had an impromptu gunfight. I had drawn the gun from its holster. The safety came off and there was a round in the chamber. Bang! Fortunately, the boy had ducked behind his dad's car and the bullet put a neat, glancing crease in the trunk instead of his head. We told his dad a pinecone had fallen on the car. I'm glad he didn't look too closely. We were lucky. Many children have not been so fortunate.

While living on the claim, I traded a Japanese sword for a Canadian Ross .303 and an old English fowling piece; a double barreled 16 gauge with rabbit ear hammers. The fellow I swapped with ran a two-handed store in Bodfish. I can't remember his name but I will never forget his idiosyncrasy of using an ink pen to stencil on his mustache. The Ross was a beautiful rifle. It was used by the Canadian armed forces. But the stock needed refinishing and I removed it intending to take it to school and do the work in the woodshop.

The old fellow I got it from only had a single round for it and I had chambered it and, forgottenly, left it in after removing the stock. It was early morning and, as my grandparents were finishing breakfast, I was seated by our old piano with the gun between my legs, muzzle against the floor, examining it without the stock. Unthinkingly, I hit the trigger with my left index finger and the gun went off with a deafening roar in the cabin. Something struck my right hand with terrific force. I felt something hit my left hand and face as well. The unexpected and mind-numbing explosion transfixed my grandparents. There are few experiences to equal the sound and concussion of a large caliber rifle in close quarters with your morning coffee.

I watched in fascination as the palm of my right hand turned all the colors of the rainbow settling on an ugly, yellowish purple. The back of my left hand was covered with a black crust that began to slowly ooze blood droplets. My face also had been powder-burned and a few grains had penetrated my eyes. I can still see a couple if I look closely, even today.

A book I was to read years later, Fate Is the Hunter, tells of the extraordinary chain of circumstances that leads up to a nearly disastrous airplane crash. As I later examined the rifle, I was to discover exactly what had happened and why this was to be one of the most fortunate accidents of my life; life-saving in fact. I discovered that the bolt of the rifle could be disassembled and reassembled incorrectly. Since the Ross was a straight-pull action design, if you reassembled it incorrectly, the locking- lugs that kept the explosion of the cartridge properly contained, would not engage. The entire force of the explosion would then blow the bolt back into the face of anyone firing the weapon, the firing pin assembly passing through the eye and brain of the shooter.

Had I fixed the stock of the rifle, assembled it and actually shot it, I would not be writing this account. The National Rifleman, just two months later, had a feature article outlining just what I had discovered for myself. The story related that some 200 Canadian soldiers had been killed in just this manner in using the gun.

The bolt of the rifle accounted for the injury to my right hand. I never recovered the firing pin assembly as it had gone through the roof of the cabin. My left hand had received the burning powder and gasses that had ruptured the base of the cartridge case. Some small amount of these had sprinkled my face as well. I sported a patch over my right eye for a while and felt quite the romantic figure (remember Brenda Star's sweetheart?).

The kids at school were fascinated by the incident as you can well imagine. But teenagers are immortal and there was never any sense of what I had actually escaped. I have the ruptured cartridge case to this very day, however, as a curious reminder of things inexplicable and how, at any time, circumstances can change things in sudden, drastic and incredible, even fatal ways. Since I had not taken the bolt of the rifle apart myself, I received it in this deadly condition. I have often wondered about the possibilities. Who had done this and why did some dumb kid have a lucky accident thus possibly preventing a tragedy? Ecclesiastes 9:11: *Time and chance happeneth to all alike.*

Having thus learned several things of value by this episode with the Ross, I decided to try the shotgun I had gotten in a "safe and sane" manner. I did know enough at this time to realize that the peculiar pattern on the barrels of the gun might mean that they were of Damascus manufacture and, therefore, unsafe with modern smokeless powder ammunition. Having nearly precipitated a couple of heart attacks by my earlier exploit and being kind and thoughtful by nature, I waited until my grandparents absented themselves before conducting my latest experiment in explosive devices.

The plan was simple. I loaded the old piece with low base bird shot and secured it to a table outside the cabin. I theorized that, unlike a rifle or pistol, a shotgun would make more than a neat, round hole in the cabin. Also, only a real idiot would fire a gun in a house, right? I then tied a string to one of the triggers and, cocking the hammers (I have often asked myself why I cocked both of them?) I proceeded to a safe position behind a big, old digger pine tree. A louder explosion than I would have expected of a single round of birdshot followed my tug on the string.

Sure enough, when I walked over to inspect the project, both barrels had gone off simultaneously. The breech of the gun was cocked slightly open and one hammer blown off by the force of the double explosion. Like the .303 case, I have managed to hang onto this old wall-hanger over the many years since (*sans* one hammer).

***

It is well known among the educated that the schools of education are an embarrassment and a laughing stock on university campuses. No wonder, since the educational establishment is typically made up of people that have no practical knowledge of real world skills or the needs of Industry they do what they do best: engage in fairyland curriculum.

This reminds me of the time the skunk went off in our cabin one night. Probably the only time I had neglected to put our old hound, Tippy, out before going to bed. I never forgot again.

It was wintertime. We had added a room to one of the old shacks that served as kitchen, living room and my bedroom. This was nice since the fireplace and wood cook stove were in this room, a reward for my labors as supplier of fuel.

One night I heard a noise and using the flashlight I kept handy discovered a skunk had gained entrance and was looking for food scraps. As any child, I was entranced by the idea of having my very own pet skunk. Thereafter, I purposely left scraps out for my secret nocturnal visitor (why should I tell my grandparents? Somehow I sensed they might disapprove). Now, the night I forgot to put Tippy out.

While we didn't see the skunk right away, it didn't take imagination to know what had happened. The smell was horrendous and a smoky, blue haze hung in the air. The point is that both the skunk and the dog had done what was natural to both. And when you mix them the outcome is easily predictable.

My grandfather was not happy about my secret visitor. He, in fact, exhibited a very uncharitable attitude toward skunks in general and my skunk in particular. So prejudicial was he, in fact, that he set about immediately planning my pet's demise. His nefarious plan was to set out cyanide-laced sardines for the skunk.

However, the skunk, probably miffed by the dog's unwillingness to be friendly, did not return. But grandad's plan did bear fruit. A few days later I discovered our pet cat stretched out stiffer than a board. I missed the cat.

There are several applications of the story to education. Our young people, parents and industry are paying the price for the skunk. The innocent, the cat, only saw a good meal. All I wanted was a pet skunk. But in befriending the skunk, I was directly to blame for an odor that lasted for weeks and, indirectly, the untimely decease of a good cat.

By apathy, greed, egotism, selfishness, too-busyness, naivete, we have allowed the educational establishment to have its own way and that way has led to an illiterate America. Certainly our civil leadership from the President on down share in the abysmal failure of education, but we get the kind of leadership we actively support.

It is not a skunk's nature to cooperate with our best interests. And if you forget to put the dog out, you precipitate crises of your own making, good intentions notwithstanding. And the cat dies.

CHAPTER TWO

This is Christmas time as I write. Fewer will celebrate the occasion in the manner they did as children. Harsh, economic realities confront us at every turn. And, of course, as a Storyteller at Large, thereby hangs a tale.

Children have been cheated of childhood in our generation. TV has supplanted reading and radio shows that allowed (demanded) the use of our most remarkable ability: imagination. And where are the people, parents and grandparents that so very much inspired children of a past generation by reading to them and telling them stories?

Without being able to exercise their imagination because of being spoonfed so- called entertainment *via* TV, children not only get fat they are easily bored and fall prey to getting into trouble. The poor excuses for toys that require no ability or challenge other than pushing buttons are a travesty. And cute as they may be, how many stuffed animals contribute to a child's learning and self-- esteem? A few stuffed "friends" are invaluable to a child, but too many is too many.

In fact, many children are being taught to be selfish and acquisitive, possessive, by their parents buying them off through multiplying "things" as if a room full of things is proof of a parent's care. A child knows better. But the message is clear: getting and having, multiplying material possessions is important.

In lieu of time with a child how much easier to simply buy another toy for the shelf, deluding yourself that you have shown a child that you care. God forbid! that you buy something that will take your time to show them how to construct something of real value, both in the building and finished product.

But we live in a culture that no longer can hand a hammer and saw to a child and teach them to build. No longer are we able to give them chores that, like tending the livestock and vegetable garden, contribute to the family table and teach the responsibility that the demands of such enterprises brings. Somehow, feeding the resident hamster or family dog or cat, putting dishes in the dishwasher or taking out the trash don't teach the necessary values.

So many of the young that our headlines herald being in want are not poor in material things alone, they are poor in spirit as well and, too often, without hope of anything better in their future. They are not only illiterate in the academic sense; they are ignorant of the things that give real value to life.

My brother, Dee Dee, (Ronald) and I called our grandmother *Tody*. I don't know why unless it was because she was so fat. My grandparents were in an auto-train accident. As a result, our grandmother swole up something fierce, to the degree that she was able to play the part of a Fat Lady in a circus and our grandfather was a Barker.

On our first day of school, dear old Mt. Vernon in East Bakersfield, Dee Dee was crying for his Tody which prompted the teacher to ask my grandfather if he couldn't let my brother bring this favorite toy of his to school the next day. Grandad, of course, declined.

I should point out that ours was not an average American home, not even in 30s and 40s Little Oklahoma. Our father left us when I was 3 and my brother 2. We never saw him again. When we got older and learned to know our mother the idea didn't seem to be such a bad one. Of course, any man that runs off from his responsibility toward children is contemptible but our mother was a real pistol.

Not that we didn't love her or she us. But her violent temper and threats to kill us occasioned by such lapses in our behavior like washing her toaster, waffle iron, clock and iron in the bathtub or cleaning the toilet with her toothbrush left us, often, in fear of our lives. My brother and I thus became very close as companions in fear when we were with our mother. The threat of death does draw people together so, if you are having trouble with your children, maybe you haven't tried this method yet.

Because of her numerous marriages, some carping critics (our grandparents) might consider our mother incapable of a firm commitment to a life partner; even a little promiscuous. Her efforts to marry into each branch of the service did provide us with a lot of war stories and different versions of how the war was being fought. There was some confusion over the fact that while "fathers" changed frequently, our grandparents remained the same.

I have often thought that our mother's rather heterodox marriage pattern added a somewhat different dimension to my brother's and my perspective of life. Certainly if a child has a nightmare and calls out for Daddy and rightly expects a stampede to assistance, he has little to fear from the lesser monsters inhabiting a dark bedroom. But this is not the only advantage our mother gave us. My spelling was much improved by having to master so many names (Pospieszynski was a real challenge).

My grandparents were not prejudiced, but the neighborhood? Whew! In fact, while my grandfather was born in the Oklahoma Indian Territory and raised in Arkansas, he escaped the ignorant and hurtful prejudice so common in those states back then. On the other hand, because he chose to marry a Blue-bellied Yankee, his mother did not speak to him to her dying day. Thus grandad rebelled against his Southern heritage and married outside the Confederacy.

Our great- grandmother was indeed a *Grand Mother*. She was grand in everything and my brother and I loved her dearly. She was a rebel of her time, being trained as a nurse and well educated. She was also a divorcee, which in those days showed a rare individualism and lack of concern with the mores of her day.

She made no secret of the fact that she married the second time for money. Unfortunately, the man had lied to her about his financial situation in order to get her to marry him. When he died, she lived with our grandparents and never remarried. God had apparently taught her a lesson.

Some of my fondest memories are of our great-grandmother reading to my brother and me. She made the stories come alive to us. I can still visualize *Tugboat Annie* and others from her reading stories from the old Saturday Evening Post and Collier's.

Children of my day had radio as a primary, entertainment media. While we always looked forward to the Sunday Funnies, and, on rare occasions, a trip to the Cartoon Matinee in Bakersfield (imagine watching two hours of great cartoons for ten cents?), it was radio that really gave us the skill to imagine.

We grew up on Captain Midnight, Jack Armstrong, the All-American Boy, Terry and the Pirates, Tom Mix, Inner Sanctum, The Cisco Kid, The Whistler, I Love a Mystery, Corliss Archer, Henry Aldrich, Lum and Abner, Duffy's Tavern, Charlie McCarthy, Baby Snooks, The Great Gildersleeve, The Life of Riley and so many more. When we moved to the mountains, we still had a battery powered Zenith radio and a wind-up gramophone for entertainment.

After we moved, some of the old programs were already passing away but I still remember Sam Spade, Mr. X, The Green Hornet, Mr. Keene, Tracer of Lost Persons, The FBI, Gang Busters, The Thin Man, The Sheriff Show, Fibber Magee and Molly, The Lone Ranger, Jack Benny, Can You Top This?, The Thin Man and so many others. Amazing how Batman, The Phantom, Mandrake the Magician and others have disappeared or changed. And how we enjoyed Li'l Abner; Al Capp sure had the number of politicians and religious charlatans.

While living on the mining claim, I tuned in a new radio show called Gunsmoke. It was unlike any other I had ever heard. Bob and Ray had already introduced a new format in humor, almost Phil Harris-like, but here was drama of an almost existential form.

The TV series was nothing like the beginning radio series. To me, looking back, it seems to have been the precursor of a very new concept in entertainment, requiring great attention to understanding a psychic plot. It was a very mysterious show to a child used to the usual, predictable and straightforward Lone Ranger format. Life was simple back then but complications were on the horizon, and the early Gunsmoke was an adumbration of these things for us children; but, back to my own plot.

My grandparents were a treasure trove of folklore and turn of the century knowledge. My grandparents had one of the first marriages performed by telephone. Grandad had enlisted in the army after leaving home at the age of 12. At 14, he joined up by lying about his age (he was truly large for his age and got away with it) and stayed in the service until a cannon ran over one leg giving him a disability discharge.

While in the army, he met my grandmother and they decided to get married. But, as the day approached, the camp (Camp Beauragarde) was placed in quarantine leading to the novel arrangement via a local judge, the governor and the camp commander.

In a curious way, my brother and I were raised a generation behind most of our age. Our grandparents were relatively young due to their marrying early in life and our mother marrying so young as well.

It was common to our Bakersfield community to live without electricity and indoor plumbing. Hand-dug wells were used for water. When electricity arrived at Little Oklahoma, ours was one of the first places to be electrified. This was due to the fact that grandad was a Jack-of-all-trades and could do house wiring himself.

The house was of simple construction (salvaged boxcar and coffin shipping crates, tarpaper, etc.). An interesting way of cleaning the kitchen floor was to simply swamp and mop, the water draining through the cracks in the boards. The combined smells of the wet wood and moist earth were marvelous, honest odors.

Washday was a communal effort in those days in Little Oklahoma. Some of the neighbor ladies would come to our place and fires would be built. Galvanized wash tubs would be placed over the fires, propped up on rocks or bricks.

Once the water was boiling, lye soap (Do any of you remember a song Grandma's Lye Soap?) and Mrs. Worth's Bluing, for white things, were added. The clothes were then placed in the tubs and constantly stirred with broom handles as the clothes boiled.

There was a festive air and the gossip flowed around us children as we played. The smell of fresh washing was pleasant to us. Once the clothes were properly boiled, the women would place them in another tub of lukewarm water for scrubbing on washboards. The final wash was a rinse in a tub of clean, cold water.

After the wash was done, the ladies would go their respective ways to hang it to dry. Looking back on it, I know that all this was a hard chore. But it seems that everyone enjoyed getting together and making it fun, especially for us children.

Grass was for cows and goats in our neighborhood, not lawns or for smoking. Over time, a few scraggly lawns appeared here and there, a few women tended plants of some variety and, of course, there were *Victory Gardens* all during WWII. But the necessities of living precluded any attempts at finery, either in housing or dress. Feed and flour sacks were common clothing material for men, women and children.

Our little Dust Bowl church, built by my grandfather, was the focal point of the community. Christmas was an especially grand time for us as children because the only toys some of the local children would receive would be through the church.

My grandparents would gather contributions from some of the Bakersfield merchants for distribution to Little Oklahoma children as well as for the Negro children across the tracks to the north of our community. Owens Toy Store was most generous. My brother and I spent many glorious moments at this wonderful treasure house with more toys than you thought could exist apart from Santa's North Pole. Any trip to the city was incomplete without us visiting this fabulous place.

I remember one Christmas, before the church was built, my grandfather dressing as Santa (though, of course, I didn't realize it was him at the time) and having the neighborhood children come to our house for gifts. It was a particularly bad winter that year, and they could be cruel in Bakersfield with bitter cold. But the children came, some without shoes, to receive their gifts. I'm sure God was pleased and honored more by this act of my grandparents than by many of the sermons that were preached in His Name.

I recall that grandad, in an attempt to help some of the older children avoid a life of crime, tried to get a youth group started. He was even able by his association with the Sheriff's department to obtain a few films and projector to show some movies. These invariably were morality plays that showed crime did not pay. How times have changed.

***

It is beautiful here in the mountains that I have come to love. The air is clear and at night you can still see the Milky Way, a profusion of stars in such glorious splendor as to leave one speechless in awe. A major distraction is the number of satellites passing overhead. Last night I counted six of them.

I love seeing shooting stars, but somehow these machines of men leave me somewhat unsettled in my mind.

When I was eleven years old, my grandparents, with whom I lived, moved from Bakersfield to Kernville. Actually, we moved to a mining claim my grandfather had acquired in return for a loan a country singer named O'Dell Johnson couldn't pay back. The only song I remember of Mr. Johnson's was Kernville California U.S.A. The only line of the song I remember is: "Snow capped mountains, ripplin streams, it's not heaven though it seems, in Kernville California U.S.A." A real toe-tapper.

The claim consisted of two, one room tarpapered shacks, a hand-dug well, and an open ditch called a *placer*, which justified it being called a "mining claim." Kernville was a thriving metropolis of 115 souls and four miles south was the little burg of Isabella, pop. 36. But Isabella had its very own mad scientist; complete with live-in housekeeper who had a boy named Larry (yes, that Larry of the Piute Bigfoot story). Larry and I became friends and this gave me enviable access to the peculiar goings on in the home.

The one decided detraction of the living conditions on the claim was the fact that electricity was non-existent (as was in-door plumbing). This meant that all heating and cooking was done on the wood stove and in the fireplace. My grandfather actually added the fireplace at a latter date.

Under such conditions, the *Saturday Night Bath* was no joke, particularly in the winter. Imagine a wash tub (clothes type) and heating water on a wood stove. Yes, the washtub and scrub board were grim realities of a pioneer lifestyle.

My grandfather was the hero of my life. But he had the preposterous notion that an eleven-year-old boy should have the sole responsibility for all the wood needed to cook and heat. While other children dreamed of bicycles, I dreamed of a chain saw. I never got one. If any of you have ever had to fell trees, saw them up and split the logs by hand with a maul and wedge, you will readily sympathize with my plight. I learned that a two- man saw worked just fine with just one boy and how to keep the pine resin cleaned off with a rag stuck in a bottle of coal oil (we never called it kerosene). Not knowing of Molotov Cocktails or needing them, coal oil was always handy since oil lamps were all we had for lighting. I also had the responsibility for cleaning the chimneys, trimming the wicks and filling the lamps.

Sam Clemens had the Mississippi; I had thousands of acres of the Sequoia National Forest as my private playground. Having been raised without the mind-stultifying effects of television and having the benefit of a background of Zane Gray, Swiss Family Robinson, The Last of the Mohicans, Robinson Crusoe, Saturday Evening Post and Colliers (1940's editions), National Geographic, and a great-grandmother that still remembered covered wagons and how the West was won, my imagination found fertile soil in the wilderness of those days.

Such was life in my forest fastness that every summer I slept outdoors under the pines. There is still no greater music than the wind sighing softly through pine needles. I would go to sleep looking up through the branches of a great old pine tree at the stars and lulled by my own, private, heavenly choir. Nor was there ever a need or thought of locked doors or crazies roaming about.

While guns were a natural part of life in the country, they were for hunting and predators, not for protection. I had my first re-loading outfit at age 14. I bought it from Guy Shultz, the local, elementary school bus driver, custodian and *Dollar a Year Man* (Fish and Game). Mr. Wallace was then the elementary principal/junior high teacher. When I became a freshman, Mr. Wallace and Guy gave me the job as the very first junior custodian for the school. I was a mean man with a broom and did my best to justify their faith in me.

I have always wished I could have provided such a Tom Sawyer and Huck Finn environment for my own children. The Kern River with its glorious wildness before the dam was built traced its way through the valley. Sloughs were home to abundant wildlife including Bullfrogs (best eating in the world), catfish, birds of every description and even deer.

It was a wondrous thing to come across undisturbed Indian camp and burial grounds, to imagine yourself the first white man to set foot on ancestral paths. Such was childish imagination, but how real it could be to a boy in such an environment.

But the point of my reminiscences begins, properly, in Weedpatch, CA. Not many people can say (or would want to) that they were born in Weedpatch, but I have a birth certificate to prove it. My one claim to fame.

I was born on a farm (Cotton patch), in a society of Dust Bowl immigrants known as Okies. Actually, My grandad was the qualified Okie and my grandmother (maternal) was a Blue-bellied Yankee. My grandfather's mother disowned him for this moral lapse and did not speak to him to her dying day as I have already mentioned.

Sometime after my third birthday, my brother was two, our father left us and we never saw him again. It was years later that I came to know my mother well enough to stop blaming him. Don't misunderstand me, I loved my mother but she went through several men before she found one, a wonderful man named Kenneth Bergstrom that could stick it out with her. She was beautiful but had a violent temper. But to this day I have no use for a parent that can simply leave their children and show no concern for their welfare.

Shortly thereafter, we moved to the corner of Cottonwood and Padre in Southeast Bakersfield, an area that carried the designation of "Little Oklahoma," settled and inhabited by (according to my grandparents) White trash and every Okie and Arkie on the lam, dirt roads and tarpaper shacks. Just across the railroad tracks (really) and North of us was the community of "Nigger Town." My grandad was one of the very few Caucasians ever accepted in that area. This because it was recognized that he was not prejudiced, even though he always said *Nigger* as a cultural expression and he was a Pentecostal preacher and jack-of-all-trades. My grandad's religion and character were color-blind, unlike many of his heritage.

Of course grandad had proven his own lack of cultural discernment and pride in the South by marrying a Northerner. It was not too surprising that he should carry his fault over to a distinct lack of any real prejudice or bigotry. He was not the stuff of a good Klansman.

Grandad's statement "God never made a beggar out of any man or His church" was accompanied with a box at the front of the pulpit and donations could be placed in that for the poor. Grandad and grandma worked regularly and hard, and took nothing for themselves from the church.

Since he built the church himself on his own property and was the sole arbiter of its function, he could pretty well call the shots. Grandma's piano playing and grandad's thunderous, hellfire and damnation preaching made them a dynamic duo. It should be pointed out that in such a culture and environment, the church was the only game in town when it came to social function. Few people had cars, the war was on, and there was no television or movie house. Greater Bakersfield with all its cultural amenities was far away, by foot for most folks.

It was fortunate for my brother and I that we were blessed with a mother, a great-grandmother and grandparents that were literate and intelligent. Schooling and reading were made important to us. But those of us old enough to remember the years of WWII as children will remember how thoroughly propagandized we were through the comic books and movies. With Superman, Captains Marvel and America, Humphrey Bogart and George Raft teaching us about the rotten Japs and stinkin' Knocksies (no child my age called them Nazis), our games were as apt to be killing the enemies of Democracy as playing cowboys and Indians.

A real drawback of the war for us boys was the fact that though you could get caps, you could not get new cap guns. Even inner tubes went to the war effort so getting rubber bands made of these for our wood guns designed to shoot them were hard to come by. Slingshots (in Little Oklahoma, properly southeast Bakersfield, in those days the slingshots were called by an ethnic epithet) were in very short supply.

It is the license of advancing age to think of the past as better than the present, to say "The old days were better," but it cannot be gainsaid that we older ones had a simpler time of it. There is also a very basic wisdom in the command that "Thou shalt not remove the ancient landmarks which thy fathers have set!"

It is also the purview of age to skip around, to ramble in reverie and forget with convenient memory, a blessing of time passing, how very harsh life could be without many of the blessings of technology mixed as they are. I would not willingly give up the wonder of flipping a switch for light and heat, nor would I trade my tap for a well with hand pump and bucket. Certainly, none of my age misses the inconvenience and stench of the old privy.

But I do admit to wishing there were more of the people that seemed to be around in time gone by; people to whom a good name was important, and a handshake was a bona fide contract. I miss the simple verities of being able to tell who the bad guys were and the black and white issues that stealing was wrong and liars were going to hell. It seems that heroes were easier to come by and identify with in that time not long past. They helped the down and out, they came to the rescue of the weak and helpless (Who was that masked man?).

Right was right and wrong was wrong. Preachers, teachers and policemen were our friends. The president was our trusted leader and our country was the ideal for an oppressed society anywhere else in the world. The Statue of Liberty stood tall and George Washington was not a liar.

I admit to being an embarrassment to my learned colleagues, those like myself with the alphabet after their names. But like a great old man, Vance Havner, I prefer Plain Vanilla. Maybe Weedpatch, Little Oklahoma and Sequoia Forest will forever prejudice me. No amount of quoting the ancient Greek philosophers will make this generation the same as those gone by. There is a difference in the music to which our young people dance. There is a difference in the amount and complexity of evil that threatens them. There is a clear warning of that generation without natural affection that presages the end, an end that carries the unmistakable hallmark of hopelessness.

The rugged mountains, the desert's sere vastness, and a clear, swift trout stream with a star-spangled canopy overhead, the critters of the deserts and forests are still my main attractions. These marvels continue to keep the best part of the miracle of childhood alive in me, to keep things in their proper perspective and priority. Perhaps the cities, while exciting in their own right, are in such chaos because city-dwellers lose sight of these things. Many children, sadly, have never experienced a smogless day or night, have never seen a live trout stream. I will never forget one young man I had taken camping putting his finger in a small stream and asking me: "Is this real water?" I didn't laugh. I understood.

***

When I was attending high school in the mountains, I played in the orchestra and band (clarinet and tenor sax). I love music.

The best hourly money I ever made at this time was playing, with Billy Mills at trumpet, for the dances at the Southfork Community Hall. Imagine! Three dollars an hour for doing something you loved to do? Fantastic! And I only made a dollar an hour at hard, manual labor (grandad was quite insistent that I engage in this kind of activity. And no, I never received any allowance or pay for the chores which were considered my duty to do. I scrounged for paying jobs wherever I could).

Billy was the son of the principal, but I had a car and he didn't; in fact I was the only boy in our high school that had his own car at that time. So, I provided transportation and the principal looked the other way at the fact that I didn't have either a driver's license or insurance. Of course, in those days many adults in our area didn't have either of these niceties of big city living.

The music of the forties and fifties was indeed music, not the cacophony of noise prevalent today. I excelled in Ballroom music suited to the clarinet, while the tenor sax was just plain fun to play.

At that time, I was driving a '38 Pontiac which deserves more attention later. I will say that my grandad was an excellent jack-of-all-trades but the automobile remained a mystery to him. Consequently, I had to learn the auto mechanic trade the hard way- by simply *doing*. A '28 Buick, a '29 Ford, a '36 Plymouth, '38 and '39 Pontiacs together with a hodgepodge of tools, a chain-fall and a huge pine tree and true grit gave me a realistic start on the mechanic trade.

Billy and I were returning from a gig on the newly opened stretch of highway between Southfork and Isabella. It was quite late and very dark. As I came around a bend in the highway where it cut through a hill, the banks ascending steeply on both sides there stood a cow broadside across the middle of the road!

To this day I do not know how I avoided plowing into the critter. There just wasn't room enough to go around either side of the animal, or so it seemed. But I did. The remarkable reflexes and coordination of youth. And guardian angels?

Turning to look at Billy, I found the seat next to me empty; he had disappeared into thin air. And then, slowly I saw a head with the largest pair of eyeballs I have ever seen begin to appear in the rear view mirror from behind the seat. He had moved so quickly while I was busy trying to prevent hamburger all over my grill that I had not even seen him move! We never know what extraordinary feats we are capable of until the exigency arises as per the saying: "Heroes are made, not born."

I took up guitar late in life. I still enjoy it but finally sold my Gretcsh Chet Atkins after many years; the inability to chord with an injured left hand (gratis an uninsured teenager and his pulling out in front of me without looking when I was riding a motorcycle. I have always wished I had been on a big hog so I could have reciprocated some of the damage that he did me). The kid was fined $17.00 for not having a driver's license or insurance and failure to yield the right of way. I spent a long time in the hospital and on crutches waiting for bones to knit, losing several thousand dollars in the process. I have always wondered what the fine would have been if he had killed me? Probably $17.50.

The moral of the story and a commentary on the system is that if you are going to be nearly killed in an accident, pick out someone with plenty to lose. My mistake was choosing the usual dead-beat with nothing and whose parents were even worse. The problem is that you, of course, cannot plan such things. And the deadbeats quickly learn that the system makes only responsible people pay. And, of course, the tragedy of drunk drivers will remain a curse until a pragmatic approach is taken to getting them off the road. How about hanging anyone convicted of murdering someone as a result of their drinking and driving?

Really got sidetracked on that one; I was talking about music.

When I first got started on clarinet, I discovered that to really become a musician took long hours of daily practice. That's a lot of self-discipline for a kid; and especially hard on my grandparents since they had to contend with all that noise of my running scales.

But, when I first performed with our little orchestra at the old Kernville Elementary school, grandad nearly busted with pride. He said: "You know, your practicing nearly drove me crazy but tonight made it all worthwhile," high praise from grandad and much needed encouragement for me.

It reminds me of the time I beat everyone in the 880 at home and Bakersfield. No one could come close to me in distance races. But I never mentioned the medals I won to grandad. I didn't want to appear to be bragging. That says something about the way I was raised. When grandad learned of it from others, he asked why I hadn't told him. I really didn't know how to answer him.

We have lost something vital in our society that used to make sense of personal accomplishment without the need of praise or monetary return. I still remember when it felt good to be a skilled craftsman.

As a machinist and tool and die maker, I thought it a matter of personal pride in doing a superior job, not for a raise or the plaudits of the foreman, but for the feeling of personal satisfaction, self-worth and self-esteem. I know these old-world values have been supplanted by an evil system that rewards incompetence and sloth. But I do miss them and the world was a better place when men and women could take justifiable pride in their work.

***

We have a storm system moving through our valley right now. The weather is turning cold and the leaves are bright and variegated colors. The clouds make marvelous shadows, dappling the mountains. The scent of a wood fire is mingled with that of the outdoor freshness of pine. It is hard not to reflect on how much has been lost to our children by the cruelties inflicted upon them.

The Ballroom music, Jazz, Dixieland, Rhythm and Blues and Fifties R & R has been supplanted by noise glorifying murder, suicide, rape, the most vulgar profanity and all manner of violence. And music is mood setting and altering.

Clark Gable is gone but his *damn* lingers on in the most savage obscenities and visual orgies of sex and violence by TV in every living room of the country. The senses of even those thinking themselves good Christians are jaded to the point of accepting the most outrageous things in both homes and churches that would have meant church expulsion scant years ago.

If I took the time to do so, I would weep for our children and nation. But I am too busy trying to do something about the situation. But even Jesus had to depart, from time to time, to some private place to keep his head together and on track.

My special need is to walk the wilderness areas, to hear the sound of the night creatures' rustle and flutter, to smell the scents of pine or sagebrush, to see the sun rise and set and the moon casting its light over unspoiled vistas, to contemplate the stars and hear the sound of the wind through the pine needles. I need the occasional sight of a waterfall through rugged granite into sparkling, crystal pools where I can see trout lazing about.

How beautiful Heaven must be. How I wish the children of the world could see the marvels I have been blessed with seeing. I can close my eyes and be there in an instant, in reality. My imagination and memory can evoke images that I have experienced, not the poor plastic, phosphor, or celluloid imitations that are the lot of most.

And the beauties of language! To recall Shakespeare, Thackeray, and a hundred others, to be able to have had the time, and ability, to devour and appreciate great art, literature, and poetry; to remember Henry, Clarke, Bacon and so many others.

But an age dooming itself by a materialistic selfishness and inability to deal honestly and pragmatically with its problems, unable to administer justice and care for its young, a society that rewards sloth and lawlessness cannot hope for poets, scientists, philosophers and artists. Like the Great Whore and Babylon of Revelation, the smoke of our nation may well rise to the lament of all other nations of the world. For who will buy their goods and services when we are gone? Who will hold a torch for life, liberty, and the pursuit of happiness in our absence?

***

It certainly doesn't help when the children see their parents in an adversarial confrontation in divorce court, often accusing each other of every heinous thing in the book. It is now common to use the charge of child molestation and abuse in an attempt to "help" the children. And, of course, there are the ever present experts (psychologists, et al.) adding their muddy conceptions to the mess. And who really cares for children anymore? This is a no-win situation, as is trying to recover damages from riff raff. What are we told? Get insurance. And what do you insure against; every contingency? With the deductibles, forget it. You would bankrupt yourself on the premiums.

I suppose these are the things that got me to thinking about Privies. Grandad really knew how to go first class when it came to building privies; you know, *out-houses*. The one on the mining claim was a masterpiece. It had a hinged seat, which you could lift to check for Black Widows before doing your business.

It was also large enough to accommodate tools as well. And, yes, slick paged, Sears and Sawbuck together with Monkey Wards was in supply. Corn was not grown locally. Care of an outhouse was simple. You threw a small amount of lime on the pile occasionally to keep the smell down and kill the maggots and that was it. A real water-saver, but sure cold in the winter; no one wasted time then sitting and dreaming of riches.

I recall one night when I looked out the back of the cabin and saw a Great Horned Owl perched on the roof of the privy. Grabbing the .410, grandad proceeded to blow the critter off his perch. Grandad had no truck with owls and one had just killed one of our turkeys the other night. Bringing the varmint into the cabin, he stretched it out on the hearth of the fireplace. It had a wingspread of about four feet, a magnificent bird (no, I would never dream of shooting one today). Because an owl had killed our turkey, grandad thought about the possibility of cooking up the owl. Seemed plausible to me, and I never questioned grandad's judgment; besides, it was an intriguing concept.

I'd never heard of anyone doing such a thing and I could see myself as the envy of my friends when I would tell them: "Hey, them owls is good eatin'."

As grandad and I discussed the proper procedures for cooking the deceased, nocturnal raptor, grandma was of a different mind. She spoiled our plan by pointing out the fact that owls were scavengers like buzzards and ground squirrels. And who would even consider eating them? But had grandma not been there and intervened? I wonder to this day if I might have missed one of life's culinary pleasures.

The .410 was a handy gun. Being full choke, it was difficult for wing shooting quail but fun to shoot. It was always kept handy for all around use against various varmints including the wild donkeys. Yes, in the old days on the claim we had to contend with a herd of wild donkeys. They were particularly attracted to the alfalfa we kept for the rabbits. They would come in at night and kick the rabbit hutches over to get at the feed. When we would hear them, out came the .410 and we would scatter the herd.

One night grandad hearing a noise out around the cages grabbed the .410 and, easing himself outside, saw a large shape squatting on one of the hutches. Thinking it might be an owl or bobcat, he let fly. The shape disappeared in the hail of shot and grandad grabbed the flashlight to examine his handiwork only to discover he had killed a gallon jug of coal oil. It took a while to clean off the rabbits that had been unexpectedly drenched in the middle of the night and grandma had a few opinions on grandad's ability to distinguish between bobcats and jugs.

I did get even with the donkey's one day. We seldom ever saw them during daylight around the place. I have no idea where they would disappear to, but one day while out with my .22 I chanced upon one of them out in the open. Only being equipped with .22 shorts that day I took aim and shot the beast in the rump. The donkey simply kicked his back leg as though the small bullet had no more effect than a fly. I shot again. Same result. The donkey continued to browse as though nothing was happening.

I must have shot him seven or eight times before giving up. But the next day, some men with a truck were seen in the area and I wandered over where I had seen them go. They were heading toward the spot where I had left the donkey. Keeping out of sight among the trees, I saw them loading a dead donkey onto the truck. I can only surmise the varmint died of lead poisoning.

Where are the great humorists when we need them so badly? We all have those *midnights's of the soul* as my old friend and mentor Dr. Charles Feinberg called them. But too many people I know personally are suffering them lately. Maybe that is why I try to intrude humor wherever possible now. It does seem that life was a lot simpler not long ago.

We had a hand dug well in Boulder Gulch. Have any of you ever heard of keeping catfish in your well to help keep it clean? Grandad swore by this and it was my happy task to supply the fish. While I didn't mind the catfish, toads would often get in also and had to be cleaned out periodically. This led to my drinking a lot of milk and coffee. The stratum was decomposed granite (DG to the cognizanti) and we had a shallow water table. Consequently, the well was only about 14 feet deep. This certainly helped as we had to use a hand pump to get water and they don't work at any real depth.

But one summer we had a drought and had to resort to hauling water from the canal about a mile away. Grandad and I soon tired of this task and he decided to deepen the well. He hit upon using dynamite as the quickest and easiest expedient for the job. Having the stuff on hand for the mining claim, we soon had our holes drilled, packed in the dynamite and proceeded to blow it out. Things went well but it was a huge job hauling the debris up from the deepened well. We did manage to hit water again and we were back in business.

Now you can't do this in L.A. I understand. Not that dynamite is in short supply, but it seems the city is not only opposed to your digging or drilling your own well in your backyard, they are fussy about who has and uses dynamite locally.

This reminds me of the time my great-grandmother was going to teach Dee Dee and me about the evils and dangers of firecrackers. Where the explosive devices came from I'm not sure. I suspect grandad had something to do with that. In any event, she had one of the infernal machines and with great fanfare about the possible loss of eyes and limbs, proceeded to light one off to demonstrate their destructive capacity. Unhappily, she planned to do this in the kitchen and toss it outside to explode (playing with explosives in the house must be in the family genes).

Now I do not know who latched the screen door. But I do know Great-grandma had not checked to see if it was unlatched. With my brother and me dutifully watching her demonstration, the sparking fuse of the firecracker in her hand mesmerized us as she struggled with the latch. We were fully appreciative of the look of seriousness on her face as we began to realize something was amiss. Great-grandma had a bad back and hip and walked with a cane. Consequently, Dee Dee and I had never known that there was such alacrity in her old body. Nor were we ever treated to her terpsichorean repertory. In other words, we had never seen her dance before. But suddenly, an otherwise unknown facet of her personality and agility was displayed in a fashion to rival an Irish Jig Master with a pocketful of bees.

Finally succeeding in getting the screen door open, she threw the sparking firecracker out when it exploded not more than two inches from her hand. My brother and I were suitably impressed by this demonstration and were very careful thereafter to: One: Try to keep firecrackers away from Great-grandma. Two: Not to let her catch us playing with them.

***

It was summer time and I had been out hunting. It was nearly dark when I got back to the cabin and my grandparents were away so the lamps had not been lit. I was barefoot as usual and, upon entering the cabin, my foot came right smack down on the middle of a snake. All I remember is the feel of the poor reptile's sudden muscular jerking coiling under my foot. I don't remember leaving the cabin, let alone how I went through the door. All I know is I was magically outside the place instantly as though I had been tele-transported.

Once my heart started up again, I lighted a pine torch and went back inside. There was no sign of the snake, so, lighting the coal oil lamp I doused my torch and made a careful survey of the cabin. Looking back on the episode, I know the snake had to have been at least as surprised as I was. But the serpent probably didn't have the propensity for heart failure.

This world is full of snakes (not only ordinary crooks and those that abuse children, but some wearing long black robes and some holding high political office), and it behooves us to tread through its darkness properly shod and light in hand.

Having been, among other things, an auto shop teacher, I have always equated MD's and mechanics. They both diagnose and have the same stock phrase to give you: "Let's try this and see if it works." In both cases you pay your money and take your chances. But the doctor, unlike the mechanic, gets to bury their mistakes. Therefore, mechanics have to be slightly more cautious. Both professions (and education) get away with malpractice because people have to trust those in such professions to an extraordinary degree. And through ignorance and forced trust on the part of the general population, unscrupulous men and women have the opportunity to take advantage.

It is sad that, after you have been around as long as I have, you feel like you are entering a room full of snakes when having to deal with many of these people. But you can shoot a snake. And, while some of these people need shooting, society still takes a dim view of judicial short cuts of this nature. Too bad though. Sure would save a lot of taxpayer money. And, it would probably encourage some of the idiots to do a better job or get out of the business. As usual, you come up with a simple answer to a complex problem and some wet blanket finds fault with it.

But, I fear the times ahead will cause people to start taking short cuts to justice. We can only stand for blatant abuse by corrupt politicians, doctors, lawyers, educators, thieves, etc. for so long. The time is fast approaching when the average citizen who is only talking about hanging and shooting will say, "Enough is enough!" and grab his rope and gun. It is both interesting and appalling to see how people respond to the violent, quick justice movies that abound. Bronson, Stallone, Norris, Seagal are far removed from the simplicity of the old John Wayne films, but they do play especially well to a thoroughly frustrated population.

As the leadership of *Let them eat cake* insulates itself more and more from the ugly realities of a vanishing middle class and the increasing population of those that are turning to crime as a viable alternative to making a legitimate living, it opens itself up to revolution and anarchy. Far too many of these leaders feel themselves safe from the wrath of an aroused populace, the Great Unwashed.

But Rambo and others are waiting in the wings; they simply need the right leadership and circumstances to take action. And then all hell is going to break loose!

***

We were just a bunch of dumb Okies in those simple days of Little Oklahoma. We took it for granted that our country would always stand, like Superman, for Truth, Justice, and The American Way. Our little church was a fun place and, as children, we felt secure in the simple lessons of David and Goliath, of Moses in the bulrushes. The Sermon on the Mount had a comforting relevance to our everyday lives and the Golden Rule was not sneered at. The old claim is now Boulder Gulch campground. But some of the huge, old boulders and a few of the great, old pines that used to sing me to sleep are still there. I go there sometimes when the camp is empty and reflect on those golden, magic times so long gone.

My grandmother and great-grandmother both died in the old cabin. Grandad passed away a few years ago. So much gone that made for love and security; that helped me believe in doing right no matter what others might do. How I wish I could have given all that was mine to my own children and the thousands of young people I have dealt with over the years. How I wish they had the security and love to dream and imagine a bright future for themselves.

CHAPTER THREE

I wonder why kids don't play marbles anymore? As a child in Little Oklahoma, I lived for shooting marbles. Any child worth his salt, to be acceptable in our company, had to have a good collection of Puries, Boulders and Stripies. A couple of Steelies had to be included as well. One had to be on the lookout for Doughies, only used by unscrupulous cheaters. How many of you remember the incantation: "Here's the river, here's the snake, here's where you make your big mistake!" while kneeling in the dirt, drawing the appropriate symbols to foil your opponent's shot? Or, do any of you remember throwing a marble over your shoulder in order to find a lost one? This was one of the hazards of playing chase.

In order to give the reader some idea of how serious I was about marbles, I came in second in the Bakersfield Championship in 1943. Such was the innocence of the times that a city could have a marble-playing championship for children while the world was plunged into war. Yes, there was a citywide championship for marbles. But, then, there was no such thing as TV or gangs of kids shooting bullets at each other. Shooting marbles was certainly preferable but, then, children had a chance to be children in those long ago, simple days.

I could read the papers, listen to Gabriel Heatter and Walter Winchell, hear news of battles over the radio, but bombs were not dropping on Little Oklahoma. Therefore, the War was an exciting and far-away thing, made real only by Superman and Captains Marvel and America doing battle against the rotten Japs and stinkin' Knocksies. Even Bugs Bunny was doing his part alongside John Wayne, Humphrey Bogart, and others.

There were the numerous military personnel in and about, the little flags in windows with blue stars indicating some loved one in the military (and, of course, an occasional tragic gold star, commemorating the ultimate sacrifice). We children could see AT-6s and an occasional P-38 overhead from Minter Field. Sometimes we were entertained by them engaging in mock combat. But God was sparing America from an enemy on our shores.

I remember another kid and I attempted a revival of playing marbles in high school at old Kern Valley High. But the times, they were a changin' and we met with little success. Too bad.

Cap and rubber band guns, marbles, slingshots, the good, warm, honest alkali dust under our bare feet. And there was a truly marvelous place called The Dump.

None of us had ever heard the word *Landfill* as children. The Dump was its progenitor. There were few as exciting places to visit as the Dump. Whenever grandad had to go to the Dump, I was quickly in the old, Ford pickup truck with him, all eagerness to explore this wonderful treasure trove of people's castoffs. Truly, one man's trash is another's treasure, but to us children it was all hidden riches only awaiting discovery.

I still remember the time I became wealthy as Croesus as a result of my finding an entire, dollar bill. Nothing escapes the sharp eye of a child. No eagle is a match for the gimlet eye of the child seeking treasure. I was making my way up a hill of paper, cans, broken wood and glass when I spied it. A fresh, crisp, new, one-dollar bill. It was folded into a square no larger than about one inch. But I saw it.

To understand the magnitude of such a find, one must remember that at that time penny candy was really a penny, bread was five cents a loaf and an entire peach pie could be bought for fifteen cents. Royal Crown Cola, Pepsi, Coke, Dr. Pepper, and Nehi were a nickel. An entire dollar was real wealth.

My strict, religious up bringing caused me to give ten cents (a tithe) of my treasure to the church (The church was the little, dirt floor Pentecostal one my grandad had built himself and pastored in Little Oklahoma in Southeast Bakersfield). But what was a dime to insure that God would undoubtedly bless me in finding even greater wealth? Such is the natural innocence, superstition and greed of children.

***

Life is a crapshoot! The philosopher who made this profound observation is forgotten to me but his point is well taken. It reminds me of the short time I lived in Las Vegas when I was a young boy. We lived within six blocks of the Golden Nugget and it was during the time of the premier of "My Friend Irma Goes West" with Jerry Lewis and Dean Martin.

I will never forget the sight of Jerry being towed on roller skates behind a Cadillac convertible down the main drag or the stand-up comedy routine with Marie Wilson. Nor will I ever forget the little ditty she gave about fishes: "Of all the fishes in the sea, my favorite is the Bass; he climbs up in the seaweed trees and slides down on his hands and knees." Children remember some of the most amazing things, often to the chagrin of their parents.

Mama was a pistol! Not to be confused with the very popular song Pistol Packin' Mama though it fairly describes my own mother. While I was raised, primarily, by my maternal grandparents I am grateful to my mother for adding an important dimension to my early childhood and teenage years.

It was during one of the periods my brother and I would visit with our mother and the latest stepfather that I enjoyed the cosmopolitan flavor of Las Vegas. The stepfather, Jim Blaine in this case, had a job as a Disc Jockey at the local radio station (KLAS). That was a most important and interesting position. My brother and I enjoyed our visits to the station and I have fond memories of that period of time in my life.

I love the desert and the combination of the excitement of Las Vegas and the desert wilderness nearby was hard to beat. Our mother always entered the equation as a promoter of excitement in her own right. While she had a violent temper and my brother and I were, many times, partners in fear because of it, she made life interesting for us.

Mom loved music, as did my grandparents, and I attribute my own ability as a musician with a wide range of musical tastes to the combination of them and Little Oklahoma and travels with mom. No matter where we lived, music was always playing and I listened with equal enjoyment to Ernest Tubbs, Fats Waller, Spike Jones, Vaughn Monroe and Benny Goodman.

But one impression of Las Vegas troubled me as a young boy. Going to the local grocery store, I watched as a young woman with a baby in her arms take the change from her purchases and deposit it in one of the ubiquitous slot machines on her way out of the store. I'm not sure why this troubled me, I only know it made a vivid, indelible impression and I still recall it clearly.

The lure of gambling is well known. I learned early on that I could never be successful at it. Given a fifty-fifty chance, I will usually pick the wrong number. Maybe I was bothered by the idea that a young mother with a baby in her arms had better ways to spend her money than throwing it into a one-armed bandit.

Sometimes, it is worth it to take a chance. We read in the Bible about an archer who drew his bow at random and struck King Ahab, mortally wounding him. (I Kings 22:34). Personally, I believe God Himself directed that shaft. If so, the bowman certainly could take no credit for marksmanship.

It may be that Augustine, the great and venerable, early theologue of the church read this story and decided to box himself in with his theory of predestination. Though he faced a lot of fancy footwork in trying to maintain this position in spite of its paradoxical conclusion, he held on, as far as we know, to the end of his life. The gamble explicit in the theory is that if men are, according to Augustine and, later, Aquinas and Calvin, predestined to election, how to make sense of any moral imperative that would be incumbent on mankind as a whole? Why not, if God has already decided who is saved and who is lost: "Eat, drink and be merry for tomorrow we die!"

Over the years, many an interesting discussion, sometimes-violent disagreement, has been waged over the issue. Predestination versus Free Will is always an interesting philosophical entertainment. But reason dictates that if God has already decided you are going to hell, then eat, drink and be merry. In fact, rob, cheat, lie, steal and do as you please; how can you make it any worse for yourself?

Ah, well, there are always those that think they have the liberty to be astute in the affairs of this world and discount reason when talking religion, and, blasphemous as the statement may appear to some, the same thing can equally apply to Augustine, Aquinas, and Calvin. What, one may well ask, did Aquinas really believe he had accomplished when he came to the end of his life and pronounced all that he had done "... nothing but straw!" If true, a whole lot of theologians built their systems of just such straw and I suspect they will make a satisfactory fire in the end leaving nothing but ashes.

***

When I was a boy and we had recently moved to the mining claim in Boulder Gulch, I had the whole Sequoia National Forest as my playground. Ecstasy! But grandad didn't quite trust me to take a gun and immediately set out to claim this wondrous domain. He knew that at eleven years of age, I had a few things to learn first.

But I knew grandad. Children are marvelous cons when they put their minds to the task. I desperately wanted to get out and explore this treasured and exciting wilderness, but I also wanted to take a gun with me in case of the usual Indian uprisings or any other practical and anticipated menace that might arise like a bear or lion attack.

My plan was elegant in its simplicity. There was much work to do to make the cabin habitable and firewood was always needed. I set to with a will to show grandad how seriously I took these responsibilities. I cut wood, fetched water from the well and even looked for other things to do. And all this without even being asked or threatened! I actually asked grandad if he had any other chores I could do! Looking back, I know I risked my grandparent's questioning my sanity, but so intent was I on my goal I didn't even stop to think how utterly disquieting my behavior must have seemed.

Now grandad didn't hold with loafers or laziness. I was always taught, and made, to carry my share of the load (there were the usual thoughts of rebellion and hazy concepts of abuse and child labor laws in my mind but, in the end, I didn't fail to carry out orders). But to actually ask if there was any work to do? That is childhood heresy! An act that would get any self-respecting kid drummed out of the corps! Fortunately there weren't any other kids around to witness my apostasy- Except my younger brother.

Now Ronnie, my nemesis (read: younger brother and fink), was not taken in by my newfound religion of obedient industry. At the end of the day, and what a day it had been, grandad made the kind of pronouncement, which all parents think is praise. He said to my grandmother and great-grandmother: "A certain young man really made me proud of him today! He did what he was supposed to do without being told and even asked if there was anything else he could do to help."

The fink then piped up: "Yeah, he just did it so you would let him take the gun out by himself!" There is no wrath such as rises up to confront the truth when you have been found out in a well-executed plan to deceive.

Now, while I have never been one to hold a grudge, and while this only happened a few decades ago, I have recently forgiven my brother his base canard against my integrity. Of course, I assume the proper degree of repentance on his part for so nefarious a calumny. If not, forget it!

In time, I was entrusted with the artillery (no thanks to you know who) and was able to claim my rightful place with Kit Carson and other worthy, mountain men, but I never forgot my attempt to deceive grandad by my good works.

As I have pointed out in other writings, much of the Bible, particularly the Old Testament, makes no sense unless we take the position that God was learning about people and they were learning about Him. That much of what God has done is only understandable in a context of His literally dealing with children as a parent should be equally obvious.

Ah, parenthood! The bitter-sweetness of raising children (too often, these days, little devils). It isn't that I think the violence of hurting a child physically is ever the right thing to do. It isn't. Hitting people is wrong, and children are people too! But the total asininity of laws that, on the one hand, makes parents responsible for their children and, on the other, deprives them of the means of exercising any authority! Such a society is obviously doomed to raising devils, not children.

Under the present laws both my mother and my grandfather would have been cooling their heels in the local gaol. But I survived and, in retrospect, deserved most of the discipline I received, though the hitting of children in the name of "discipline" only teaches them that violence is an approved means of discipline and settling differences in our society. While it is true that I would gladly put the noose around the neck of any monster that truly abused and hurt a child to satisfy some diabolical sadism of such a monster, we have inherited the whirlwind in going so far in allowing the State to dictate to parents.

It was during WWII and another episode with our mother that Ronnie (you know, the fink?) and I, with the usual child's love and familial affection decided to do a really nice thing for Mom. We were living in San Pedro at the time and it was exciting to watch the great, gray ships of war going through the harbor.

Mom was a late riser, and without adult supervision two little boys can be quite creative. It occurred to us that it would be a very kind thing to show her our appreciation for all she had done for (and to) us. Now how were two, small children to be able to do something really grand for their momma, early in the morning, with no adults around? Boggles the mind, doesn't it?

Inventive and imaginative little chaps that we were we finally hit on doing the dishes. Now, gentle reader, I was about six years old and my brother, five. If you have had the inexpressible joy of raising children through those early years, you might wonder how two children, six and five years of age, do the dishes without adult supervision? I will, of course, explain.

There were the usual plates and silverware, but those items were simply too pedestrian to warrant our genius and industry; simply too unworthy of the zeal we had to really impress our mother with our good works. And so it was that, filling the bathtub, we submerged Mom's toaster and waffle iron in its depths along with a copious amount of bubble bath. Of course, there was a lot of water and soap and the two appliances hardly made a dent in the tub's capacity.

Casting about for more items that were obviously in need of cleaning, we tossed in a clock and electric iron. I think a curling iron also made the tub and some other miscellaneous items too mundane to recall. Lastly, how to do the actual washing? Well, nothing but climbing into the tub ourselves seemed reasonable.

And thus it was that Mom, finally awakened by the joyful sounds of her little darlings splashing and laughing, hard at work in their worthy occupation, and came into the bathroom.

The scene in my mind's eye after lo these many years shifts somewhat. I seem to recall our mother's jaw hanging open, the most amazing look of horror on her face as I raised the waffle iron from its soapy depths in salute to our labor of love. I do recall, specifically, that one of her girlfriends had spent the night and mother, to her undying credit, asked her to please take a hairbrush to us, as she was afraid to.

Love's Labor Lost is more than the title of a musty, old novel; it was quite real to my brother and me. Not only didn't Mom appreciate our act of affection, she actually seemed to respond in a very negative way. That we survived intact was a miracle.

But our intentions were honorable (well, partly, at least) and we were slow to show such industry again. There was my scrubbing the toilet with her toothbrush, but I have found that a rather common misstep among the more responsible children. In retrospect, maybe it isn't so hard to understand why I was raised, primarily, by my grandparents?

Well, what is God to do with such children? If earthly parents are any example, and I believe they are, God has a tough row to hoe. His children often mean well, but good intentions are worthless.

It certainly complicates matters when professing Christians make God look foolish with childish attempts at the work He wants done. Often, such work is simply religious and is recognized as such. Most of this stuff is rightly seen as relatively harmless, like the charismatics waving their arms and hollering gibberish, but some of these things, like churches contemplating, in some cases actually, ordaining homosexuals is downright destructive and spitting into the face of God Himself!

***

People, especially children, like a good story. A good storyteller has to have all the attributes of a ham actor, the ego, the flair and the obvious enjoyment of moving and manipulating the emotions of his listeners and readers.

Having had more than the ordinary childhood, I love to entertain children and adults with my humor, which is often directed at my earliest years. Take, for example, the time the whole family had a real donnybrook involving my grandad, grandma, great-grandma, and the principal character, our latest stepfather, Dan Pospieszynski (what a time Ronnie and I had trying to learn to spell that name). But he was an excellent mechanic and he loved building model planes. I am grateful for his teaching me some of these skills.

We had just returned to California after an abortive attempt to live in Cleveland Ohio with our stepdad's parents. We just didn't take to the Polish Ghetto and the snow and ice of Cleveland after the sunny clime and culture of Bakersfield.

I will never forget the train trip from Bakersfield to Cleveland. It was wintertime, VE day was only just past and there were many military personnel on board. Of the many things children of today have missed is the glory of travel by train. There are few methods of travel to rival the trains of the past. To watch miles of varying scenery slip by to the clickety-clack, clickety-clack of the rails, the gentle, swaying motion that lulled you to sleep in the comfortable and snug Pullman births- Sheer luxury.

Eating in the dining car was marvelous; the sparkling cleanliness and beauty of the table settings, the courteousness of the waiters, all to the constant rocking motion of the cars and the variety of the scenes slipping by. The aura of it all was beyond description. Fellow travelers were friendly and companionable. It was a whole different world.

We arrived at Cleveland in a blizzard. Ronnie and I had never experienced any degree of snow and were entranced by the sight. As with life in general, I have bittersweet memories of our short tenure living in Ohio. My brother and I saw our first fireflies there, wonderful little insects with their entrancing ability to flick their lights on and off. We also celebrated VJ day in Cleveland; whistles blowing and people running out into the streets shouting and hollering up a storm.

Since the stepdad and all his relatives were Old-world, Polish Catholics, meaning they were more Catholic than the Pope, nothing else would do but that Ronnie and I should become indoctrinated into the Roman Church as well. I suspect some motivation on our mother's part in rebellion to her parent's religious persuasion. It was quite educational and certainly a contrast to our experience with our grandparents' Pentecostal fundamentalism in Little Oklahoma.

It was in Florida (St. Joseph's Military Academy, a place that parents dumped their kids so as not to be bothered with them) that Ronnie and I were catechized into Catholicism; quite a change from the boisterous Pentecostalism of Little Oklahoma. Culture shock; but a more convenient religion you couldn't ask for. More of that at another time.

WWII Vets faced a difficult problem of jobs and housing. I wonder if any of you recall a song called "No Vacancy." Even after all these years, I still remember some of the lyrics:

Not so long ago when the bullets screamed, many were the happy dreams I dreamed, of the little nest where I could rest when the world was free.

Now the mighty war over there is won, troubles in thousands just begun, as I face that terrible enemy sign No Vacancy!

No vacancy, no vacancy, all along the line just the same old sign 'a waiting for me.

No vacancy, no vacancy, and my heart beats slow as I read on the door No Vacancy!

Since the stepdad was a returning veteran with a family, housing and jobs were a real problem. So, California and the grandparents beckoned. Because the stepdad was a mechanic, my grandparents were persuaded that he could make a go of a garage in Little Oklahoma. After purchasing a venerable Terraplane, we were on our way back to California. Unhappily, Ronnie and I now had a baby brother and the trip was made in the summer to the aromatic accompaniment of dirty diapers and the proclivity of the Terraplane for breaking down in every state we passed through. This was particularly difficult as we tried to get through desert climes. I'm sure this is why mom still hates the desert.

Never let it be said that my maternal family didn't know how to have a good time. I say maternal because my father, Oliver Glendell Heath, left us when I was three and my brother, two. We never saw him again. As a result, I never knew any of the relatives on my father's side of the family.

My grandad was a big man, over six-foot tall, large boned, real linebacker material and about 225 pounds. He was also a Special Deputy for Kern County. As a result of that car-train accident Tody weighed about 300 pounds, and she was only five-foot tall. Great-grandma, saintly old lady who walked with a cane due to a bad hip, was also only about five-foot tall and probably weighed 95 pounds. Our step-dad was six-foot and about 180 pounds. Height and weight stats are important to the story about to unfold.

I must have been about ten years old at the time and my brother, Ronnie, nine, when this sordid event took place. And what an event it was. It is said "It takes uh heap uh-livin' ta make uh house uh heap." And the folks sure knew how to heap it up somethin' fierce; fun and frolic all the time. But, I digress.

Ronnie and I were awakened by tremendous crashing sounds accompanied by shouting and screaming from the participants of the family disagreement. It wasn't Sunday so I knew it couldn't be church practice by the congregation of my grandad's little Pentecostal flock.

Even at our tender ages, my brother and I had become accustomed to a certain degree of mayhem and life threatening interchanges between mom, our grandparents and various lesser contenders, acquaintances and stepfathers. All this and World War Two at the same time made for a good deal of excitement in our young lives; never a dull moment.

By the time Ronnie and I were out of bed and at the doorway of the living room where the action was in progress, it was obvious that our current stepdad was getting the worst end of the discussion. He was on the floor, grandma was sitting on top of him (all 300 pounds), grandad was struggling to get handcuffs on him, great-grandma was flailing away with her cane (and great-grandma could really wield a mean cane) and managing to hit grandad more often than Pospieszynski. The stepdad was screaming, "I surrender, I surrender!" at the top of his lungs. Small wonder; I bet a lot of you folks have had just the same kind of thing happen to you. Well, at least close to it.

It was all very interesting and Ronnie and I were careful not to intrude our presence into such a spirited and enthusiastic display of adult entertainment. But we did wonder where mom was. It wasn't like her to miss out on one of these exchanges of differing viewpoints (particularly when she was often the prime instigator of them).

Finally the battle was ended, the cuffs were on the miscreant and grandad hauled him off to the pokey. Ronnie and I learned later that he had landed a sucker punch on grandad's nose and this precipitated the wholesale battle. To this day I don't know where mom was at the time or what part she played in the whole affair. I do recall Ronnie's and my fascination at the amount of blood and hair all about the battleground afterward as we examined the floor and broken furniture. It was all quite interesting to our young minds. My brother and I were suitably impressed with the enthusiasm of the participants; it isn't every day that kids get to observe grown-ups at play in such spirited fashion and children greatly need adult role models.

I have often found myself pitying those that have been deprived of the cultural advantages my brother and I have enjoyed. It is a truism that there are two kinds of people: Okies and those that wish they were. And, while I am only an honorary Okie, I take great pride in my nativity of Weedpatch and raisin' in Little Oklahoma (Southeast Bakersfield, to the uninitiated) with all its refugees straight out of the *Grapes of Wrath* from the Dust Bowl and the Great Depression. The Joads would have been right at home with us. It is easy to feel sorry for those that have been denied such a rich and interesting heritage.

I have to wonder what families without the necessary survival skills are going to do. It makes me think of some of the old songs of my own Dust Bowl days. For example: "Dear Okie, if you see Arkie tell 'im Tex has got job way out in California; pickin' up prunes, they're all out of oranges."

As I sit writing this winter, warmed by a good, wood fire, (Still in the Kern River Valley at this point) I can gaze out my windows at the snow-capped mountains all about. There are snow flurries and the whole scene is one of contentment, particularly since I don't have to be out in the cold.

We've had a series of storms that promise a goodly amount of water in the lake, and with an improved snow-pack in the high country, good fishing in the river and streams this spring and summer and plenty of quail and deer and I'm reminded of that famous song by O'Dell Johnson: Kernville California U.S.A. "Snow-capped mountains, ripplin streams, it's not heaven though it seems, in Kernville California, U.S.A." (Ok, so it's not so famous; but it ought to be).

I have taken some friends out to my secret Indian campground and introduced them to the fascinating search for artifacts, primarily arrowheads and fragments of obsidian. I have even found some in Kelso Valley. I have enjoyed seeing them get the bug; they walk around now, permanent crick in their necks, looking at the ground wherever they go, hoping to see that wondrous glint of light that betrays the marvelous, smoky, volcanic glass the natives worked with such consummate skill.

It is a shame that the government, in its infinite wisdom, had so little regard for this site when they decided the old mining claim would be a dandy place for a campground. So much for government's real regard for the riches of a culture that was so much more attentive to God's creation. But, sadly, if the Indians had had the advantages of the conquering hordes, I doubt we would have found them much more conscientious about preserving their own heritage. Oh, well.

It takes time to learn wisdom. There was a time as a young boy that I would shoot those beautiful, gray tree squirrels. They were good eating and I hunted for the family pot. It's quite something to eat squirrel and frog legs until you're swole up like a pizened pup. I can still enjoy a good platter of frog legs, but I now just enjoy watching the gray squirrels. The ground squirrels I still shoot. I have never known vermin with so many fleas or so industrious in procreating and digging holes, often killing trees.

Of course, for those of you with the unhappy experience of learning how quickly you can be up to your neck in hamsters, the ground squirrel is a eunuch by comparison. You would think that any animal with a gestation period of 16 days would one day rule the world. Fortunately, it is also true, that any animal that thinks running an endless wheel endlessly is its calling in life cannot be too great a threat to civilization. On the other hand, look at what most people do for a living! Maybe the hamster isn't so stupid after all. At least he doesn't punch a clock or worry about the rent. The flip side is being eaten by the family cat. Alas, it seems there is no Utopia.

The snow has been falling heavier as I write, some of the flakes as large as silver dollars- The angels having a pillow-fight. The area is now a winter wonderland as the feathery flakes drift softly down, filling the quiet air. It's enchanting and thoroughly delightful as long as you don't have to be out in it. I recall making snow ice cream as a kid. We simply scooped up a bowl of fresh snow, added a small amount of vanilla extract, cream, and sprinkled in sugar, mixed and ate. Marvelous; might do that now. Simple folks got simple ways.

And speaking of frog legs, I'll never forget the time I almost caused mom to croak. Therein lies a frog-tale.

Our second stepdad, MaHoney, a soldier, was courtin' mom at the time. He had picked us up and taken us to a nice restaurant. When Ronnie and I were told to order what we wanted, I ordered frog legs. I'm sure the poor man didn't suspect what elegant taste I had for a poor, unsophisticated, little Okie kid. But in truth, frog legs were common Bill of Fare for me. How was I to know that they were frightfully expensive when ordered in a high-tone restaurant? Us simple folks were used to eating the critters and certainly couldn't understand anyone placing them in some high-falutin Epicurean category. Certainly I wouldn't have understood their being the most expensive dish on the menu.

MaHoney took it like a man and over my mother's protestations, said, "Ah, let the kid have 'em." And I had 'em. I'm not sure what the bill came to, but judging by the soldier's and my mother's expressions I'm sure he was sorry he let me have 'em. I'm sure mom would have liked to have let me have it. I do recall that after he and mom married, I never ordered frog legs in a restaurant again. And in truth, restaurant frog legs lacked something. They just weren't as good as fresh-gigged.

I'm not sure how I got started on this line of reminiscences and I'm having trouble making some profound, philosophical or theological point of frog legs. Maybe God enjoys stories also?

As a little Dust Bowl Okie, it was my privilege to attend old Mt. Vernon Elementary in Bakersfield. The second grade teacher as I recall had a few problems, one of which was that she had trouble with some pronunciations. This caused her and the class a real disaster on one occasion.

We were having a class Spelling Bee. I was an excellent speller and often won these events. However, this time the teacher created a terrible situation because the word she asked for, *accept*, kept coming out of her mouth *except*. Now there were several other excellent spellers in our class. When the first one tried to answer her with the correct spelling of except, exactly the way the teacher pronounced it, the kid was told it was wrong. The next kid did the very same thing, and so did a third. It was my turn and I didn't know what was going on. In spite of the fact that each of us was told to sit down as soon as the *ex* came out of our mouths, none of us could think of any other way to spell the word she was so obviously saying. I failed to answer and the teacher was tearing at her hair by this time. It never occurred to her that she might be to blame due to her poor pronunciation.

And, so, as with many things, we think we are saying things easily understood and only succeeding in exasperating our listeners and ourselves. As a teacher, I learned that some lessons can only be mastered by the repetitive method, saying the same thing over and over like learning the multiplication tables. But I have never forgotten that episode in second grade. When something is so obviously clear to you and others are not getting it, you better re-examine your teaching.

However, I did get even, though not through any motive of revenge; some things just seem to work out that way- Happy circumstance; serendipity.

The school was having a talent show. As one of the better singers I was volunteered by this teacher to sing in front of the whole school. She had a few selections for me to choose from but none of them seemed to hit me quite right. They just didn't fit my mood. Bakersfield radio stations carried many good musical programs and I was always listening to music from the radio, the church, and mom's records. I had memorized many old favorites such as "Cocaine Blues." As a result, I had an extensive repertoire of widely diverse songs and decided to do one of my own favorites. But I failed to share this decision with the teacher. And so it was that good, old Mt. Vernon was treated to my rendition of that great and famous ballad: "Cold Icy Fingers."

> Now Bill Jackson was a fellow that believed in hainted sights
> He used to dream about them when he went to bed at night
> And when he dreamed about them you could nearly always tell
> He'd just pull back his covers and jump right up and yell
> Keep them cold icy fingers off 'a me
> Keep them cold icy fingers off 'a me
> I don't mind your naked bones
> Don't mind your hollers and your groans
> But keep them cold icy fingers off 'a me
>
> One night as Bill was passin' a graveyard on a hill
> Somethin' dressed in white jumped out and made a grab at Bill
> Bill said you may not catch me but I'll make you do your best
> But for we start to travel, I'll make one last request
> Keep them cold icy fingers off 'a me
> Keep them cold icy fingers off 'a me
> You can chase me out of breath
> You can scare me half to death
> But keep them cold icy fingers off 'a me
>
> Bill went to see a doctor with a misery in his chest
> The doctor looked at Bill and said take off your coat and vest
> He started tappin' on Bill's wrist and gave Bill such a shock
> That Bill just jumped right back and said now wait a minute Doc
> Keep them cold icy fingers off 'a me
> Keep them cold icy fingers off 'a me
> You can cure my aches and ills
> With your powders and your pills
> But keep them cold icy fingers off 'a me

The teacher was most unforgiving. Little did she realize how lucky she was that I didn't treat the school to Cocaine Blues (circa 1942), my alternate choice. Looking back, I think it was the reference to naked bones that got to her. She was quite the old maid. However, if any of you want the lyrics to that other old favorite I'm afraid it's now hidden somewhere in the drawer of my mind and will not readily show itself except for bits and pieces like "Took a shot of cocaine and I shot my woman dead," but it's quite a rouser. My cultured tastes and refinement knows no bounds and I am always anxious to share the bounty of my childhood with others who have similar, discriminating tastes.

Children today face things that I certainly never had to deal with and neither, probably, did you. The single most important thing is the consistency of the love they need to see in their parents for them. It takes a lot of effort for parents to be consistent in both love and discipline, but it's the only chance the children have. My brother and I were blessed by a loving environment among people that cared for one another and for us. In spite of the turmoil of incidents such as I have described with that one stepfather, we were never left in doubt of these people's love for us. We can't help wishing things were different, that our children didn't have to face the ugly realities with which they have to deal. But wishing won't make it so.

***

It was a dark and stormy night. It wasn't, really, I've just always wanted to start a story with the infamous line. In reality, it was a beautiful, balmy, summer evening.

My brother, Ronnie, along with a friend and I were on our way up the Canyon on 178 out of Bakersfield to Bull Run Creek to get in some trout fishing. I was driving the friend's dad's truck, a '40 Studebaker. I hit the first S curve at the mouth of the canyon a tad fast and we managed a four-wheel slide through it. Fortunately, there wasn't any other traffic. It did not bode well for our journey but we were young and, hence, indestructible and laughed about it.

It was great to be young and single in the Fifties in America and, especially, in California. Tax-fattened hyenas, otherwise known as politicians, hadn't yet perfected their methods of robbing responsible, working folks blind, teachers were still trying to educate, welfare wasn't yet an approved life-style, you could buy a house for $3,000, gas was fifteen cents a gallon and Jimmy Swaggart and Jim Bakker were still virtual unknowns; all in all, a pretty good time to be alive in the good, old U.S. of A.

It was a beautiful night, filled with the aroma of the marvelous scents of the river and the vegetation as the road wound along its banks, climbing toward Isabella and Kernville. Mice scurried across the road in the beam of our headlights, we could hear the croaking of frogs and the occasional, soft, soggy balloon pop as a tire would roll over a toad, his tongue, eyeballs and sundry juices squirting out, tracing an intricate pattern over the warm asphalt. Once in awhile a hawk or owl would make an appearance as they chased their dinners of the smaller critters. We passed road-kills of snakes, mice and one skunk. Don't mind the smell as long as the little fellows keep it at a respectable distance.

In addition to our fishing and camping gear, I had with me one of the first new-issue, Single-Action Army Colts, a beautiful work of art in .38 Special caliber. Colt hadn't yet put it out in .357 or any of the other, larger calibers. I bought a .357 later and kept it for years; my favorite sport shooter; 100 rounds and one rabbit, fast-draw. That's fun and easy on the rabbits. But you have to be a hand loader to afford it and, fortunately, I had been one since I was 14 years old while living on the old, mining claim in Boulder Gulch.

The holster for the Colt was a professional Hollywood rig with steel insert. I had been taught by a real pro and thereby avoided the Clutch and Grab gang that was popularizing the sport of shooting themselves in the foot by trying to imitate Hopalong Cassidy. Actually knew a kid that had managed to put four holes in his leg and thigh with one bullet trying this trick; wouldn't have believed it possible if I hadn't seen the holes in him. Fortunately, he was using a .22 and the small slug missed the bones; but to get back to the story.

We arrived in Kernville about 9:00 p.m. and took off on Burlando Road. In those days, you could drive past the pavement on the dirt road clear up to the old smelter. Awful rough road even then and you had to know where you were going. A short distance in we could hear the Creek, the swift water making its own music. The stars were shining brightly, trout were waiting for us and we could smell the pines and lupine. Marvelous!

Then, disaster! There was one stretch of the road that cut into the side of a hill, was quite steep and overgrown with branches and often wet from a spring that flowed across it. Breaking brush and branches, I tried to barrel through when the rear wheels of the old Stude hit a slick spot and slipped off the side. So there we were; the right rear wheel jammed against the brush and branches, dangling off the road and no means of getting it back on track. We couldn't go backward, forward or sidewise- Stuck.

Exchanging the appropriate comments and good-natured pleasantries the situation demanded there was nothing to do but start hoofing it back to Kernville in the hope of finding an adventurous tow-truck driver at the local gas-up. Not wishing to leave the Colt unattended, I stuck it under my shirt in the waist of my Levi's.

After an hour's hike through the darkness, we reached Kernville. It was now about eleven o'clock. The only place still doing business was the local cuttin' 'n' shootin' joint, the saloon. Not knowing what else to do, we went in. I was mindful of the Colt snug in my waist, but the place was peaceful and no one was being rowdy.

We asked the bartender if he knew of a tow truck operator available at that time of night. He didn't but a couple of guys, feeling no pain, were intrigued by our tale of woe. They were up from L.A. and had been fishing the Kern and getting plastered, alternating pastimes.

Nothing else would do but that they were going to take us up the road and get the blankety-blank Stude back on the trail. Sloshed as they were, common sense was a no-go. Of course, we were in no real circumstances to argue against even a remote possibility. In a spirit of liquid camaraderie, they left the bar and ushered us out on our quest. And then I saw their car: It was a spanking, brand new, Plymouth station wagon.

Now you really have to see the trail up to the smelter to understand what was going on in my mind. It is a twisting, jagged, boulder-strewn, pot-holed path hardly deserving of the name road. Pan-bustin' rocks jut up from its surface here and there and, in some places large boulders line both sides of the narrow trail. In other places, tree limbs and brush rake the sides of any vehicle going through. An occasional muffler or pipe will be found to give mute testimony to its ruggedness. And a couple of drunks were going to take us up this so-called "road" in their brand new vehicle! And we were going to let them!

Piling into the Plymouth, we hit the highway. Long live truth, justice and the American way! We got to the end of the pavement without incident. Fortunately, there was no traffic on Burlando at midnight as we took our half out of the middle and both sides going. Then we hit the dirt at the end of the pavement with a cloud of dust and a hearty *High Ho, Silver!*

A deep trough of sand in the road helped slow us down as we got to the first boulders. *Crash* as the Plymouth bounced off one and *Crash* it went against one on the other side. *Bang! Crash! Bang!* we caromed off the rocks. *Wham!* into a hole. *Clang!* went a rock against the pan. By now, drunk as he was, a note of genuine doubt and concern began to creep into our driver's voice. A pine limb scraped against the windshield carrying away a wiper blade as another large boulder banged against the left, rear door and he hit a large hole at the same time. "I don't think she'll make it boys!" the guy said. We were sure she wouldn't make it.

To the accompaniment of loud and colorful language together with gut-wrenching impacts of the wagon against various obstacles, he managed to get the poor, hapless Plymouth turned the other direction. He was going considerably slower now. Even so, we added a few more dings in the skin of the used to be new vehicle heading back.

There was a pronounced shimmy to the wagon as we got back onto the pavement. We could hear the roar of the exhaust where the pipe must have been dismembered and a loose shock was knocking against a back axle. There was also a scraping noise as a fender was chewing rubber off one of the tires.

We managed to get back to Kernville and I discovered I couldn't get the door of the wagon to open on my side. Ronnie and the kid got out ok, but I had to roll the window down and crawl out it on my side. The poor Plymouth looked like it had been through the wars, as indeed it had. We didn't wait around to exchange pleasantries, but beat a hasty retreat after quickly surveying the damage. I've often wondered how those good Samaritans felt when they sobered up and could clearly discern the carnage. Not good, I suspect.

Well, here we were with no answer to our dilemma. We trudged across the bridge in the hope of seeing something open on the other side of town. Suddenly, our luck changed. The local sheriff pulled up to us.

"What's the story, fellows?" the deputy asked somewhat guardedly. We explained our predicament and the constable, a young fellow also, was a good Joe and invited us to hop into the squad car saying he thought he knew someone in Isabella that might be able to help us out. I crawled in front with him and Ronnie and the kid got into the back seat. It was only then sitting next to the deputy that I thought about the Colt in the waist of my Levi's; an interesting situation.

I considered the reaction of this minion of the law if he knew I was sporting a loaded Hogleg under my shirt. My emotions were mixed as I tried to keep from laughing out loud at the possibilities. Fortunately for all concerned we got to Isabella without incident and the deputy found a fellow with a truck who was willing to help us. He was a little dubious about our telling him we had gotten the old pickup in as far as we said. He knew the road. So bidding a fond *adieu* to the deputy, we set out into the warm and balmy summer night back to Kernville.

To make a long story short, he got us there and managed to get the Stude out of its predicament and, after giving him twenty bucks, a princely sum back then, went on his way. It was now about 3 a.m. and we finally crashed in our sleeping bags.

We were up early and the trout were obliging. Some of the pools at Bull Run are as much as twenty feet deep with beautiful waterfalls emptying into them. I've caught five-pounders here. Some years ago, Forestry put up a gate at the end of the paved road to keep the riff-raff out. I'm glad they did as some bums had begun to litter the place with trash. Let's face it folks, if it's easy to get to idiots will ruin it.

It was later that I found out that my brother had a Triple-A card and could have used it to pay the tow truck driver. I was not happy. But my brother has never been noted for his quick wit in a crunch. Oh well, if you are a real fisherman and know Bull Run, you know in spite of our minor setbacks the fishing made it all worthwhile. Now, many years later, I have almost forgiven my brother his oversight about that Triple-A card and the whole incident is a, mostly, pleasurable memory of simpler times and thankfulness that that poor, unsuspecting deputy never learned of the Colt.

***

It's a good thing God has a sense of humor or I believe we'd all be dust by now. I'm reminded of the time that I was weeding the yard next to one of our cabins on the old mining claim.

Kids being kids, weeding was not high on my list of enjoyable activities, especially when there were more important things to do like hunting quail. And, being a kid, work was a matter of interpretation; if I had to do it, it was work; if I wanted to do it, it wasn't; funny how that never changes. And, being a kid, I looked for the easiest way to get the job done. So it was that I nearly burned one of the cabins down.

It was summer and the weeds were really dry; a real fire threat. But I figured I was smart enough to keep the fire from getting too close to the cabin. And think of all the time and energy I would save in the process. So, striking a match I lit the stuff off.

It's truly amazing how fast fire travels in dry weeds. In no time at all it had reached the tarpaper side of the cabin and took hold. It's equally amazing how fast a kid can move when inspired by the image of a grandfather with a piece of firewood in his hand, ready to administer the appropriate punishment for catastrophic lazy foolishness.

Inspired by the threat of certain death at the hands of grandad, I immediately, with my bare hands, began to throw copious amounts of sand and dirt against the flaming tarpaper. My effort would have shamed the most industrious badger going after a ground squirrel. Helped along by a legion of guardian angels, I managed to extinguish the impending holocaust. Only then did I wonder why, in my "planning," I didn't have the presence of mind to have a bucket of water handy? Simple; the stupid cabin wasn't supposed to catch fire! Also, lacking the niceties of electricity and indoor plumbing I would have had to pump the water from the well by hand, and you just didn't pump a bucket of water unless you really needed it. I was the innocent victim of a plan gone awry. I chopped the rest of the weeds with sore and bloody hands and, by God's grace, grandad never did discover how close we came to losing the cabin and my entire back end.

***

We have just experienced a marvelous thunderstorm here in the Valley. The air is clean and fresh and the mountains are beautiful. How grateful I am to be here in this country and have time to enjoy it.

I just got back from a trip to my gold mine with one of my old students, George Taylor. A beautiful trout stream runs through the claim and in spite of drought, the stream was running nicely and we caught trout. I cooked them on the blade of my machete and ate them right beside the stream. Now how can you beat that for quality living! The country is so rough that it keeps the riff-raff out and only other noble souls (fishermen) frequent the spot.

The first time I ever visited the place in 1948 was at the invitation of an old man (probably my age now). He was the stereotypical prospector; grizzled, gray beard, gnarled hands, stooped back, faded and well-worn Levi's, patched flannel shirt, slouch hat, etc. He happened by our cabin one day and was invited to lunch. While eating, he learned of my passion for fishing. He described where he was living and how to get there. He said there was a great trout stream with waterfalls and deep pools and plenty of large trout begging to be caught.

The old fellow lived in an old tin shack on the claim by the stream. He made enough panning the creek to supply his few needs and came down to town (Kernville) only when absolutely necessary. He recognized in me a kindred spirit and the first chance I got I took the rough map he had drawn for me and, with tackle in hand, went calling.

The stream was everything he said it was. A few other tales might have been embellished though. He showed me a dent in the shack at the side of the doorway that he said he made chunking a rock at a bear. According to him, the mine was last worked about 1928. It was a Lode claim and every winter the stream would flood it out. There were some old model T or A engines, and an old straight eight that they had used to try to keep the shaft, a stope, pumped out. He told me the old miners quit when they couldn't keep up with the water.

I filed on the claim, naming it the *Laura Jean*, some years later. Only then did I discover that the old boys that had worked the mine had never bothered with this nicety. They simply took the gold and didn't bother notifying Uncle Sam of their enterprise.

As a high school teacher, I have taken several of my pupils back to this pristine, wilderness site and given them the chance to share the wondrous joy of an unspoiled, mountain trout stream and the wildlife. So many magic hours with young people, my own children especially, in this truly magnificent setting.

It has seemed a sacred trust to maintain this spot. Its very ruggedness has, thus far, kept it so. Only the hardiest can make the hike in and these are, invariably, kindred souls. It is in such settings that we clean out our minds and souls and get our priorities right. There is no other counsel or medicine its equal. However, that might be my Choctaw Cherokee blood on grandad's side speaking- Strong feelings for the land and critters there.

CHAPTER FOUR

Over the years, I've noticed some differences between men and women. Now some will applaud the sagacity and profundity of that statement while others, those without a sense of humor or lacking Attic Wit, will say, "It's about time!"

Even the philosopher and poet need the guidance of the Little Woman in matters like dress. For instance, when I think my outfit of chartreuse shirt, plaid pants, and two-toned, perforated shoes with argyle socks appropriate for dinner at Burger King, it takes the little woman to notice the possible clash in my sartorial choices.

It's true that men and women have many, different priorities and notice different things. That's often a good thing. If only they could cooperate rather than making such things a chip on the shoulder or a line in the dirt where each dares the other one to cross.

I've also noticed that when it comes to fishing, men and women simply don't communicate on the same level. The real importance of fishing is lost to most women, but is obvious to men. That's why no amount of explanation to a woman will suffice. Now I know some women who like to fish. But they don't comprehend the religious significance, the true worship of the devout angler. The ritual of adorning one's self with the liturgical vestments and equipment of Holy Office is, mostly, nonsense to a woman.

I have asked women if they have something as peculiar to their gender as fishing is to men. So far, none have been able to come up with anything. If you have any ideas on the subject, please let me know. It seems quite a conundrum at the present. I believe we could all profit from a thorough research of the question. If women do have something of a like nature that speaks to their souls, as fishing does to men, it seems an elusive thing for the time being. Remember one thing; if such a thing exists only women, as with men and fishing, will be able to understand it. If it does not, I have to wonder why?

In conversations with women, it is admitted that fear is one legitimate concern that deprives them of the wilderness experience. It may be, that, while the peculiar distinction between men and women that results in men being, for the most part, the real romantics, explorers, artists, inventors, risk-takers, etc. exists, it cannot be denied that women have every reason to be afraid to wander in the wild. Imagine what must go through a woman's mind if she finds herself alone at some distant stream and three, strange men approach.

While in today's evil society even men must be on guard against one another, it is women who bear the brunt of having to be constantly vigilant against the depredations of two-legged monsters. And this has been the case throughout history. It goes a long way toward explaining the resentment, animosity, and need that women have toward, and for, men.

I know it's unkind, but I can't help but be reminded of that old saw: "Beauty may only be skin deep, but ugly goes clear to the bone." Old brother J. Vernon McGee was correct. In reference to the use of cosmetics among the saints he said, "Some women need all the help they can get." My personal objection to such use is warranted by the plastic, painted look of the likes of women TV evangelists. They look like they have been done up by a Geisha school dropout. Since this whole dangerous subject should be the focus of a much larger work, I return to the safer theme of fishing.

A man seems to have an instinct for what is acceptable worship when embarking on Pilgrimage to the trout stream. He knows that to enter the Holy of Holies, the Cathedral of the wilderness requires the proper attire, sacrifices, and attitude of worship or God will not bless his quest.

The first, and most important, sacrifice is time. It takes real grit and determination, real honesty and integrity, to make the time available from his busy schedule for the true believer to go to church. He must do this at the possible risk of incurring the wrath of those less devout; like the little woman. She may think it more important to clean the garage or cut the grass. Heresy! But the true believer will not let such inconsequential things stay him from his course.

It's unfortunate that women don't seem to understand the significance of having a man who loves to fish. If they knew that the time he spends at the lake, river or stream might be the one thing that makes him different from a man who would punch her lights out, she might be properly grateful.

If you are a woman with a man who loves to fish, it would help you to accept the fact that, like a woman with PMS, he will suffer the same symptoms when deprived of his soul's need of the supply of a pool of trout or catfish. When that time comes upon him, you'd better let him go or be prepared to suffer the headaches, crabbiness, lethargy and other complaints common to the malady. And, of course, nothing you say or do during such a time will be right.

Keep in mind the fact, that, if a man denies the spirit and does not go fishing when it is his clear duty to do so, it will only create a situation at home. His inner battle will result in all kinds of inharmonious behavior; he will wander aimlessly and listlessly, he will seem to be distant and not hear when spoken to (Some women will say I have just described their man whether he loves to fish or not). In some of the worst cases, he may resort to watching football or basketball on TV. If he takes up golf or watching bowling on TV, the situation is irreversible; terminal. You have lost him: A word to the wise.

Now we all know that there is a difference between the true believer and the fanatic. When I first received the call to fish, I was a small boy equipped with cane pole, string and rusty hook. A hapless angleworm dangled from the end. But the Damascus Light struck with my first fish off the muddy bank of the old, Kern River. I say the *old* Kern because that sacred spot is now under the waters of Lake Isabella. Sacrilege!

It was a marvelously sunny, warm summer day. My grandparents had taken me to the river soon after we moved to the old mining claim in Boulder Gulch. The river, its surface mirror-like between the rapids, glistening in the sunlight and moving slowly around large granite boulders, its banks shaded by rows of leafy old Cottonwoods looked and smelled like heaven on earth. The good warm honest mud and grasses of the riverbank squirmed up between my toes; heavenly. The water was crystal clear, the bottoms of the pools with their rock-strewn and sandy terrain easily visible. Fish could be seen moving about. Electric excitement!

I don't recall that grandad had given me any specific instruction in the art of angling, but being an Okie he probably knew it was in my genes. His own equipment and dress were little different than my own.

That first fish and I were both hooked irretrievably. Even though my tackle was the most rudimentary imaginable, even though I was barefoot, shirtless, and had on bib overalls I was doing the best I could with the light I had and God rewarded me accordingly. Even though that first fish was the lowliest of the low, a seemingly worthless mud-sucker, it had done its task; the dew of The Chosen sprinkled my feverish brow. It remained for time to do its work in establishing a systematic theology, a doctrine of belief and acceptable Worship and Service of Devotion.

But, for the sacred moment, holding aloft my wriggling treasure of the deep, the sun sparkling, glistening from its iridescent scales, Isaac Walton, split-bamboo rods and Royal Coachmen, hand-tied, were yet future unknowns. I had much to learn, was ignorant of so much, but I had entered upon the Pilgrimage and my calling and election were sure.

Time has passed, and while the elastic spring of youth has long gone from my steps and my pilgrimages to Mecca (the trout stream) are now less frequent, my memories serve to take me there whenever I choose. Pity those who know nothing about such things.

***

A note to the non-cognizanti about Poets: In the Greek, the word Poet means a "Maker." These were the men who made stories. They created characters, some of heroic proportion, and wove tales to relate history, to make moral points, to uplift the spirits of those in need. I try to do the same thing by the use of the simple, honest verities; the work and sincere ethic that so distinguishes such people and my early character formation which was so passionately ingrained by my birthplace of Weedpatch and tenure in Little Oklahoma in Southeast Bakersfield and later in the Sequoia National Forest.

The most important thing of literary significance in my life was my early acquaintance with the King James Bible. The early reading in this literary masterpiece contributed the single most helpful thing to my education and appreciation of the English language.

A poet does not always have a popular following. If he is true to the craft, he deals with the truth and the truth is not always a pleasant thing. Recent Russian poets are more readily attuned to this than those of the West. They, correctly, recognize the fact that America has become a nation without a soul. And while the line between prose and poetry is often merged, and, at times, indistinguishable, both are vehicles of the expressions of the soul. It is a tragic thing that the souls of so many are so shrunken, so impoverished and mean in our society; so many are afraid of the truth and lack the conviction of truth.

It is a mind-numbing task to wrench myself from thoughts of a trout stream to deal with such things. How much more desirable to my soul to meditate on the forest or desert, far removed from such affairs of this evil world system. But it is not enough to discern evil; action is required: But what action?

Thoreau, in his excellent and thought-provoking work on Civil Disobedience would, doubtless, have much to say on the subject. I am, presently, at work at emulating his Walden experience in the hope that it will grant me some of his insight (without his ego). Though much of this was gained during my childhood while living on the mining claim in Sequoia National Forest, I am much older now and in need of a refresher course in the simplicity of living. In the process it may be that I, like he, will have the opportunity to spend some time in gaol as I confront the local bureaucracy which is not disposed to the independence of kerosene lamps, wood stove, and privies as a lifestyle.

But I feel, keenly, the need to, once more, wield hammer and saw. There is nothing that takes the place of a man doing for himself. My cabin will be of the simplest design and construction. But, surrounded by the large pines and boulders, the quail, squirrels, and other critters, the wind making its peculiar music through the trees, I hope to recapture some of the magic of the independence of spirit and soul that is so vital to maintaining a correct perspective of what is important and what is not. Essential to this is, of course, the proximity of the trout stream.

I plan to construct a small pond on the property, certainly nothing of the magnitude of Walden, but it will suffice to satisfy the deer, quail and squirrels, without which the place would certainly be lacking in the proper companions suitable to a gray-bearded curmudgeon. I'll keep you all informed on the progress of this experiment in "If you don't want much, you don't need much" and "A wise man lives simply." It should prove to be most interesting.

Since the price of liberty is eternal vigilance, we can no longer depend on our leadership to pay the price. For most, their only "vigilance" is the next election and lining their own pockets.

Even the experts are in agreement that government, at virtually every level, is out of control. Crime is rampant, people are being taxed beyond the ability to pay and the "fixes" are proving worse than the problems in too many cases. I mourn for those, trapped by their circumstances, unable to even dream any longer, unable to entertain any thought that things will be any better for their children.

These people never thought about planning for their lives; they must have thought that somehow, everything would work out. But life is not like that. The world is a rewarder of results, not wishful thinking.

As I travel the open highways of the San Joaquin, passing through Weedpatch, Arvin, Lamont, Pumpkin Center, Taft, Shafter, I wonder? The open fields of cotton, beans, onions, and the orchards of almonds, oranges and grapefruit, the vast vineyards filled with the promise of plenty, I wonder? I'm sure Steinbeck and Saroyan wondered as well.

People in California are awakening to the harsh reality of the scarcity of water together with the huge influx of Mexican illegal aliens that are colonizing the area. Jobs are being lost in Silicon Valley clear down to San Diego, companies are revising their plans for expansion, and builders have to contend with agriculture that is much in jeopardy.

I skirt the east side of Bakersfield, now a teeming metropolis, the air discolored and heat waves wriggling up from the asphalt, concrete, and arid alkali soil, distorting the view. I travel through the oil fields and watch the Iron Birds, heads bobbing rhythmically as they sip black nectar through steel straws. I drive up the canyon, marveling at the rugged, granite monuments and the Kern River beckoning the fisherman, cutting through the magnificent, solid rock formations, unchanged since childhood. I delight in the grass-carpeted foothills- smooth, rounded, undulating, and inviting tender caress.

How very horrible that so many human beings must live like rats in a cage in places like Los Angeles, deprived of fresh air or a view of the stars, where young people have no hope of anything better and join gangs in search of something that they think will make their lives relevant and purposeful, will give them a sense of "belonging." And what of a society that seems unable to offer them any better hope?

As I sit by a campfire of Juniper, stirring the coals and watching the coffee boil, absorbed in the aroma of its richness and enjoying a cigarette, and I do enjoy smoking, I can't help but think about the skewed priorities of humankind. The black silhouettes of the mountains outlined against a star-bright night speak peace to my soul. The hoot of an owl, the bark of a coyote, the scratch of some other night creature nearby all tell me that people were never meant to pass their time in this vale of tears in a constant attempt to "have" at the expense of their own souls. I'm sure David got to the point where he would have gladly traded the palace for the peace and tranquility of the sheepfold, bears and lions notwithstanding.

Just had an interruption in my writing; Missy, one of the resident gray tree squirrels, was at the door demanding nuts. She prefers pecans but had to settle for walnuts. She now takes them from my fingers. She is fun to spoil. A momma and papa Valley quail spend most of their time in the yard now. Something to do with the ready availability of fresh seed I'm sure.

I used to be an avid pilot and have my share of war stories as all pilots do. I even owned a couple of birds at various times; an Alon, a real kiddy car to fly, very simple, and a venerable Stinson, not so simple as a taildragger but built like the proverbial brick outhouse. I only mention this as an aside to the real story of life at Minter Field outside of Bakersfield shortly after WWII.

The barracks on the old Army Air Corps base had been opened to veteran housing. The only authority in residence was the base fire department. This meant that all us kids had the entire facility to explore, and explore we did. Many stories to tell about our tenure there like discovering the mortuary; what our imaginations found to entertain there!

One of our favorite toys was the parachute-training rig. A facsimile of a fighter had been placed at the top of a high scaffold, and a tall derrick with parachute harness attached was alongside. The idea was to climb into the cockpit of the fighter, put on the harness and, swinging out of the plane, pretend to be jumping from a disabled aircraft; really great fun. It's a wonder none of us were killed.

One day, a biplane landed at the base. I don't know why the pilot landed there, but he had left the plane and wandered off somewhere. We kids had watched the plane come in and, with the aircraft unattended, it acted as a magnet, drawing us to its wondrous, mysterious and magnificent presence.

What a sight! It sat gleaming in the middle of the vast empty airstrip, its siren call beckoning our attention.

Now we were all avid model builders, but apart from the mock fighter none of had actually ever touched a real plane. And here was the real thing just begging us to examine its mysteries. Off we ran toward it.

There were only four of us, and when we reached the plane we circled it, enwrapt in awe at its magnificent closeness. Tentatively, fearfully, we touched the smoothness of its fabric wings and fuselage. Somewhere, I found the courage to climb up on a wing and stared, entranced, into the open cockpit. My eyes consumed the intricate array of inscrutable instruments, the rudder pedals, the actual seat where the pilot sat; the joystick that gave him control of this magic carpet.

In my mind's eye I was transported far above the mundane, earthbound cares and concerns of earth, I was free as an eagle, carving paths through the ether, dodging clouds and enemy aircraft; I was Pappy Boyington, the Red Baron, and Eddie Rickenbacker, I was Errol Flynn, and John Wayne of The Flying Leathernecks and Flying Tigers.

And then, disaster! As I stood on the wing of the plane, enraptured, the stick began to oscillate side to side. Now I hadn't touched anything in the plane, but since I knew, intuitively, I had no business being on that plane or even touching it when that stick began to move of its own accord I just knew I had done something terrible! I had somehow incurred the wrath of the Genie of the machine. Those of you that grew up with the knowledge of Gremlins know what I am talking about. I was terrified!

I jumped from the wing like a turpentined cat and hit the asphalt at a full run, never looking back. It would be some time later that I would deduce the obvious: one of the other kids had to have been moving one of the ailerons, rudder or stabilizer causing the stick to move. But don't bother trying to explain that to a kid who believes in Gremlins or has enough conscience to know when he has been doing something he shouldn't.

***

They say romance is dead! Just look at what we are getting on Western music stations. Between jammin' eighteen wheelers and someone done me wrong songs there is romance enough for the most discriminating. Given the "genius" of music today it's no wonder kids are confused. They have a choice of music that treats guitars like loaded weapons and lyrics that make truck driving equal to becoming rocket scientists accompanied by noise that makes salamanders impotent and scrambles the brains of amoebas.

And today's dancing? It reminds me of the time a visiting idiot was trying to pry a jammed .22 out of a rifle with a screwdriver in a flood- damaged house my son Michael, and daughter Karen and I were rebuilding. A nine year old girl who was visiting happened to cross the line of fire when the round exploded and the slug punched a hole through her leg. Talk about timing! She put on a dance that would have shamed a Hottentot or Comanche warrior, all accompanied with the appropriate music of howls, squirting blood and screams together with the urging encouragement of general, good-natured, shouted curses. But it wasn't all fun and games working on that house. We worked our backsides off and I helped the kids learn that nothing is impossible if you know what you are doing and are willing to sweat.

Thursday, May 30. I have just returned from starting work on the cabin up at Erskine Creek. Muscles I haven't used in too long a time ache. I got the floor joists in and spent the night in the old, Dodge wagon. Cold; but it was a beautiful, moonlit night, the wind soughing through the pines, lulling me to sleep.

Make no mistake; building without water and power on site is nothing to write home about. Breakfast consisted of boiled coffee, eggs and hotdogs scrambled together in the cast-iron frying pan. But that is the price of some degree of solitude among the rocks, pines, and critters. I will have to condescend to getting a portable generator eventually.

The sun really warmed up toward noon. Knocked off and took a drive over to Boulder Gulch before heading back down the Canyon. We have to contend with the roadwork and I would have to wait until 4 p.m. to get through.

As I sipped coffee from my disreputable and omnipresent cup and mused of my childhood on the old claim, my mind was flooded with the memories of the simple life I had enjoyed here with grandad, grandma and great-grandma. Grandma and great-grandma died in their beds here in one of the old cabins. I miss all of them sorely.

Sadly, the campground was littered with trash. The Styrofoam Generation with its uncaring and selfish attitude was well represented. Incongruously, a gray tree squirrel scampered about and a Valley quail perched on the limb of an old pine calling lustily to the covey. But the noise of the traffic on the highway and the litter profaned the moment.

At some distance, I noticed a young woman and a small boy going about looking through the trash. It became obvious that they were looking for aluminum cans. The young woman was clearly handicapped; she walked with a difficult, wrenching stride from some kind of hip problem. Their clothes were dirty and they needed a bath.

Since I was going to be heading back down the canyon in a little while, I called them over to me. I asked if I could give them some of the food I had left in my ice chest. They gratefully accepted a loaf of bread, some hotdogs and a large, blueberry muffin. The little boy's eyes really lit up over that treat. Grandad, grandma and great-grandma would have helped and I honored their memory.

As I walked about the place, I could see a young man with the boy and girl. It seems that they were staying at the camp and trying to stick together in extreme circumstances; homeless and jobless, depending on the warm weather and the castoffs of campers.

Here was a young couple in their twenties with a boy about five. It made me want to weep. I thought of the growing number of signs held in the hands of young people "Will work for food!" Bangladesh, Kurdistan and Ethiopia may be far away but these things are here at home, in the Land of Plenty! The shame and disgrace of it all!

People, as I have said many times, do not plan to be destitute, uneducated, drunkards and drug addicts, jobless, welfare mothers and wards of the courts and jailbirds. But, as I have also said many times, without a plan for success, a plan for failure is already assured.

***

Perhaps God did not make a mistake in making the seeds so large in Avocados. But I do find fault with Him in not providing more trout streams. To me, there is nothing closer to heaven on earth than the crystal clear waters of a pristine, wilderness stream with deep pools, waterfalls and splashing, rock-studded, short rapids, the sunlight glancing all about with the brilliance of countless diamonds from the splashing play of the cold waters rippling and spraying off the rocks.

Put all this with the rugged country of huge, granite mountains, scented pines, a clear blue sky, the call of quail and the rustle of deer among the trees, trout lazing in deep, cool pools of crystal water and you have the closest thing to perfection for body, soul, and spirit you can find on earth.

I have fished the ocean, lakes and rivers but these lack the gem-like perfection of the forest fastness of a wilderness trout stream; to drink in the beauty of sun-dappled pools as the concentric rings spread toward the banks from a trout taking some insect on the surface. There is magic in the electric strike of the fish taking a hand-tied fly of your own creation or a simple bait of redworm or salmon egg.

It has been my happy lot to have enjoyed the vastness of the Mojave Desert and Death Valley. There is a peculiar beauty in the rugged, unspoiled (then) bigness of these Lonesomes, particularly at night when the air is so clear that each star stands out with sapphire quality and beauty and you can tell the grains of sand in the moonlight. I have watched from sunrise to sunset, in rapturous silence, the variegated, subtle changes of myriad colors reflected from the grim rocks and mountains of places like Cuddeback and Fremont Peak.

The openness of the majestic spiked Tetons, the grandeur of Bryce, the romance of Colorado, Wyoming and the Dakotas, all these I have relished in my travels. I will never forget my taking the summer, long years ago, to tour in my '54 Chevy station wagon, every national park between the Twin Cities and California. I have seldom spent my time in a better way. No crowds of people, no trash or beer cans, no traffic, only the scenic grandeur of things the way God left them. The irreplaceable memories in my night visions are beyond price. How I wish children today could have had their souls enlarged by such experiences.

Like Thoreau, I can settle for a special tree where I can sit on a granite boulder and, watching and listening, commune with God in an often-wishful state of mind that wishes things were different in the world. I prefer the rugged beauty of my trout stream where, in sacred solitude, my line in the gleaming water, I lift my soul to the granite peaks and rest in the coolness of a great, old pine and am free.

I walk the pine needle carpet and, plucking a couple from a handy branch, crush them between my fingers and drink in the perfume of them. I take a pinch of resin, the beautiful, translucent, amber, aromatic blood of the pine from the bark and savor its aroma, then, placing it in my mouth, relish the pungent tang of the unadulterated taste of the forest. I will cook the fresh trout by the side of the stream and, with pinion nuts and berries, Indian coffee and tobacco, enjoy life in a fashion that no Wall Street tycoon could buy for any amount of money, and those too busy with the affairs of this world might envy but never emulate. Tom Sawyer and Huckleberry Finn would understand.

It often makes me wonder what others are striving for, what they think they really want of life that drives them to rob, cheat and steal, to work even honestly for some unidentified "something" that they think will satisfy that itch they can't seem to scratch. It does seem that people do, indeed, live lives of quiet desperation. Too busy to what purpose? No time to do what? The tragedy of lives lived to the flick of a switch and escape into the world of TV.

It's too bad religion gave place to the devil in making hell more exciting and enticing than heaven. If there is supposed to be joy in our salvation the churches have certainly missed the boat. The silliness of such people like the charlatans on TV notwithstanding, trying in the flesh to make religion exciting, I will take my trout stream or the Great Empty of the Chocolate Mountains, of a six-gun on my hip, chasing that 500 pound Jackrabbit. I'll never forget my beautiful daughter Karen telling me that as a little girl she was afraid for me because of believing there actually was such a monster. We should be careful what we tell our children.

The old towns of Isabella and Kernville used to be heaven on earth. The Kern flowed, unrestricted through the valley. Numerous sloughs were home to abundant wildlife. Catfish and frogs made for great sport as, Indian fashion; you sneaked up on them for your breakfast or dinner. The outdoor aroma of the water and vegetation, mixing into some kind of mental satisfaction and joy that plastic would profane.

It's no wonder I feel trapped in a city environment. Concrete, asphalt and plastic make a prison to me. It just isn't natural for people to live in cities. Like rats in a maze, I see folks trying to get by in circumstances animals show more sense by avoiding. In fact, only people are capable of building their own prisons. Animals would never build nests with no escape.

But animals have the enviable attribute of instinct. They don't have to plan. People have to think and plan. Most don't, of course, and since they don't plan for success, a plan for failure is assured.

***

I have recently passed through the Canyon, the Grapevine and Holiday Valley. The "March Miracle" of abundant rain has resulted in turning the fields and hills into brilliance of colors DeMeer would envy. Against a carpet of emerald green, God has painted fiery beds of glorious orange with poppies, the shimmering, subtle purples of Lupine and the wild, yellow sulfur of mustard blossoms. When mixed together, the effect is breathtaking! While it is, at times, difficult to make the transition between the lyrics of "There's a tear in my beer when I cry over you," the idiocy that produces noise from hard rock guitars that sterilizes frogs at 300 yards and such mentally uplifting "literature" like Playboy and such lesser works like Shakespeare, it is still incumbent on us to make the distinction between trash and treasure.

But a society that teaches its young that sex is a commodity to be bartered, of value only as a trade item, as long as women popularize pornography by deeming themselves as pieces of meat to be exchanged for money to satisfy the ungodly lust of men, such a society is doomed. What value can men place on something women treat as of no real worth, as they go from one man after another and divorce no longer carries the stigma of failure to commit faithfully to a life partner? It is tragic that such people openly lie to God and society as they take vows to be faithful to one another. What a sordid, even obscene travesty in today's culture. However, I don't believe God thinks it's funny. And there are the idiotic religious professionals still talking about praying mothers while Dad is made to look ridiculous! No wonder women are giving up in disgust when real men are so hard to find!

Mom and my grandparents were of incalculable value to me in giving me a broad background that could make do, could appreciate the value of even the most transitory things; could take joy in such varied circumstances as Las Vegas or Little Oklahoma. I can, in my imagination, enjoy such magic as to be the envy of the most skilled sorcerer or conjuror. To be able to appreciate the shaping and forming of metal by lathe or mill, to turn walnut and ash into something of beauty and practical value, to wire or plumb a house, to get an engine humming sweetly and teach these things to others, these are things that fulfill a man, that tells him It has meaning and is worthwhile, these are the whispered promises of immortality.

A mother teaching the little one to do dishes, sweep the floor or do laundry might not speak as loudly for the present, but when that little one learns she is contributing something of value to the family, it has eternal potential. When that boy is taught to take on the obligation for disposing of the trash, cutting the lawn or washing the car, he is learning lessons for living a productive life.

Pity the child that learns not to obey until the pitch of his mother's or father's voice reaches the correct crescendo, that is confused by orders that result in threats of bodily harm or death unless followed. Such children do not dream of the joy of fulfilled expectations while marveling at the industry of ants or the glinting beauty of a butterfly. They, too often, are shoved in front of the tube and treated as the unwanted liability they in actuality are to such parents.

***

It was early afternoon on a mild, summer day. The forest was quiet. I had been outside doing some chore and came into the cabin through the door to my grandparent's bedroom. My grandmother had become bed-ridden, and grandad was out front doing laundry with scrub board and washtub by the well. There were only the three of us now since great-grandma had passed away.

As soon as I entered the cabin I sensed something was wrong. Looking down at the face of my grandmother I knew, instantly, she was dead. She looked still and peaceful; a thin line of foam had formed at her lips.

I walked slowly, trance-like, out to where grandad was rubbing sheets against the wash board. He had an apron tied around his waist and his shirtsleeves were rolled up above his elbows. All I could do was say, quietly in a near whisper "Grandad." He turned, and one look at my face together with that one, softly uttered word was all that was needed. We stood looking at each other for a moment, then slowly he dried his hands on the apron, and with reluctant, halting steps he began to walk toward the door of the cabin,

73

knowing and not wanting to know, what awaited him. I followed. I was sixteen years old.

Grandad was crying softly by the time we reached my grandmother. Bending over her, he used the corner of the apron to wipe the spittle from her lips, his tears dropping down on her.

We do not attain any sum of years without confronting the finality of death. Nor do we reach much age without some moment crashing down on us that so indelibly impacts our senses as to imprint itself beyond any forgetting. Some are so dreadful as to render the victim incapable of any further attempt to cope with life in any sense of normality. Insanity is often an escape to an unreachable world, far removed from the impossible dread of some things that are too horrible to bear by mere rationality.

And, some others, like walking into that cabin on that day one summer, or watching my eldest daughter die and my eldest son Daniel trying to deal with it, forcing yourself to live after an adulterous wife has, without any conscience, hurt and twisted your children, your children making disastrous choices, will forever be there, intruding and insistent, making a difference that works itself out in countless ways, decisions and actions throughout your life.

My grandparents loved each other. Grandad had cared for grandma like a baby throughout her invalid, bed-ridden, short remainder of life. He washed her, he did the laundry, and he cooked and did all he could to make her comfortable. Here was the proof that fidelity and commitment were not just grand words.

Love covers a multitude of sins. My grandad was far from a perfect human being. He had a violent temper, so much so, that my mother, with a temper to match his, married early to escape it and my grandparents had had some terrible fights over the years. Theirs was not a storybook marriage. But among my store of precious memories there will always be the sight of grandad, bending over grandma, wiping her now silent lips and his tears falling on her. There was love in its most raw, mind searing, most redeeming and priceless form and truth!

I suppose most people realize that families, as such, are no longer the mainstay of America for, in truth, there isn't that many left. Marriages and vows are a meaningless form, the parties generally entering the relationship without the slightest intention of fidelity or genuine commitment. Homosexuals are partnered with the state's blessing. Children are a liability more often than a blessing and treated as such.

And, so, I retreat with some few like Thoreau. I write, travel, and build. Knowing what I know, how can I do differently? "To him that knoweth to do right and doeth it not, to him it is sin." And I know as I sink sixteen's in those two-by-fours and wipe the sweat from my eyes, that this is right.

***

At least Sam Clemens didn't have to deal with perversion on a national scale. He and Bret Harte could do battle with the more seemly sins of their day like political corruption and religious and scientific chicanery. Henry James could content himself with innocuous and wordy novels. Sam could, safely, take to task the Boston Girl with her ungrammatical attack on his misuse of the adverb and tautological tendencies. Some things, as Sam pointed out, are simply unlearnable; and "rose up" continues to be a good, acceptable Southern phrase.

"I have a friend," Sam said, "who has kept his razors in the top drawer and his strop in the bottom drawer for years; when he wants his razors, he always pulls out the bottom drawer - and swears. Change? Could one imagine he never thought of that? He did change; he has changed a dozen times. It didn't do any good; his afflicted mind was able to keep up with the changes and make the proper mistake every time!" And so it is that we are, in some ways, doomed by bent of mental curiosity, to make some of the proper mistakes every time. Some things are, simply, unlearnable.

But I did learn, early, not to gamble on games of chance. Though I agree with Sam and Bret that the scholarly pursuit of poker and a thorough knowledge of the refinements of the game are at least equal to the pretentiousness of chess, and I further agree with Sam "... for the instruction of the young, we have introduced a game of poker. There are few things that are so unpardonably neglected in our country as poker. The upper class knows very little about it. Now and then you find ambassadors who have a sort of general knowledge of the game, but the ignorance of the people is fearful. Why, I have known clergymen, good men, kind-hearted, liberal, sincere and all that, who did not know the meaning of a 'flush.' It is enough to make one ashamed of one's species."

It never crossed my mind, throughout my entire childhood, to ever steal anything from my mother or grandparents. Purses could be left open and in plain sight with impunity, and never a stirring of larceny in my thoughts. It was, in my case, simply unthinkable. Until Poker!

Now my brother and I could, and did, draw blood over games like Canasta and Monopoly in our childhood. But we did not learn to play poker. If we had, the nefarious incident may not have taken place and sullied an otherwise perfect and pure conscience in this regard.

An older child, much wiser in the affairs of this world (and not so pure when it came to theft) was visiting. He knew how to play poker and, deeming me deficient in knowledge of such things and being ever so solicitous for my education, was more than willing to introduce me to this worldly refinement.

After a few hands, it was determined by my "mentor" that I was ready for the real thing. Of course, this meant using real money.

Needless to say, my teacher soon exhausted my small supply of pennies and nickels. But my brain was hooked by the possibility of easy riches through the simple mechanism of the turn of a card. It was an intoxicating thought. And I just knew my luck had to change.

Beats there a heart, anywhere in the land, no matter how seemingly pure, that does not shelter, in the darkest recesses of its innermost closet, some shameful thing, the common knowledge of which would cause the perpetrator of the dreadful act to die of terminal mortification? NO! We are all of the same, common clay.

And so it was that I betook myself to my grandparent's bedroom and stole the thirty pieces of silver (a couple of half-dollars, some quarters, dimes and nickels) from their supply of change they kept on a shelf.

It didn't take my tormentor long to clean me out of my ill-gotten coins. The shame of my nefarious act began to burn into my mind and soul. But the dastardly deed was done and was not to be undone.

I never confessed my crime. The shame and betrayal of trust were too much for me to do so. But neither was I ever tempted to repeat it. Between that experience and my short tenure in Las Vegas not long after, I was forever cured of any propensity for gambling apart from some relatively innocuous turns in adulthood at slot machines that had more to do with "When in Rome" than any thought of "easy riches," and I do believe God is opposed to gambling as well. Whisky was another thing entirely. I liked it.

Strong drink and tobacco (and gambling) were an absolute taboo of my grandparents. Not so with my mother. She both smoked and drank. Between the popularizing of such sports via silver screen, the license of society because of WWII and rebellion to her parent's mores, Mom heartily engaged in both of the fascinating and sinfully attractive practices. Then, as now, one of my favorite odors is acquired by sticking my nose into a pack of cigarettes or pouch of pipe tobacco. I even enjoy an occasional cigar.

It was while living at Minter Field with my mother and Stepdad #3 that so many things of great interest occurred, among them, my introduction to drunken debauchery at the tender age of ten.

My brother and I had discovered the "wine cellar," a stash of booze Mom and the stepdad thought they had well hidden. A bottle of whisky was among the forbidden fruit. There are some things that just have a natural attraction for kids; along with blood, guts, guns, explosive devices and sundry items of mayhem and destruction there is booze.

Now no child with any self respect can deny a righteous dare. And when one's younger brother advances the dare, well, you can imagine for yourself the humility of not meeting the challenge. And I was up to the mark.

My brother: "Bet you can't drink any of this stuff." Me: "Of course I can!" I did. In fact, I liked it. No challenge at all. It was so good and impressed my brother so much that there was nothing to do but have another snort. I felt good. I felt real good. I was thoroughly drunk.

I recall basking in the hero admiration of my little brother, going into the bedroom, and getting up on the bed beginning to jump up and down like crazy. What great fun!

But suddenly I was lying on my back, staring at the ceiling, watching it swirl in a hazy circle above me. "This is not right," my mind was saying. My stomach knew it was not right, in fact, my stomach was plumbing new dimensions of never before felt uneasiness. No, not uneasiness; my stomach knew I had purposely tried to assassinate it! Well, my stomach was not going to take that lying down you can bet. It didn't.

You've heard the one about the passenger found bending over the rail of the ship, whom when told that no one had ever died of seasickness replied, "Please don't tell me that. It's only the hope of dying that's keeping me alive!" I discovered the absolute truth of that statement. I had never known such sickness, never believed anyone could live through such living death! But I lived. It wouldn't be until some fifteen years later that I could even endure the smell of whisky. However, once overcome ... but I leave the sordid details of that stage of my youth for another time.

CHAPTER FIVE

These past few days I managed to get the roof trusses built and get the roof sheathed and covered on the cabin; hard work but a welcome respite from the cares of this poor old world's sorrows. But, how I longed to be able to take a righteous shower! While there is nothing wrong with honest toil and dirt, there is nothing wrong with wanting to be clean either. Hopefully, Walden Puddle will come about in the near future. Then, at least I can immerse myself in the pool until I figure out shower facilities.

While the sun was beating my brains out as I was nailing CDX sheets to the trusses, I recalled the Quilting Parties. These are a fond memory of my childhood when we lived on the corner of Cottonwood and Padre in Little Oklahoma during the late 30's and early 40's.

As an aside, my mother tells me that they found Amelia Earhart's kidnapped husband in this house while it was under construction. I need to check this out. Maybe the archives of the Bakersfield Californian have the story. She says my second stepdad was in the Army Messenger Pigeon Corps. Now how about that?

Another curiosity; my grandparents, due to circumstances I have described in my book, were married by telephone; an extremely rare occurrence during that era and, reputedly, the first done, with the governor's blessing, in Louisiana. These were inventive people.

My grandparents had a quilting frame that hung from the ceiling of the living room. At times the neighbor women, mostly members of grandad's little congregation of Faith Tabernacle, would get together and make quilts.

It was something my brother Dee Dee and I always enjoyed. Bakersfield, as you may know, is noted for its sometimes balmy, often very hot summers and pungent odors. My earliest memories of the smells of the packing plant down the road, mingled with the oil wells and holding ponds, outdoor privies, the various flora of our little neighborhood, are deeply imprinted in my mind.

But the thing that made the quilting parties so much fun was the fact that, as the ladies all gathered around the apparatus Dee Dee and I could crawl under the thing and, in the coolness of our shadowed sanctuary, listen to the genteel gossip. We were far too young to understand much of what the women said, but it was pleasant to hear their lulling voices and share the enjoyment they obviously were having as they sewed the various pieces of fabric into fascinating mosaics of a quilt.

Quilting was a communal thing. Grandma and great-grandma were precious to my brother and me. It made us feel good whenever they and all the neighbor ladies got together and had fun. Like crawling into our private preserve of the cannas in the yard, there was some kind of magic in the warmth and security of just being around good people and a shaded place during the hot summer days, of listening to Jack Armstrong; the All American Boy, Captain Midnight, Amos and Andy, Duffey's Tavern and so many more that kept our imaginations alive and made us laugh. The old Saturday Evening Post, Colliers, and National Geographic- Great-grandma would read to us by kerosene lamp and make Tugboat Annie come alive.

You know, women and children have lost a lot to an ephemeral "equality." When women were responsible for the home and little ones, when they gathered in community, as for quilting and wash day, they shared the work, they talked, children felt secure. It was hard work but by working and sharing together, they and their families gained a great deal. Women and men had clearly defined roles.

But now it takes two paychecks to make ends meet. Children, in droves, suffer the consequences. All our modern conveniences have left us with less and less time for the really important things in life. Thanks to pornography like Playboy, Hustler and Penthouse, men think they are being cheated when they look at their wives or girlfriends. And, because sex is no longer a sacred trust, because women have devalued themselves so much, men are always looking for something, someone else. And concerning trust, women are just as bad or worse.

But this way is too hard. I'm too old to long maintain such anger. It depletes my strength. I would far rather look back to that time of simple verities, to once more in my imagination, live again the magic that used to be childhood. Like the magic of digging holes.

Now children are naturally born with some Badger blood. There is nothing more natural to a child than digging holes. Throw away the Nintendo and give a kid a shovel. He doesn't need any instructions with this implement. He knows, intuitively, what that thing is for. And, unless you say he has to dig a hole for some real purpose, like planting a tree, thus making a fun thing work, he will set to with a will and make holes. And what do you do with the hill of earth removed during the project? Well, naturally, you play on it. You roll down it; you play King of the Hill and, in general, make productive use of the material. Honestly! Adults just have to have these things explained.

Ronnie and I, and some of the neighbor children, were prodigious diggers. The rich, yielding, rock-free soil of our neighborhood was designed of God for just such a purpose. We didn't just dig, we excavated. A truly marvelous hole was made in the side yard next to the church once.

We had a Victory garden there. Acting on instinct alone, we must have realized the church and garden would shield our efforts from the prying eyes of the resident and prone to misunderstanding adults.

Like Topsy, the thing just grew. What started out as just your ordinary hole soon became two large holes with a connecting tunnel. Somewhere, a couple of pieces of plywood came to us; covering the project with them and a thin layer of soil gave us an underground house safely concealed from the prying eyes of adults. With a candle for light, we had a marvelously mysterious hide-a-way of our very own.

Sadly, the enterprise came to an end due to the common occurrence of a fire. A storage shed caught fire and the fire truck, in an attempt to get close to it, decided to use the side yard. There was some consternation among the adults, particularly the firemen, when the truck's wheels disappeared up to the axle in our secret house. Fortunately for us, no one was home at the time.

In retrospect, it is a wonder that none of us kids died as a result of such activities. Small wonder, as we get older and have children of our own, that we live in fear for them.

Negroes played an important role in my childhood while living in Little Oklahoma. The Dust Bowl migrants of our neighborhood not only brought their simple, generally honest viewpoints with them; there were also the prejudices and bigotry so common to ignorance and superstition.

The railroad tracks separated Little Oklahoma from Nigger Town, as it was called back then. Grandad, in spite of his Southern background and because of his calling as a Pentecostal preacher, was one of the few Caucasians acceptable to the inhabitants of Nigger Town and we frequently traveled in the area. As with all human relationships, you can generally expect to be treated as you treat others regardless of race. This stood me in good stead during my tenure as a high school teacher in Watts. Has it really been that long since the riots and the burning and looting of this area? And what has really changed for the better for these people since that time?

Thoreau's dictum that "A wise man lives simply" is a truth impossible of improvement. There must be a place where people can dream and hope, where they can clean out their minds and gain a fresh perspective of what is really meaningful in life. You simply cannot do it while drowning in smog and staring at the asphalt, steel, and concrete jungle.

For those of you who can, get that place and teach your children how to do for themselves. It simply cannot be beat as a family exercise and an invaluable investment in theirs and your future. Like the title of a recent and popular book: Do It!

There were many times, as a child, that my grandad let me just do it. The *It* didn't always work out; but in no instance did I fail to learn something of value, even from the failures.

Now Grandad was the idol of my childhood. He could do things. He could build a house, do wiring and plumbing, in short, he was a jack-of-all-trades as many of his generation were. But the automobile remained a mystery to him all his life. Grandad was never a mechanic.

Sometime after moving to the mining claim in Sequoia National Forest, I came of age to have my own car, about fifteen years old. From somewhere in that mysterious gene pool, there lay the genius of the mechanic and machinist in my own make-up. The essential missing ingredients were knowledge and experience.

I cut my teeth driving the family pick-up, a venerable old Ford, and a '28 Buick. Grandad, being a firm believer in that maxim of hard work never killed anyone had me earning money digging septic tank holes by hand and every other job requiring a strong back. I was a mean kid with a pick and shovel (not to mention the fact that I supplied all the fuel for our stove and fireplace). But a regular job came my way when I became the Junior Custodian for old Kernville Elementary.

For once, I had a real job and a steady income; the magnificent sum of $35 a month for cleaning classrooms every day after school. I was ready to commit to the American Dream, going into debt on the installment plan.

And so it was that Grandad and I took off to the Big City of Bakersfield where I bought a '39 Pontiac for $100 payable $10 a month (I think it was the amber fog lights that attracted me to this particular car). The fact that it had a pronounced knock from the bowels of the engine didn't seem to perturb Grandad. I drove the old car, slowly, all the way up the canyon with the engine knocking the whole time.

An acquaintance, Gus Suhre, who was a mechanic, upon hearing the knock in the engine pronounced it a bad rod bearing. Now neither Grandad nor I had any ideas about the mysteries of the internal combustion engine. But I was determined to learn. And we all know a little knowledge is a dangerous thing.

Gus explained the procedure for curing the Pontiac's illness. It was utterly incomprehensible to me. What was a crank, a micrometer, a rod bearing? I was going to find out.

With the tools available, I was able to pull the head and pan on the car. With its innards exposed, I was finally face to face with the complexities of the engine. There were things called valves, pistons, rods, and I began to operate. With Gus' explanation I was able to locate the loose rod and pull the cap off and remove the rod and piston. However, what to do with this micrometer thing-a-ma-jig? Gus had uttered some mysterious words about something like "miking" the crank. I was supposed to use this glorified C-clamp to find out if the crank was out of round, whatever that meant.

Following his mysterious instructions, I dutifully screwed the thing to fit the crank journal and moved it around like he said to do. The problem was that I simply did not know what the purpose of this maneuver was supposed to accomplish. Somehow, the fit of the contraption was supposed to tell me if there was anything wrong with the journal. It didn't. Mainly because I didn't know how to read a micrometer or what, exactly, I was looking for.

But I manfully checked to see if the device moved around the crank at a certain setting and called the case closed. Looked all right to me. It was smooth and there wasn't any burning or galling as Gus had warned me to look for. And I had the rod and piston out. I was ready for the fix.

Now, as Gus had said, I was supposed to get another rod and piston (Gus never bothered to explain why he thought I needed another piston; perhaps he didn't want to go through the drill of explaining how to remove and replace just the rod). This necessitated another trip to Bakersfield where I was soon to be introduced to the exciting world of Auto Junk Yards.

At the earliest opportunity, Grandad and I took off and I was soon examining bins of pistons and rods at one of the yards. All I knew was that I was to get a replacement for the offending '39 engine rod. But the bins had mysterious markings designating the assemblies with hieroglyphic markings like .010, .020 and .030.

Now I have already said automobiles were a mystery to Grandad. It never seemed to occur to him or me to ask what these mysterious markings meant. As a result, I simply took the one that looked the best from a bin marked with the hieroglyph .010 and off we went.

On arriving back at the claim, I inserted the new rod and piston in the cylinder. Seemed a tad tight. What to do? Of course! Get a bigger hammer! Which I proceeded to do. With a little persuasion from the hammer handle, I managed to pound the recalcitrant piston into the cylinder and the rod down over the crank. Replacing all the parts in the order in which I removed them (no new gaskets; why waste money?) I was finally ready to crank the sucker up!

Now for those of us that were raised with the old six-volt systems, we know how difficult it can be to get an engine started, particularly if it has had major surgery, with those old, six-volt batteries. With great foresight, I had parked the car on the convenient hill at the side of our cabin.

Getting in the car, I performed the maneuver all us oldsters were familiar with back in the old days; I put the car in second gear, put in the clutch, let off the parking brake and let her roll. At a fairly good clip downhill I popped the clutch and the engine fired. Once. With a horrendous bang!

Rolling to a stop at the bottom of the hill, I jumped out to see what had happened. From the place the engine had fired, there was a long trail of oil in the dirt. Looking under the car I saw a truly magnificent, jagged hole in the pan. At the place where the trail of oil started, I found what remained of the rod cap. Interesting.

And so, my early introduction to auto mechanics was an explosive success. Knowing how to read helped. I discovered what "oversize" meant regarding pistons, and engine cylinders were actually bored at times when majored. The experience was of incalculable value to me in later years when I taught auto shop to high schoolers. If I could be so dumb, why couldn't they?

I latter acquired a junk '38 Pontiac with a reasonably good engine and, with true grit, a convenient pine tree and chain-fall, managed the Herculean task of swapping out the engines. I was about fifteen years old and didn't even have a driver's license, let alone insurance. Few of us mountain kids and not a few adults bothered with such niceties in those days. Besides, there were no Chippies or other minions of the law to contend with. And very little traffic.

While the trans and engine bolted together nicely, the clutch linkage was not as cooperative between the '38 and '39. A short length of chain took care of this minor problem. I actually drove this car to L.A. when I left the claim in '53 and subsequently traded it in on a magnificent '41 DeSoto convertible.

A great deal of learning took place in my life on the mining claim. But it took the proper environment for such opportunities. And, while the episode of the Pontiac is fraught (freighted to use Sam's favorite word) with all kinds of morals, points, etc., that I had such gumption, ignorance and all, was due to the fact of that environment and the support of loving elders who would encourage such a task.

As I think of all the things and people that contributed so much to my own ability to dream, to do, to plan and build and teach others, I have a debt to pass these things on to others, young people especially. How I wish I could give them the same opportunities to learn, plan, dream and do that it was my blessed good fortune to experience. And after all these years, with all the disappointments and failures, I still strive to do.

It is a tragedy of our times that children are cheated, robbed, of the opportunities I enjoyed as a child, that even the most caring parents seem unable to grasp the eternal significance of teaching the kinds of things that can only be learned in such an environment as that which I enjoyed can supply. Young people especially need examples of "Can Do." They are losing hope in droves because of the mind-set that the future holds nothing for them.

However, put that child in an environment with caring elders, where he or she can do, and watch them blossom into individuals with values, self-esteem and real-world skills that will serve them a lifetime.

When I visit the old claim (now Boulder Gulch Campground), when I survey the ancient familiar mountains and travel Bull Run, Fay Canyon and so many other places of my childhood, I sometimes talk things over with Grandad, Grandma, and Great-grandma. Do they hear me? I have no idea. But I find comfort in the conversations. I think they are proud of me, and the fact that I am still doing. I believe they know what really counts in life by now. Somehow I think these are still the same things they thought really counted when they taught me as a child.

It is too easy, at my age, to slip back into that time of simple verities long past, to escape the ugliness all around by dwelling with those gone on whose love and support are all too lacking for children today.

***

As I write this, I'm not sure where Christmas will find me. It's hard not having a family anymore, especially during the holidays. I certainly understand the depression this brings on in others in similar circumstances.

We've had some showers in the Valley and the nights have turned cold. A light dusting of snow shows on the surrounding mountains. The Canyon is resplendent in the variegated colors of the leaves of the trees and the sun shines with crystal clarity. The air is sweet and crisp.

With so much happening throughout the world, I'm apt to suffer information overload. Also, so much of what is happening is bad news that I have to stretch to get some humor to share with you and lighten the load. So, I went out to the cabin and took a walk among the pines and rocks and concluded that my best source of humor is still myself. I love to tell stories on me. And a great source of humor is in life's embarrassing moments.

An adolescent can endure just about anything but embarrassment. If I didn't know this as a youngster, I certainly learned it as a high school teacher. Its judicious use as a teaching mechanism proved useful. But, you walked a fine line in its application. Never did I exercise this option without recalling an incident in my junior high years.

Girls, at this innocent period of my life, were strange creatures indeed. They were not unlike Martians, intriguing, but suspect. And, for all my acquaintance with the fair sex, they may as well have come from outer space for all I knew about them. They smelled nice, seemed to be preoccupied with their appearance and cleanliness and I never saw one of them spit. Altogether peculiar.

They traveled in groups and spent a lot of time whispering to each other and giggling. They would look at a certain boy in a peculiar fashion, go into a huddle and giggle. Bizarre behavior but fascinating.

Those of you who have read my book, Confessions and Reflections of an Okie Intellectual, will recall my talking about my raisin' by my grandparents. Sex was never mentioned. Much of my reading was Victorian and novels like The Last of the Mohicans, The Talisman, and other such works led to my thinking of the opposite sex in terms of mystery and purity. My moral code in this regard was worthy of a Knight seeking the Holy Grail. Utterly chaste, naive, and ignorant.

My favorite sport in school was baseball. It was lunchtime and three or four of the boys and I were having our usual, loose game of pitch and hit. I happened to be pitching at the time.

Three of the strange, alien creatures wandered onto the infield and, in their inexplicable humor, called out to me: (They seem, like sharks sensing blood, to intuit who is easy prey) "What do you want to be when you grow up?" In a vain attempt at nonchalance, I was actually quaking at being singled out for their attentions, I replied: "Useless!" There, I thought, that ought to get rid of them.

To my utter dismay, they broke out laughing and giggling, and one of them, I would swear, was actually blushing (Some girls really did that a long time ago). Now, as sharp as my retort had been, I could find nothing in it to warrant such a reaction. But, as I've said, they were strange creatures; one never knew how they would respond to anything. Some things, at least, have never changed in that regard since time immemorial.

But, to my further consternation, the afternoon found several of the girls and boys looking at me and smiling in a peculiar fashion. What in the world was going on? There was, obviously, a joke being shared about me of which I had no knowledge.

During the afternoon recess a buddy, J.L., took me aside, and with admiration said, "You really have a lot of guts. You really put those girls in their place." Now, while I was not immune to praise, I hadn't the slightest idea of what in the ever-loving-blue-eyed-world he was talking about. So, I asked: "What in the ever-loving-blue-eyed-world are you talking about?"

J.L.: "You know; when those girls asked you what you were going to be when you grow up and you said 'A NUDIST!' " That marvelous computer known as my brain suddenly went into a crash mode. Whether in the body or out of the body, I could not tell. To a painfully shy youngster, to have to come to grips with such a story going around the entire school among his peers was too much for me to grasp.

How I got through the mercifully few last minutes of the afternoon I don't know. I remained in mortified shock, unable to look at anyone. Eventually, as I maintained my innocence and defended myself at such vile calumny best I could, it was too good a story for everyone else and I remained a reluctant hero to my buddies and the girls continued to look at me with new eyes of interest thereafter.

Having had more than a casual education in the mechanisms of the female mind lo these many years, I have come to the conclusion that either God has a perverse sense of humor reflected in His creature's appreciation of practical jokes and slapstick humor or He wishes He had done some things differently in His creation of men and women. I don't allow of any middle ground such as the religious nonsense that God is incapable of error. His own Word bears testimony of the opposite case. My religious friends have the burden of proof on their own heads as they try to fancy-dance their way to an apologetic for Jesus' command that we are to be perfect just as God is perfect and, that, if any two agree they can ask and God will bring it to pass. As I have said many times, He must have something else in mind when it comes to a definition of perfection than how religious people construe it.

***

When asked who the first two Apostles were, Tom Sawyer replied: "Adam and Eve?" We may laugh at Tom's desperate answer but it reminds me of many a similar answer to Bible questions. My great-grandma was fond of showing off my Bible knowledge as a child to others. She would ask: "What was Noah's Ark made of?" and I would dutifully reply: "Gopher wood."

Now my grandparents, my great-grandma and I had no idea that the Hebrew word translated Gopher wood was an uncertain translation. In the NIV it is given as Cypress. But we knew our King James Bible was God's Word and would defend Gopher wood to the death. I don't think anyone in Little Oklahoma knew there were any other versions or translations of the Bible and we would have branded anyone a heretic and blasphemer who suggested such a thing. The Old Time Religion was good for Paul and Silas and it was good enough for all of us. And anyone that had a lick of sense or cared anything for God knew Paul and Silas used the King James Bible!

As I often reach back in my memory to that simple time of my childhood among simple and honest folks, the women in grain or flour sack dresses and us boys in our bib overalls and barefoot, I long for the plainness and openness of our dirt-poor community in old Southeast Bakersfield; a time before drugs and a collapse of morality were destroying our nation. A time when the bad guys really did wear black and the good guys wore white and, sensibly, kissed the horse instead of the girl (I know, but the aberration of Hopalong Cassidy didn't count. Maybe he was the forerunner of the anti-hero, in attire at least. But I'd hate to hang that on Hopalong. In any event, there was never any question about his being a good guy and our hero).

But, by the end of WWII, there was a quick change of culture in our nation. The boys came back from overseas where so many had gained a cosmopolitan view of things, and that together with the nation having become the preeminent world power, an industrial giant, the Atomic Bomb, women working at men's jobs, the abandoning of the simple, agricultural way of life, so many, many changes. As with the Old South after the Civil War, gone forever, the way of life we knew as children.

I have lived long enough to look back far enough. I grieve for the loss of so much for our children. It seems a tragedy that young people know more about the local Mall than an animal trail along some shimmering, singing, mountain stream or a clear night sky, bejeweled by countless stars, that their ears are accustomed to raucous noise as opposed to the bark of a squirrel, the call of quail or the hoot of an owl.

It is incredible, thoroughly implausible, that a Dust bowl, Weedpatch, Little Oklahoma Okie like me should one day be sitting at a computer, a Ph. D. hanging on the end of his name and reaching back to such a simple time of life in order to make sense of it all. It's all a little fantastic. It does bring to mind the statement in the Bible that God uses the foolish things of this world to confound the wise.

I just returned from a hike in Fay Canyon. The recent snow and rain has been sufficient to cause the streams in the area to be running nicely. This is a particularly beautiful area and while walking through the forest I lived again some of the fun my children, Karen and Michael, and I did have there. I am sure that someday they will treasure the memory of the time just as I do.

As I walked along one of the streams, my eye caught a glimpse of a piece of obsidian. Sure enough, it was part of an arrowhead. This area has a lot of game and, judging from the shape and size of the fragment, I'm sure some Indian had shot at something, probably a deer or maybe a rabbit and this was the remains of his attempt at dinner.

A couple of hours later when I was returning to my car I came across a place where it was obvious some folks had been cutting trees for firewood. I spied some shell casings, .45 auto. Being a re-loader from many years' back, I have a habit of picking up brass. Someone must have emptied a clip from the number I found. As I was gathering the cases, I found a 1985 penny. I'm gray and my eyes are growing dim but I still see obsidian, shell casings, and money on the ground.

I sat on a granite boulder beneath a big, old Digger pine beside the stream; and with my ever-present cup of coffee and a cigarette, examined my artifacts.

It must be my Choctaw Cherokee blood that responds so to such an environment. I could well imagine the Indian and what he had to contend with in living off the land. My thoughts ran to what it must have been like here before the intrusion of the White-Eyes. Then I looked at the .45 casings and the penny. The Indian could never have imagined the culture that would produce such marvels. What a difference between that arrowhead and the .45, and his wampum and the penny with the technology that produced such things.

And I thought about someone like me who has taken it upon him to question the teachings of the great scholars of the Bible. But I also thought about what that Indian understood in his own culture and environment. His knowledge was certainly extremely limited compared with what European nations possessed. But he functioned well enough in the world he knew. And, as in the allegory of the cave, thought he knew a great deal.

However, the Indian's knowledge and expertise were to prove no match for the superior learning and technology of the more advanced cultures of Western Civilization. An arrow is no match for a .45 auto. But imagine, if you will, the tremendous difference between the time and the world that existed for both the Indian that shot his arrow and the person that stood in the same place firing that .45! Who do you suppose God holds more accountable for knowing what is best?

While I long for a simpler way I once knew as a child, while I know that much of what I was blessed with as a child was denied my own children, I, like the Indian, will learn and adapt or perish.

The Indian may well have had a profound belief in The Great Spirit, but it did not save him or his way of life when opposed by a greater power. That he was ignorant of things like systematic theology, having his own equivalent in his own system of superstitions and beliefs, was to prove no match for the great learning and better ways of his conquerors.

I was impressed once more by the seeming accident of birth that made me the beneficiary of being a citizen of the United States, and that I was born in a time of such vast advances in the sciences.

And so it is that so many things twist and turn through our lives that bring us to moments of decision that can so thoroughly change things for good or evil. So it is that I began to question so many of the things that I had simply accepted as Articles of Faith that had no sound basis in either Scripture or reason, confusing like so many do beliefs with knowledge.

I do not have any longer the excuse of the Indian or, even, a simple product of Little Oklahoma for my ignorance. I became educated. More, I have a wealth of experience for which I am both responsible before God and, from which, I am to draw for examples of my own blind orthodoxy and childishness. I can envy my Indian ancestor for his freedom from technology, for his escaping having to pay a mortgage and fight traffic. But I cannot envy his ignorance and superstitions. I loved my grandparents dearly, but I cannot envy their own ignorance and superstitions.

I do believe, however, that, as with the Indian, had they known better they would have done better. They did the best they could based on what they had; and they were honest in those things. I hope I can do as well.

CHAPTER SIX

Grandad and I had decided to make a killin' on rabbit hides. My grandparents had the largest rabbitry in Kern County during WWII; 600 breeding does. I remember it well because it was my job to keep the critters watered and fed. Some of the hutches were three tiers high. During the Bakersfield summers, I had to keep the burlap on the hutches wet to cool the bunnies.

When we moved to the mining claim near old Kernville some of the livestock went with us, including a selection of rabbits. I had come of age to be totally responsible for the firewood and the breeding and care of the furry creatures. Being an avid woodsman, reading Field and Stream and Outdoorsman, The National Rifleman, etc., I asked my grandad one day: "Why don't we send some of the rabbit hides to one of these places that advertise in the magazines for pelts?" Grandad agreed it sounded like a plan.

It never occurred to me to ask what Grandad did with all the pelts he accumulated in Bakersfield. But, after butchering a rabbit, I would dutifully stretch the hide over a wire frame for drying. I had read articles on curing pelts and had followed the instructions well as I could. At the time of this experiment in fur entrepreneurial activity, about sixty pounds of pelts sat at the ready.

Selecting one of the advertisers, we boxed and shipped off the hides. The cost of shipping came to $1.64. This was a long time ago. Anticipating sudden riches, I waited impatiently for the check to come in the mail. In about six weeks it did; in the amount of 68 cents. We had lost 96 cents on the deal, not to mention all the time and trouble of skinning, stretching, curing, boxing and shipping. It was at this point that a good vocational counselor should have recognized my genius and groomed me for work in the Pentagon or Congress. Another of life's opportunities missed because of the failure of the schools to help the best and the brightest.

It was about this same time that I was learning taxidermy by correspondence school (another sure-fire scheme gleaned from one of the outdoor magazines). I managed a trout and a squirrel, Frankenstein couldn't have done better, and then I tried a dove. The grandparents raised pigeons and doves and, as children, one of our favorite treats was fried pigeon or dove eggs sunny side up. Such cookery required a delicate touch. The squab was good also.

I had read that birds had to be soaked in kerosene before peeling the skin from the critters. Obtaining one deceased dove, I obediently followed the procedure for soaking it. In about five hours, following the taxidermy directions, I removed it from the bucket of kerosene and set it out to dry, and went squirrel hunting.

Occasionally, grandma had a hankering for roasted dove. I returned from the hunt to discover my dove plucked and my grandma complaining of a strong odor of kerosene on the bird. Her first thought was of grandad who had doused the rabbits one night by mistaking a gallon jug of kerosene on the top of a hutch for a bobcat. The .410 had done a satisfactory job of killing the jug and drenching the inhabitants. For whatever reason, I never did get around to stuffing birds.

***

Our grandparents had taken Dee Dee and me to a Christmas program at The American Legion Hall in Bakersfield. I was about four and my brother three years old. Some lady was on stage singing when I turned to Dee Dee and exclaimed in a loud voice: "Dee Dee, I think that lady is a painted hussy!" Dee Dee replied: "I think she's a painted hussy too!" One can only imagine the embarrassment of our grandparents as everyone within hearing range burst out laughing at Dee Dee's and my somber pronouncement concerning the character of the lady in question.

Now neither Ronnie nor I had any idea what a "painted hussy" was. Having heard the phrase a number of times, perhaps we had learned to equate it with any woman who dressed in a certain way and wore makeup. However, living a generation behind the times with our maternal grandparents, we children were exposed to a morality that society has long since abandoned. However, such has not been to the benefit of civilization.

***

I envy the guy in Colorado that is making a business of sucking prairie dogs out of their holes with a large vacuum device and releasing them on federal lands. The critter doesn't know what happens to him. "He's a little dazed, but otherwise ok," says Mr. Balfour, the genius who came up with this scheme.

Some years ago, I went to Colorado to start a private school for a group of folks in Wiggins. When it came time to return to California, the family flew back, but I was left with the task of driving the largest rental truck available and towing the family station wagon behind; a big, Chevy Kingswood Estate. Since this occurred in January, I called for weather conditions and was assured they were ok. Wrong! I was only a few hours on the road and hit a blizzard that remained with me all the way to California. At times I was creeping through blinding snow at five mph. When I began to see big rigs that had slid off the road, I knew I was in trouble. If the pros were losing it, what were my chances, especially in the biggest, fully loaded truck I could rent with that big wagon pushing me down the long grades?

I knew, in many instances, that just one push on my brakes would be the end of it. Ice formed on the windshield and, freezing my backside off, I was forced to keep my head out the window at times to see where the road was, as I would creep slowly down the steep hills.

The trip was made more interesting by the fact that I was transporting a Colorado Cottontail rabbit my daughter, Karen, had caught (God only knows how?) shortly before our departure together with a cage of parakeets and a white momma cat. I was able to keep the birds warm by placing the cage on the floor in front of the heater when I had to have the window open. The Cottontail proved no problem because when I put it in the truck and took off, he ricocheted around the cab like a ping pong ball for a minute then disappeared under the seat not to be seen again till I reached my destination in California. The momma cat didn't seem to care about anything but sleeping and eating.

But a funny thing occurred on my way that still brings a smile to my face. I reached Boomtown the second night, dead tired and ready to crash in bed. I hadn't shaved or bathed for two days and looked like death warmed over. Bundled in my overcoat, gloves, muffler and stocking cap, birdcage with its inhabitants and a grocery bag in arm, I entered the motel-casino to get a room for the night.

I know I had to have made quite an impression in the splendor of the gaming establishment. There were all those high rollers, dressed to the nines, and this desperado appears in their midst. Security guards abounded and I attracted no little interest from them. It didn't occur to me until I, dead tired, was sitting on a stool, birdcage at my feet, waiting for the clerk to do the paper work for my room, that the bag I was holding contained five pistols that I instinctively didn't leave in the truck. Tired as I was, the humor of the situation impressed me. If those guards only knew I was armed to the teeth! Suppose one asked to check my bag? What a stir that would make! Another opportunity to make film at eleven; but by God's grace (and sense of humor I suppose) no one checked me out, though I am certain no more disreputable looking character had ever appeared in their glittering midst, and I got the needed night's rest.

I promised him to share some of Dee Dee's and my experiences in the Dust Bowl labor camps when we, as children, traveled across the country. Please bear with some repetition as I fulfill this promise.

While we had the luxury of going to Cleveland Ohio by train, our mother and stepdad decided to make the return trip to California by car. The current stepfather, Dan Pospieszynski, was a mechanic and it was decided, with the grandparent's help, to set up shop in Little Oklahoma. The trip occurred in the summer of 1946. We were packed into a venerable Terraplane, and we now had a baby half-brother, Johnny, to accompany and amuse us and off we went: Westward HO!

The Terraplane had a disconcerting habit of breaking down in every state we passed through. Somehow, our stepdad managed to get it fired back up each time but it did pose problems. One breakdown occurred in the Arizona desert. I still attribute our mother's dislike of the desert to this particular episode of adventures in travel. I know we baked for a while to the accompaniment of our baby brother's cries of discontent and malodorous diapers. Perhaps my brother and I added some to the unpleasant experience, but memory being so kind in such matters I don't recall our doing anything, as with any well-mannered little boys, but exercising great forbearance and patience in the situation. Our mother may remember it differently.

Anyhow, I do recall a truck stopping, an empty car-carrier rig, and the driver and our stepdad trying to get the Terraplane onto it without success. My childhood memory includes a few vultures circling overhead and someone making a threat about "there was going to be one more death in Death Valley" during these pleasant hours in this Big Empty which may just be fanciful. But every time I think about the incident, the vultures are there.

Somehow, the car wound up in some town where the stepdad could make the necessary repairs throughout the night and the next day: On the road again! The road was good old Route 66 with its fascinating Old West museums and their displays of rattlesnakes, Gila monsters, meteorites and other desert memorabilia. One even had a mummified bandit complete with rope around his neck and rusted, iron bracelets hanging from one withered wrist; fascinating to childish imagination. I remember one exhibit with two Gila monsters in a circle of death; each with the other's tail chomped in its jaws. I have never lost my fondness for lizards and horny toads; but I still shoot rattlesnakes.

I marveled at the Painted Desert with its magnificent, splendid vista and grand array of subtle shades of colors. I so very much wanted one of the glass jars that were filled with layers of the colored sands, but the folks couldn't afford souvenirs.

It was undoubtedly this early, nomadic life that helped prepare me as a child for the loss of my family through an unexpected divorce (the woman deciding she wanted another man) and the fact that I have had no home or certain dwelling place these past few years and learn the hard lesson of "abased and abound." Still, I would not have chosen such a life. I will always be a family man at heart but not many women would be able to stand for such a life as I now lead. And, too, on those occasions when I have had to eat dirt and coexist with cockroaches, I found that it was worse being considered inconvenient or tiresome to friends. The cockroaches have proven to be better company, even preferable, on some occasions.

There have been times, though, when I needed a blanket and floor space in lieu of the road. I am properly grateful for such and never considered it being for my benefit alone. People have needed my company and visits many times that they weren't even aware of. I have also learned the luxury of being able to close a door for privacy; something I will never again take for granted.

It was in our travels cross-country that brought us into contact with the labor camps and the people that Steinbeck and Guthrie immortalized. The simple living conditions and the simple ways of the people touched me as a child as did those early Okies and Arkies of our Little Oklahoma neighborhood.

As I have said several times, these folks didn't know they were underprivileged and culturally deprived because there didn't exist, then, the host of bureaucrats and officials telling them they were underprivileged and culturally deprived; there didn't exist a legion of social services that catered to the poor in order to build their own bureaucratic empires, keep scoundrels in office and fill their pockets at the expense of the working middle class. Certainly, without the demonic instrumentation of television, we had no idea of what we were being deprived of.

It seemed reasonable to me as a child that Santa only came at Christmas. You worked for anything you wanted the rest of the year. I will never forget selling Cloverine Salve, flower and garden seeds door to door in order to earn my Red Ryder BB carbine. Of what great value such a noble possession when I had earned it by my own industry!

The real tyranny of poverty is accomplished not by being poor, but by a society's emphasis upon what constitutes *poor*. And, while, as Topol so well put it: "It's no disgrace to be poor, but it isn't any great honor either" it took the bureaucrats and the welfare state to make being poor a disgrace and dishonor humble, simple living and, even the opportunity, freedom and liberty to choose such a lifestyle. The streets, ghettos and barrios are a poor substitute; a cruel trade.

There have been times in my life when a dollar in my pocket or a can of peaches was wealth. But it took the government to make me feel poor and underprivileged, to make me feel that, in some ephemeral and disquieting, vague way that I was being cheated of something that I hadn't earned by the sweat of my own brow.

It is just such misanthropic, dinosaur thinking that makes the new generation consign me to the elephant's graveyard of those old world values where things like honor, duty, integrity, commitment and a man's word and name had relevance. However, it seems characteristic of a man who has a complete collection of Pogo books, loves opera, Thoreau, and disdains affectations by freely admitting that he can't stand ballet.

The camps of the forties we experienced couldn't have been too different from those of a few years past. Certainly they were peopled by the same kind of folks. The war had left its impress and much talk surrounded this great event of American history. We children still played war games along with Cowboys and Indians. Cap and rubber band guns were equal to both occasions. The conversations were still held by grownups with the ubiquitous chew or snuff doing good service in punctuating speech. There were even a few Mammy Yokums complete with corncob pipes.

Some camps had running water, some didn't. Some had cabins, some had tents or half-tents, a floor and board structure halfway up and topped by tent material. A few had wood stoves. One of the best was nestled in a grove of magnificent trees. Being summer time, I was entranced by the huge, marvelously colored moths, along with June bugs and other assorted insects that would be attracted to the camp lights at night. I had never seen such amazing behemoths of mothdom; some were the size of hummingbirds!

One of the great inventions of civilization is the Mason jar. These were obviously designed for children to keep a variety of insects and lizards with which to keep such treasures captured for the handy and close inspection of budding, inquiring, prospective scientists; the future entomologists and herpetologists; also, you could, if you had a mind to, get some interesting reactions from assorted mothers and little girls with some such collection of varied arachnids, moths, flies, etc.

The occasional lizard or small garter snake served admirably in such experimentation of human behavior, especially if the incarcerant(s) somehow, inexplicably, got loose in a bedroom (your mother's or a sister's, if you played your cards right and the fates cooperated).

A parent with such a child is helped in their own growth processes by finding an empty jar and stimulated in their minds by having to imagine what might have been set loose in the house. I am convinced that one of the major obligations of children toward their parents is just such activity. It keeps the grownups on their toes.

Speaking of lizards reminds me of Bob MaHoney, our second stepdad who served in the Army Carrier Pigeon Corps during WWII. Bob was a good guy. It was during one of his visits to our place in Little Oklahoma that he decided to help Dee Dee and I catch lizards.

The place at Cottonwood and Padre in those days was surrounded by an alkali wasteland; great for the inhabitant lizards and other assorted reptiles. Bob's plan was simple. He took a length of material like a fishing rod and, making eyes of thin, copper wire along its length and passing the thin copper line through them fashioned a noose at the other end. The idea was to get this noose over the hapless creature's head and jerk it tight, thus capturing the poor thing. Fortunately, like putting salt on a bird's tail feathers, no lizard was to be had that exhibited the necessary degree of cooperation in the procedure. Looking back on it, I still wonder why it didn't occur to MaHoney that had we ever gotten such a device over a lizard's head the contraption would have successfully garroted or even decapitated the little varmint. Maybe Bob didn't really like lizards?

The subject always reminds me of the heady days of my Iguana ranch and bronzed bullfrog schemes, raising gnus for fun and profit and the time I dropped the mouse down the back of the dress of one of mom's friends while they were talking.

Seemed like a good idea at the time but I lost the small, white rodent amidst the confusion, ear-rending shrieks and what has to be a world's record for the Shimmy. Since I was raising the little creatures at the time, the mouse was easily replaced. Don't know about mom's friend. Don't recall any further visits though.

One thing leads to another. This happened when my college roomie was a Black Irishman, and the vilest human being it has ever been my privilege to know.

I was courting the kid's mother at the time. She worked as a cashier for the old Roxie Theater in downtown Whittier. Nixon's birthplace, if you know anything about it, was a lily-white, staid, conservative town of upper class folk; boutiqueish shops and manicured lawns; Rodeo Drive environment.

It was a warm, summer evening when I decided, with my partner's encouragement in evil, to pull this stunt. I had a straw sombrero, which I had adorned with the spike from a German, WWI helmet. Putting on a pair of ragged Levi's, a weathered and corrupt flannel shirt and a pair of Firestone, radial sandals (no socks) and draping a large, polka-dotted bandanna around my neck together with a heavy necklace of large beads, and a scroungy serape over my shoulder, a two-days growth of dark beard and sporting a pair of dark sunglasses, I would have been the envy of Pancho Villa. My buddy managed to make up an outfit that is best described as a lumberjack down on his luck. Thus it was, properly attired to terrorize, or, at the very least, properly offend the locals in our sartorial splendor we assayed a nonchalant evening stroll through downtown Whittier. Destination: The Roxie!

With the polite citizens of the town crossing the street to avoid contact with us (My buddy had the presence of mind to carry a tin cup in case we got close enough to anyone to panhandle), we made our inexorable way to the theater. As luck would have it, we made it all the way without encountering the local constabulary and being detained from our quest. It was only the recognition of my buddy that kept, I'm sure, the kid's mother from fainting or screaming at our sudden appearance in the front of her. I don't think Whittier ever forgot us. No, we didn't get to see the movie that night.

***

It has been my privilege to spend years working for an honest living, to work with the folks that have kept this nation going, the mechanics, machinists, laborers, construction workers as well as the doctors, lawyers and teachers, a few of which, I have found to be honest. But my heart is still, largely, with those poor folks of my Dust Bowl era like my grandad whose philosophies of life, as with Thoreau, were based on such simple verities but proved so profound in the working out.

One of the earliest jobs I had that paid a wage was on a rock crusher in Old Isabella. The rig had been set up along a stretch of the river where the rock and sand could be processed for building materials. I was about fifteen years old and was paid a whole dollar an hour for lubing the machinery, keeping the ditch clear for the shovel and tossing boulders into the massive, iron crusher jaws. Being summer time, a 55-gallon steel drum was available to immerse my body when the heat got to me.

It was marvelous to watch what those great iron jaws would do to the rocks I threw to them, slamming, busting and chewing into the various parts of aggregate with horrendous noise, which would drop through the screens for sizing. The long shovel, dragged by cables, would reach out and drag a mammoth mouthful of material up to the crusher and spill it into its jaws, there to be hammered unmercifully to pieces.

Once, while clearing the ditch for the shovel the operator, not paying attention to the fact that I was still in the ditch, shoved the contraption into gear. The slack, steel cables suddenly whipped tight and caught me in the chest flinging me bodily into the air and out of the ditch. I was fortunate enough to escape with no more grievous injury than the loss of my shirt and a full-chest cable burn oozing blood droplets. A dunk in the water drum and I was back at work. A slight mishap was not going to deprive me of the opportunity of a dollar an hour.

If such a thing were to happen in today's society, some lawyer would have had me owning the rig. Not to mention the possibility of some kind of Workman's Compensation scam, apart from my age. Why, I might have wound up one of those forty-five percent getting some form of government assistance. Of course, where would a fifteen-year-old get a chance to do such work today? No insurance! In spite of the potential for accidents, I mourn the loss of opportunities for young people to do the kinds of work that were open to my generation due to the exhaustive controls government has placed on jobs; another case of government overkill. It's not that workers do not need protection in the workplace, but excessive, bureaucratic intrusion with its attendant litigation has emasculated industry. They have protected (read: Enslaved!) us to death.

I do not, however, suffer the delusion of a William Ellery Channing, a champion of The Elevation of the Laboring Class: There are those who, in the face of all history, of the great changes wrought in the condition of humankind, and of the new principles which are now acting on society, maintain that the future is to be a copy of the past, and probably a faded rather than bright copy. I am far more the weekday preacher of Thackeray, the Harlequin who, filled with sorrow for the human condition, nevertheless, knows the absolute need for humor.

In keeping with a balanced perspective, I am Thoreau's Saunterer. I don't take walks; I saunter. The word derived from the French, *Sainte-Terrer*, a Holy-Lander, meant in the Middle Ages one on pilgrimage. I do not take walks; each walk is a pilgrimage. My walks are more of Thoreau's choice of *sans terre*, without land or home, for, although we may at times have a bed for awhile, we know it is not our home.

A further condition to Sauntering is the freedom of Thoreau's cautionary word: "A man is rich in proportion to the number of things that he can afford to let alone." Therefore, like Thoreau, I draw strength from familiar commune with the mountains, rocks, trees and streams of God's creation and being thus wild, pity those wage slaves who, because of tyrants and their own greed in wanting ever more and more, all suffer, more or less, the tyranny of poverty no matter what their material possessions and wonder, as Thoreau, that they have not all committed suicide long ago. However, we are willing to credit them with some fortitude, even heroism that they remain by their lasts and anvils.

Thackeray described Swift as "Wild, witty and poor." I have suffered somewhat the same description of my own choice of lifestyle the past few years. But, though the lengthening shadows of the evening of life approach, as long as I can saunter I will continue to draw my strength from commune with my friends like Emerson, Thoreau, and Cooper; together with the critters, the pines and rocks of the mountains and the fenceless, cleanness of a desert panorama.

I still find comfort and joy in examining the skin of an old pine and the lichen, mica-mottled, shape and strength of a huge, granite boulder; of staring up through the branches of a tree to a clear blue sky. There is joy and the sense that we are not alone, that there is eternal purpose, when staring at the star-studded canopy of the night, listening to the flutter and scratchings of night creatures or in the blazing heat and light of Midsummer Day in the middle of the Mojave. I still thrill to the sun and a full moonrise; I'm still moved at their setting. A good thunderstorm is a delicious joy to my soul. Though the scars of battle, those lifelines, etch ever more deeply into my face, I have never lost or traded the wonder of a child at it all. These things I share with all such men and women irrespective of education, race or geography.

Men owe it to women and children to never lose the best part of the child in them. It is the wonder and magic of childhood that, retained in the man, evokes the tenderness and understanding, even the strength, so necessary to any weaker. It is that best part of man, in God's image, that becomes the poet and artist. That which began with lying on the grass or sandy loam and watching the ants in their fascinating industry or, if you were fortunate, a doodle bug (ant lion) working his way into the soil creating a marvelous cone in the process. Looking at the sun and your surroundings through a piece of colored glass or a clear colored marble, a purie, of believing anything is possible if you are honest and true, of believing in a world of adventure that would reward thrift and honest toil.

My life in Little Oklahoma and on the mining claim in Sequoia National Forest, my reading the classics of Cooper and others forever and indelibly molded the values and ideals I carry with me today. No amount of betrayal of them has diluted them, only tempered them by the ugly realities of the baser natures of men and women.

Thus it is that my need of Walkabouts in what I can find of that Great Empty keeps my mind in tune and the real issues and values of life, as I see them, in perspective and the best part of the child alive. This helps keep me from the mere sentimentality of Meet John Doe and the overly simplistic fixes of hugely, complex problems that only lead, ultimately, to Hitlerian solutions while, at the same time, able to enjoy Nelson Eddy and Jeannette MacDonald and grieve over what others choose to listen to.

I am indeed fortunate that I can escape to the mountains occasionally. I fervently wish I could remain in my cabin among the pines and the critters. Writing is a great emotional drain as well as on my physical resources; it's hard work. Far better to seek the wily trout or simply sit on my screen porch and listen to the music of the wind sighing through the pine needles and rustling through the leaves of the oaks; to watch the lizards sunning themselves on the granite boulders and listen to the call of the quail and the barking of the squirrels.

I never think of God's judgment but what the discipline of my own children comes to mind. We read in Proverbs that foolishness is bound up in the heart of a child but the rod and reproof will drive it far from him, that he that spares the rod hates his own child and not to spare our own hearts in the chastening.

No one could love his or her children more than I do mine. Before God, I lie not, if He should ask me what, in this life, was my greatest regret I would immediately reply: "Not sparing the rod!" It comes down to: "Hitting children is wrong! And children are people too!" Knowing what I do now, the rod would never have had any place in disciplining any of my children. And I would preach against its use against any child! Many the nights that I had to go to bed hating myself for what I mistakenly believed I had to do in barbaric attempts to discipline my children; particularly my son Michael. There are other methods of discipline that hurt parents just as much. I had to leave him at home once when I went fishing due to a very destructive thing he had done. I can't describe my own hurt at leaving him crying because he could not go with me. My heart was certainly not in the trip without him. I had to go, nonetheless, or the point couldn't have been made.

I know God must feel just as we do in disciplining and judging His children. There is more hurt in the heart of the loving parent than any suffering the child endures. But, sadly, it takes growing up to realize this. The lone parent who loves his children enough to prove that he cares about how they will grow up thus often finds himself consigned to the children's outer reaches. However, I repeat, to a chorus of Amens by parents, only until they have children of their own!

Is it any wonder that when given the option between urbane and domesticated I would choose the wild and untamed? But I am of the same conviction of Thoreau and London that a man draws his real values and strength from the Garden of pines and mountains, the desert and the sea, rather than from the neatly manicured lawns and shrubs of his comfortable prisons. It is natural in our hearts to admire the wild which excites and equate the tame with dull. I concede the need of being with people and my own proclivity for musty books. I open a book, stick my nose, literally, into it, and breathe its perfume of the printer and binder's craft before I even begin reading. I draw strength from such a wild source as well as that of naturally and unrestricted flowing streams and rivers.

CHAPTER SEVEN

Like so many others there was a first real romance in my own life, a love that makes all art and poetry real. I would have cheerfully slain dragons, reached for the moon and stars, lived a life devoted to the happiness of that One I cherished who became the definition for my whole life, my reason for being, for existing. I was able, shortly before her death, to share this experience with my eldest daughter Diana. I hope I can do so with Karen also someday. Somehow, in the telling of it, a bond was established that was never before possible. I will never forget her putting her arms around me afterward, kissing me and saying, in a way that made it sacramental, "Dad, I really do love you." In that moment, as a result of my own, true, love story, I had managed to communicate that thing that makes life worthwhile to the young; and the old have lost, traded for the cares and concerns of the world.

I am not leaving my sons Daniel and Michael out of this in my thinking. Daniel was there at the side of his sister when I told her about this. I know he understood what I was trying to say just as, I'm sure, the other children will also someday. It took many years for me to understand and find the words for it; I don't expect them, or anyone, to come to a full realization of it without paying the price.

Perhaps it was the reality of first love that made me a successful teacher of young people. I never recovered from the reality of that first love and I became understanding of its operation in the lives of my pupils. But it is the thing that makes me grieve so for the poor exchange our young people have settled for. "How do I love thee? Let me count the ways" has been traded for the glorification of evil in the raucous noise they call "music" and the sexual abandon of this generation. The needs are the same, but the poor substitutes for real love leave nothing but destruction and hopelessness in their wake.

I do have one important point of understanding in this tragedy. Young people are giving up any hope of love at a younger and younger point in their lives. Divorce, together with pornography, violence, corruption, illiteracy and drugs have taken their toll in the dreams of young people. Chastity is passe and the devil has substituted mere lust in its place. What our young people cannot possibly realize is that knights in shining armor and sleeping beauty are only possible in terms of chastity and morality, in that best part of the child that one loses in betrayal of what really is of value in our lives.

Our present Civil War of values rages. Norman Lear and PAW vie with moral principles and Kipling's IF. The lessons of James Dean, Natalie Wood, and Sal Mineo in *Rebel Without a Cause* are still to be learned. The poetry of the movie lost in the grim reality of "It's only a story." I sorrow for the loss of "The sad, silken rustle of each purple curtain while each slowly dying ember wrought its ghost upon the floor," traded for Stephen King, and, Madonna in exchange for "The Lady of the Lake." Who among our young people can now distinguish the child in Gatsby and fathom Fitzgerald's own yearning for immortality in the love of that One? Who among them knows the dark nobility of the singleness of the goal, the final bonding in mad purpose, in the hunt for "Ye damn-ed whale?"

The thumping, mindless and sense-destroying, animalistic noise of the music my youngest daughter and son listen to is a counterpoint to my choice of Red Sails in the Sunset. Not because I have not tried to teach them better, but because an entire society is telling them that their poor, deluded and antiquated father just doesn't understand. They can't possibly know what they are losing in the process; for that, they would have to accept the wisdom and experience of their father and society tells them that I am an anachronism. What chance do such young people have of ever coming to an understanding of real love, of that thing that makes it all worthwhile, when they don't even realize that MTV and the noise they are listening to, the violence they are being taught is the antithesis of all that is lovely, is anathema to truth, beauty, hopes and dreams, a mind-destroying, numbing analgesic to living a real life of eternal purpose!

There were several, large old pines on our mining claim. I was able to build a platform in the branches of one of these not far from our cabin. Thither I would resort to do my schoolwork on occasion and, in addition to the usual math and English, I would often take some books for pleasure. Sitting on the planks in the branches of the old tree, I would look out to the dun-colored, sere hills of the east and, moving my eyes north to north-westward, to the majestic, forested and granite grandeur of the mountains, master of all I surveyed from my aerie. What child could help but imagine all things were possible in such surroundings?

It may well be that the most profound and vital questions of life are the purview of youth. It is in adolescence that all the extremes of life come crashing in on our minds and bodies. It is at this time that we begin to question, for ourselves, what is of real worth and how to begin pursuing our usually vague goals.

Were April Love and Sixteen Candles the last vestiges of what our parents had left of the best of their own experiences? When I was forced to leave my playground of the entire Sequoia National Forest for the culture shock of the

SouthBay of SoCal, I was seventeen years old. Admittedly, I was ill prepared for the transition. Not that I hadn't lived in metropolitan areas before or was not, to some degree, cosmopolitan in my travel experiences and mixing with society. But the forest and desert, the hunting and fishing had been my choice of lifestyle. The rocks, trees, streams, and critters were my soul mates, my community.

To leave my forest fastness and a high school of 72 for the beach cities and a school of 3,000 was a tad difficult. But the music went with me. It was the same and American Bandstand and the Top Forty were there to greet me. I played clarinet and saxophone in the band and continued to do so at Mira Costa in Manhattan Beach. I still have my clarinet.

But I was not really prepared to meet the society of my new school. Thanks to my, even then, antiquated ideals of romance and chivalry and the morality of my grandparents and James Fenimoore Cooper, I was easy prey to the excitement of my new surroundings. My senior year was attended by events of major proportion; I had full-time employment at Floyd and Gill's Body Shop and got married; pretty fast for a kid in his senior year back in 1954. You might say I acculturated at an accelerated pace.

Even in those incomparably simpler times, an eighteen-year-old boy and a sixteen-year old girl still had the deck stacked against them. So it is not surprising that, continuing my fast pace, I found myself a father of two, divorced and introduced to child-support payments by the time I turned 21.

Manhattan, Redondo and Hermosa Beaches were my Camelot, a fairy-tale world that only exists in the imagination unless you were fortunate enough to have been young and lived in them in the fifties. The sheer magic of such an environment made anything possible in a slightly different way than the possibilities of my other life in the mountains.

I was young, had a full-time job and a car, a DeSoto convertible. I had my music and my books. The ultimate fulfillment of my contentment and excitement was realized in holding a lovely, soft, warm girl in my arms as we sat in the open convertible watching the waves roll in on an immaculate, uncrowded beach to the music of Ebb Tide on the car radio. Gas was twelve cents a gallon, an apartment by the beach was thirty-five dollars a month and you could buy a brand new Chevy convertible for less than eighteen hundred dollars; a house for four thousand at four per cent interest. A dollar or a dollar and twenty-five cents an hour job was sufficient to live a life about which the rest of the world could only dream or watch movies of it.

Far removed from any real want or care, we lived lives of Lotus-Eaters in an oasis from any turmoil or strife due to drugs or crime. Dean Martin and Jerry Lewis were supplanting Abbot and Costello and TV was an interesting, but not all-pervasive, demanding drain on our time and senses. Andre Kostelanetz, Oscar Levant, Morris Stolof, Jackie Gleason, and Frank Chacksfield were not a betrayal of Gershwin, Benny Goodman or Glenn Miller. They were most certainly not *elevator music* to a generation that still retained hope of the future and any heritage of real love and romance in their souls.

What does a man who remembers a first kiss say to a generation that has done it all by the time they are fourteen? What does the poet have to offer young women who are "things" and young men who are emasculated of any manhood? How do you explain the magic of being able to sit for hours, content to simply hold one another while listening to the strains of Billy Butterfield or Mantovani? What tragic, grievous loss!

With that kind of music in the background as I write, I am young once again, I am with that girl and we share the secrets of the universe, the secrets of lovers who blindly trust and have faith that all must be well. We are the true believers in life, a life where you can commit to one another and never for a moment doubt that trust will ever be betrayed. Better to have loved and lost than never to have loved at all? Yes! A thousand times better!

The girls have gone but the memories linger on. They, in fact, have never left that better part of the child in me. They are still the innocent and pure, sweet-scented softness of the best part of the man that now lives in my children. How I wish I could impart to them my store of precious memories. But how to impart that which is so intensely personal as looking deeply into the eyes of that one you cherish and would cheerfully die for and being able to see into their very heart and soul? And how do you explain the mechanism by which that first love becomes a foul spirit of competition, then combativeness, selfishness, and in its final death-throes, bitterness and hatred?

A society that makes divorce easy and adultery a joke cannot hope for anything better than we now live with. The poet's pen cannot hope to scratch the flint-like, hardened callousness to virtue, the insulated shell that refuses sacrificial love. As an admitted heretic I have come to the conclusion that God, Who is Love, had to first learn to love. I admit further that such a conclusion was aided in part from my" ...pouring over many a quaint and curious volume of forgotten lore." However, the conclusion was far more the result of my acquaintance of God Himself through Creation, including Nature Red in Tooth and Claw and by giving myself to the loving of others.

If would-be theologians would only be as honest in their own approaches to Nature as some eastern philosophers, they would admit they have failed, miserably, to convey the love of God to others in any intelligible way. In spite of the equally miserable failure of eastern philosophies to deal with the subject in all honesty, they, at least, are willing to impart some degree of humanity into it, much as the Egyptians and Greeks. It is a perversion of God's love to dress it in black, stand it in a pulpit for display and endow it with the hypocritical garb and language of liturgy and religiosity. Such will never entertain the notion, let alone honestly ask: "Lord, is it I?"

Can I hope to understand the wounding of God's own heart unless I have experienced the same thing by looking into that girl's eyes and seeing my own love reflected by hers for me only to have it turned into betrayal? Can the real perversion of what is holy and good by a Judas be reconciled in any other fashion, let alone be made intelligible in any degree? I think not! When, in this temple of clay, we give ourselves to others, there is always the risk that the one loved will turn out to be a betrayer, an impostor. We must take that chance if we are to have any hope of understanding what life is all about. To clothe such a profound truth in religious verbiage is to profane it, to prostitute it to the designs of evil men and women who would put a price on it for which our weak flesh can find the coin without personal sacrifice.

I have found God and the Muses to be far more understanding and forgiving than most of my religious colleagues. It takes much to admit of ignorance, let alone hypocrisy. If that girl and boy could have kept the candle of love lit, what a difference it would have made. But to trade it for the meanness of what this world offers in its place? How very foolish.

The world is a cruel taskmaster. There is no place in it for the idle or foolish dreamers. It rewards industry on the most pragmatic of terms. Even Thoreau had to accept the necessity of making pencils. But, he had the advantage of being able to make it a noble occupation. The secret is being able to do what is required while never losing sight of what is of real value, of keeping the child with his and her magic and dreams alive while earning the adult's wage by honest toil.

When I held that girl, I was hers and she was mine; the two had become one. And so it should have been in that ideal world of true love and romance. But the times were already changing. The truth of the statement "... when lust hath conceived, it bringeth forth sin and sin, when it is finished, bringeth forth death" was lurking in wait for any unwary challenger. When lust is the motive to begin with, how avoid its inevitable result?

What our children have inherited is lust, not love. Glorified by the universities, Hollywood and TV, by government itself, lust is the operant condition of their lives and they know no other. It may be a most unique legacy to my children that their father knew what it was to love; that he held a girl in his arms without any thought but the exquisite joy of sharing the closeness of one another and that was enough. It took an entire society's cruel devaluation of the fine gold and silver of real love and romance to make the trade for the tawdry brass of lust as the goal rather than the seeking of the other's happiness and a lifetime commitment.

In that definitive treatise on love, the thirteenth chapter of First Corinthians, we are told that love seeks the welfare of the other, not your own. It seems much easier to say what love is not than to explain what it is. Nevertheless, it is defined for us so perfectly in sacrificial love that only those with no interest can miss the meaning.

My daughter Karen and I were sharing some thoughts and prayer was mentioned. It has been a curiosity to me that prayer is so natural to people yet little that is intelligible has been written on the subject. If my presumption that few religionists have much real knowledge about the true nature of God, then this is not surprising. Too often clothed in the language of religion, prayer is made to be a mystery and I don't believe God is purposely hiding from those that seek Him.

Because of my conversation with Karen, I was reminded of something that came to me many years ago. We like to teach our children to say their *Now I lay me's* early on. It is good to kneel with our little ones and come before God in prayer. We hope they will continue, as they grow older. But, a curious thing about prayer became clear as I began to speak with others about the subject; the fact that many of us fall asleep as we lay in our beds talking the day over with God. Most expressed concern about being rude to God in doing so.

As I have done with others, I did the other night with Karen; I tried to explain what makes a great deal of sense to me. If God is our Heavenly Father, why should He react any differently than an earthly father who loves his child? I don't think He does. As a father, I can think of few things that would give me more pleasure than to have my little one fall asleep in my arms while telling me all about their day's activities, their hopes, dreams and plans. For lo, these many years, I have found it the perfect end of the day to fall asleep talking with God. Many times it has been the only means of finding peace at the end of a dreadful day and the only means of finding badly needed sleep and rest. I'm certain God looks forward to that special time with each of us.

I don't doubt the Psalmist found himself falling asleep in prayer as he communed on his bed with God. What a fine way to find surcease and comfort from the evil of the day.

I have a tremendous advantage in having known so many loving people. Beginning with our maternal great-grandmother, our grandparents and our mother, my brother and I grew up in the warm security of people committed to one another. While mom and our grandparents fought like the proverbial cats and dogs, Ronnie and I never doubted their love for either us or for each other. Why? Because, when the chips were down, they were there for one another and for us. Somehow, in spite of the fussing and fighting, the commitment and genuine love came through. These days, the first disagreement easily ends in divorce.

I have a great debt of love to these people. I owe mom so much for the music in my life, to my stepdad, Ken, for caring for her and Ronnie, Johnny and me. It has been my great good fortune to know so many loving people throughout my life. In spite of all the grief and tragedy so common to the human condition my memories of those dear ones shines through any gloom and I still hold converse with those gone on before me whose wisdom is, now, I choose to believe, so certain.

As I listen to the music of the fifties, I am once more cruising in my beautiful '53 Cadillac convertible, top down, sun shining and ocean breeze clean and perfumed with the scent of the sea, through Manhattan, Hermosa and Redondo toward Palos Verdes and Portuguese Bend on Pacific Coast Highway. When I reach the cut toward PV I'll take the shore road. I'm now divorced but the world still holds promise of love and beauty. I've left Floyd and Gill's and sanding cars with 320 wetordry by hand until my fingertips bled and am employed at North American Aviation as a machinist; I have the Caddy and a bachelor apartment in Redondo. I'm now meeting other people and, especially, girls.

Ronnie also has his own place but he is going steady with Susan. They will marry, have two children, Jennifer and David, and Susan will divorce him. Danny and Diana are with their mother in Hawaii where, after our divorce, she went to be with her parents. Oh, well. There is still magic and romance in the latter fifties SouthBay; especially if you're young, have a good job, the music and a Caddy convertible.

But Camelot can be a dangerous place for a poet looking for love in all the wrong places. In spite of all the betrayals, no poet worth his salt is going to forego the experience and hurt and chance the loss of the greater goal of an illusive ideal. Surely, he says, these things are temporary and will pass; the Truth must be out there somewhere along with someone with whom to share it. Don Quixote will find his windmills. It is the world that is out of step and tune. I know in my bones that Atlantis's of the Sands like Ubar are still to be discovered, that there is truth in the mythic of the Arabian Nights and The Talisman and Good Guys still win! Purity and Virtue will still triumph over evil!

In defense of our children listening to the noise they call music today, I know the music we were listening to in the fifties, much of it from the thirties and forties as well, was based on a culture and society that still lived in hope that things would only get better and better; jobs were plentiful, America was the preeminent world power, we were a nation on the go and a phone call or cup of coffee was a nickel.

In contrast to the songs of love, hope and a better future of my time, our children turn to the mind-numbing noise they call "music" glorifying suicide, violence, sex and drugs as an escape from having to hope in the face of hopelessness. Such noise is a mechanism for tuning out the mind and giving in to the animalistic senses that have no responsibility or accountability; an anti-establishment protest against being robbed and cheated of hope. A generation that has lost hope in eternal verities of love and goodness, the triumph of good over evil must opt for the glorification of evil as it gains the ascendance. At least it promises change and excitement and, therefore, must be better than the status quo, which dooms them in any event.

A large part of the American Dream still existed in the fifties. I could have gone to Lake Isabella and built my cabin on a few acres without the defeating and strangling codes that now have succeeded in destroying any hope of people being able to do for themselves and provide for their children without becoming slaves to Big Brother and the Bankers. No one to date has ever done the requisite study on this subject which figures so prominently in a nation's fall from its ideals and greatness and virtually enslaves its citizens in perpetual debt through exorbitant property taxes and mortgages which can never be paid off.

It would seem to be obvious that a man must be able to have hope of providing for a wife and children in order for love and romance to survive, to enable that girl to commit herself to a husband and children. The basis of this is a home of their own no matter how humble; remove this hope and you have the generation and the society we presently have; a generation that knows it has been betrayed and is ripe for rebellion and revolution or at the worse, anarchy.

In my reverie, there is a definite need for the old SouthBay of clean air and beaches, no graffiti in sight, of the excitement of being young and the whole world waiting your impress upon it. I need to remember the first issue of Mad Magazine appearing and seeing Shane in downtown L.A. (got my first parking ticket then). There was the quaint florist shop at the end of Pier Avenue where I could get orchids and roses for the girls and the marvelous coffee shop next to the beach with its windows giving us a view of the ocean, where we all shared so many profound experiences and the wisdom of youth.

Such things are more than a catharsis and reaching back to the sanity of simpler times and values. They are some of the best we have to offer our own children in the hope that they will understand the way things are supposed to be. Perhaps, in sharing some of these things, some young people may be encouraged to take the reins, get involved and seize opportunities. Not all of it is gathering rosebuds while ye may. There is work to do. If their own store of precious memories is to be of value to their children, they must be given hope that not all is lost to them. It is the poet's task to encourage them and face the evil with determination to overcome it!

Even in Camelot, there are inescapable realities. Dragons need slaying and damsels need rescue. The young knight must know his enemy and keep his sword sharp. A betraying Guinevere or Lancelot should never cause the loss of a crown and the Grail must be sought no matter the cost. Arthur must be true though all others play him false. While it is, as my old friend pointed out, women, who, predominantly and historically get sex and religion all confused, it is still the responsibility of the Moths to draw near the Flame and its Keepers, upon whom, Love's Labors are not lost.

What a time it has been! From that small boy's bare feet kicking the gray, summer noon-heatened, alkali dust of Weedpatch and Little Oklahoma to cross-country trips by train, bus, and auto, grandad and grandma meeting us at the top of the old Grapevine in the '28 Buick, to the mining claim in the forest and, thence, to sun-kissed Lotus Land. Things learned in Cleveland, Las Vegas and Henderson, lakes Mead and Isabella. The times in WWII San Pedro, San Francisco and Oakland, a collage, vignettes here and there, that makes up the tapestry of a life.

Even though Jacob's Staff has been traded for written language, it is still the responsibility of the poet-historian to keep the legends alive and make his marks on Aaron's Rod. Truth will always sort through the myth and make what is vital real. In the most clouded of memories, sharp spikes of light along with Thoreau's flakes of light dart here and there, illuminating what is of real value in the keeping and the sharing with others. We can never guess what is taking root in the minds of our children that will become their own epics.

In the twilight of life, we begin to sort through, even unconsciously, the things that make it all worthwhile, the faces and places, even demons that come often unbidden to mind. I would make more of fiction were that needed. But reality has been more than enough to pauperize any attempt to clothe it with more than an occasional lapse of memory, which in its kindness, covers many hurts. We are all builders and makers regardless of the type of architecture.

I have a love of all kinds of architecture, from the most garish of Gothic and Baroque to the most sterile monuments of glass and steel. Roman or Oriental, it all fascinates me as an expression of cultures. The simplest forms of bare studs and the aroma of clean, new lumber always excite something in me. I recently saw a civic center building that had an entryway of a wall of glass brick. How many my age remember when those marvelous blocks of translucent glass adorned so many buildings? When the sun strikes through them, they have the most entrancing array of shades of light. What a glorious touch the veined hues of the different marble and granite used in some of our own creations like Grand Central Station. Such Cathedrals invite worship.

Even tents in the wilderness had to have their ribbons of color. The nomad needs something to draw his eye and tell him he is a man. Few things attract a man, as Thoreau made so plain, as his honest toil resulting in a structure, no matter how humble, which evidences his ability to do with his mind, back and hands. And, if the effort is directed toward the welfare of his family, what a worker he is! We are inveterate builders but even the cave will show signs of something more than utilitarian shelter. We will hang our pictures and bric-a-brac to declare our personness. The most humble of abodes will show some indication that building is more than providing a roof over our heads. This is the reason for my making so much of removing the onerous bureaucracy that precludes a man doing for himself. You must turn from the seemingly, meaningless disarray of twisted threads and knots of the back of the carpet and look at the grand design of its true face.

In one of my wilderness forays, I came across an old mining shack of rough lumber. The bare, wood walls of the interior were covered over with the comics (funny papers to us oldsters) of a long defunct newspaper. Now any part of the newspapers would have served as well against drafts, but the comics? They were the needed color.

We are suffering the noisome pangs of politicians, once more, telling us what they are going to do for (more properly to) us. They will talk of building for the future. My grandad built a better privy than what these scoundrels are likely to produce and it smelled better than the stench of these charlatans.

Pencils and Walden may, at times, become confusing but the doing for others never does; they should all work together for good. If we are to build with other than wood, hay, and stubble they must. The Ancient Landmarks will stand no matter how evil men and women try to remove them. But, Oh! The grief and the loss that the attacks on them cause!

Somewhere along the way, we got too busy for the things that really count. The work, books and beauty, the others are there but they want for attendance. As rich as the endowment may be, it profits nothing to those that will not take heed and invest it properly.

"You have forsaken your first love... I would that you were either hot or cold but because you are lukewarm, I will spew you out of my mouth!" What a word of warning that should be to all! However, it falls on deaf ears of those who are more concerned for the cares and riches of the false than a reality where love conquers all. God's love goes begging as the professionals either prostitute it as religion or mysticize it to some ethereal realm out of existence.

I might have as easily settled for the counterfeit if I hadn't held that girl in my arms, listened to the music and watched the waves roll in. If a true lover's and father's heart hadn't grown out of all these things, I would be no better off than the religious and political charlatans that abound unable to distinguish between Heaven and Hell and opting for the glory of evil.

Children should never lose Christmas or Halloween. That young girl and boy must never lose their first love.

> But my white pow, nae kindly thowe
> Shall melt the snaws of Age
> My trunk of eild, but buss or beild,
> Sinks in Time's wintry rage.
> Oh, Age has weary days,
> And nights o' sleepless pain:
> Thou golden time, o' Youthfu' prime,
> Why comes thou not again!
>   Robert Burns

But my dear Robert, you surely knew that the youth that learned to love never went away and you proved the truth of it in your own life.

The Way of All Flesh does not have to be the only way. There are precedents aplenty for something better that will carry us through and, in the end be able to say: It was worth it! What will you say?

It's beginning to feel like summer here in my hometown, Bakersfield. I don't like being removed, even temporarily, from the trees, rocks and critters, but for the time being I am in town and doing my best to keep my spirits up in the heart of the Asphalt Jungle.

There are a lot worse places to be. We read of them and watch what's happening in our country and around the world and have to admit: Yes indeed, there are worse places to be than Bakersfield, even in summer.

At least the mountains are nearby and I can look east and remember the old days when, as a child, I would look at the purple hills through the haze and imagine marvelous things and adventures while listening to Jack Armstrong, The All-American Boy on the radio. A little later in the evening, Grandad would put Dusty Skies on the wind-up Victrola and I would, unconsciously, memorize the lyrics to this old tune.

Weedpatch and Little Oklahoma are not the same places of my childhood. Gone are most of the empty fields where you could catch luckless lizards. I still like the little fellows but a surprising thing has happened over the years; they run faster than they used to! I know this is true because I can't catch them as well as I could when I was a kid; probably something to do with the hole in the ozone layer or air pollution. Maybe the dinosaurs will make a comeback when we foolish humans get through fouling our own nest and killin' each other off- Just a thought.

But it was magic, drinking a bottle of strawberry Nehi, and, kicking back in the shade of Faith Grocery's porch at Cottonwood and Padre, watching the sun shine through the glass tank of the Mohawk gas pump in front of the store. The war in Europe and Asia was still going strong and our comic book collections were filled with Superman, Captain Marvel and other heroes fighting the Japs and Knocksies.

Dee Dee and I had our picture taken sitting in the new Jeep that we kids at Mt. Vernon Elementary had bought with our war stamps. That made Ronnie and me big shots since the picture appeared in the Bakersfield Californian.

Purple mountain's majesty and Amber waves of grain were, like, Columbia, the gem of the ocean, still popular tunes and without a hint of hypocrisy attached; simple times and precious memories.

There are few companions in my life like Thoreau despite his ego. Like he, I would fain have planted ... sincerity, truth, simplicity, faith, innocence, and the like rather than beans. There is time for beans and pencils and they should not be in competition with those heart's longings for that which encourages the spirit and gives hope of better than meeting only physical needs or gaining the wealth of this world.

Like Thoreau, I sow in hope. While much of what I write has been called inflammatory I do not write in order to promote anarchy but love and understanding. I am not an incendiary but do hope to ignite hearts to a better calling than the evil system that does promote lawlessness and greed. And if, as was the case of my soul brother Henry, I provide some of the friction to an evil machine so much the better. In some cases, the system is of such a complexity that the simplest solution may well be to take an ax to such a Gordian Knot.

Unhappily the Knot has its guardians who, unless they be subdued first, will inveigh with all their might against all who oppose them. It will take a good many ax-men to win such a battle.

The good man and woman are called to Civil Disobedience against unjust laws. They had rather obey God, though their god be only to do what is right that separates good and evil, than men when the choice is presented. For that reason, they must cry out against injustice and fight for an end to those laws that would murder the innocent whether by the mechanism of legal abortion or adultery and divorce by whim. They are called to confront evil from within the home and at their work place. Their very lives must testify of the Godly steel in their backbones that will not tolerate injustice and murder, or blind obedience to the State that requires the sacrifice of their children to the slavery of the State.

The very complexity of the evil system of government leads directly to the attempt at simple solutions. This is an historical imperative and most often leads to slavery or revolution. It is an historical imperative for the very reason that too many men's hearts seldom seek the welfare of others but are motivated by the desire to live without honest toil; by the desire to steal, lie, cheat and engage in every form of immorality freely and without restraint.

So it was early recognized that Law was an absolute necessity to restrain evil and punish the evildoer. Though this would seem to be self-evident, it is still required for each generation to teach the next. Our failure to educate our young people to the facts of our national history and the great men and women who sacrificed so much to give us the greatest and freest nation the world has ever seen has led to a generation that neither knows Joseph nor the God of Joseph.

***

I walked into a time machine May 29th. I went to the first school reunion I have ever attended and saw a group of people I had not seen in forty years; my special thanks to you Ann and Arlene for making it most memorable. My thanks to so many others for what had to be a Herculean effort to put the whole thing together. While I was only able to attend the function Saturday morning at the park, it was more than worth it.

The past forty years had taken its toll on all of us. It's a good thing we had nametags. However, as we became re-acquainted, the years slipped away and we were all, once more, transported back to an age of innocence in the late forties and early fifties. I could recognize Ann and Arlene but, I have to confess, it took a little while to see, in the mature bodies and faces, the children of those bygone years; however, once recognition took hold, the kids were there after all.

As a loner way back then, and now, I contented myself with meeting a few of you like Jim, Lee, Bob and Lois, J.L., Ann and Arlene; the rest of the time sitting by myself, watching and listening, and letting my imagination take me back so far in time to the magic of the old Kern River Valley and the old schools. I had been in touch with Henry, Tom, and Russell in recent years. I wish they could have been there at the park. In spite of the absence of a few, I was surprised by how well represented my group from that far away time was. I was told Myrtez and Donna were there but I didn't see them. No one seemed to know what became of Ethel.

Of course, the great majority of those that attended were strangers to me. By force of circumstances I removed from the valley in 1953 and lost all contact with you folks. But I never forgot any of you. Because of the construction of the lake, many newcomers were not really known to me at all.

I focused on Ann and Arlene because they, more than anyone, epitomized what changes with time and what doesn't. I was a painfully shy boy during those years of school. It was a fascinating thing to examine my thoughts and emotions as I spoke freely with two girls I would have hidden from back then. Girls were strange and interesting creatures, but totally alien to my sphere of abilities. Talk to one? Terrifying thought! Not on your life!

Oh, it wasn't because I didn't want to, I simply couldn't. For only the briefest time, shortly before my departure to the South Bay, was I just beginning to find the courage to even think of speaking to you girls. I would apologize for the many, seeming, slights of that time, but it wasn't that I wasn't interested; I simply lacked the ability to communicate with the opposite sex.

Like many of us, I fell in love with a couple of you but could never say so. The romance of the valley and the music we all shared, the poetry of the time and place, could not have but resulted in all of us being in love at some time in our young lives back then. But, I was a loner because I was not able to communicate those desperate longings and feelings to any but the forest, mountains and creatures with which I felt at ease. While most of you were managing your adolescence in more normal ways, I was hiking the mountains with rifle or shotgun and note pad or fishing Bull Run Creek.

Part of the problem was the fact that I was living with my grandparents and, thus, raised a generation behind times. I was reading Sir Walter Scott, Brett Harte and Cooper while many of you were into literature of much more contemporary usage. The band and orchestra were more my forte and interest than mixing in the more usual interplay between most of you. Thus, self-excluded for the most part, I didn't really get to know many of you as I wished I could.

Even being one of the few kids with his own car and the magnificent job as the old Elementary School's first Junior Custodian (remember Guy Schultz?), I still bluffed my way past, denying the fact that I was simply too shy to really communicate my real feelings for some of you. I could deal with the guys, in that I could be hard as nails, but you girls? Not a chance. Terrifying! I fell apart inside and nothing but confused and twisted verbiage was at my disposal in your presence- Totally mortifying.

That is what was so intensely interesting in speaking with Ann and Arlene. The painfully shy boy was still trying to think of something to say. The 56-year-old man with a Ph.D. in Human Behavior was discussing and analyzing the situation- Fascinating.

In no time at all, the boy saw you girls forty years back. We were all, as with some of you guys, teenagers once more. The years rolled away and the magic of that simple era was there once more. The jarring impact was the talk of children and families. Not possible! I thought to myself. We're supposed to be talking about the latest hit song by Rosemary Clooney or some track meet with Johnsondale, not jobs, careers, husbands, wives and children. No! I wanted to be back at the old schools when we were all young, strong, invincible and so full of hope for the future, excited by the possibilities of life, surrounded by the pristine, majestic mountains filled with wild life, deliciously clean air and water, so far removed from the stress, hatred and strife of the metropolitan areas.

Nostalgia and melancholy may find a voice in the magic recesses of memories, in the longing for those simpler times; but our eyes and faces bear testimony to the fact that we have lived, each one of us, lives that have had to deal with the grief that comes with the passing years, of realities far removed from the simple joys of adolescence spent in our valley.

I tried to share some of the magic we had then with my own children as they were growing. I would often take them camping, shooting and fishing in the area over the years. When I started teaching in the Antelope Valley, I would bring many of my pupils here as well. Over the years, I maintained a kind of presence in the area. I must confess I did not care for the growth that, little by little, began to restrict and destroy much of what used to be wide, open country. Too many foreigners began to invade. I remember when the gate had to be installed at the end of Burlando Road to keep the riff raff out and prevent them from trashing the Bull Run area.

Also, it seemed that real estate agents were breeding like lice everywhere. Now I have always placed real estate agents just a notch above judges and TV ministers and a notch below winos and used car salesmen; I haven't met one yet I would trust; they have always seemed a blight on the valley.

But how good it was to have a chance to run away from the present of a world gone mad to those days of yesteryear, when we all dreamed dreams and all things were possible to those that believed.

One of the things that nagged at the corners of my mind was the fact that we were; back then, before the TV generation, readers. Reading was important to all of us regardless of the genre. Our teachers helped make it important. Two things seem to correlate in our present, dismal society, a society that doesn't offer much to the young people of today; seems bent on, rather than offering hope, destroying them.

Dear Dan, Karen, and Michael,

It is hard to write the things I feel compelled to say. I wish I could spend my time in whimsy and tell more of the stories I used to share with you children. However, the world you and the grandchildren are inheriting is an evil one and the evil must be confronted. I would far rather write of the tumbling Hawk, gamboling in his ethereal aerie, of critters, mountain streams and the joys of reveling in Creation.

But in case you are worried about Dear old Dad becoming overly morose through the somber subject matter I must treat; I present you the following:

It was a dark, but not stormy, night. It was, actually, a beautiful and balmy, summer evening when the Indian and grandad decided it would be a good time to jacklight some deer. The Indian had a brand new Hudson and was anxious to show what it could do. Thus, nothing would work but to take Jack Ranch Road up into Wagy Flat where the deer were plentiful and the road was a challenge. I would go along as spotter in the back seat, my eyes being exceptionally sharp and well-suited, almost cat-like, to night vision.

Loading various weapons for the nefarious purpose into the Indian's new car, we were off in a cloud of night-dust. For some reason the only gun I had in the back seat was an H&R .22 nine-shot revolver. I suppose it was for killing a rattler if we spotted one in the road.

For those unaccustomed to the delights of Jack Ranch Road, suffice it to say the Hudson was in for a workout. A dirt track with sudden switchbacks, numerous pot holes and sundry rocks, steep hills, trees that grew close enough to scratch fenders, the road is not to be dignified with the label, rather one should call it a glorified animal track, only marginally better than the road up to Bull Run Creek. The Indian was soon cursing a merry tune in his unique dialect (a few Anglo-Saxon, four letter words were easily distinguishable) and wondering at what insanity had brought him to this sorry pass in his new car.

The right, front wheel slammed into a hole and we were treated to the caressing sound of the dirt track screeching against the bottom of the car and impacting with the differential as the rear end was bounced, forcefully, into the air jolting the joints of the occupants. My head hit the roof of the car. The Indian added a couple of lyrics to his tune- Some fun.

Coming around a curve in the track, the headlights picked up a small herd of about half-a-dozen deer lying down against the side of the hill. There was some confusion with the occupants of the front seat trying to stop the car and get one of the guns unlimbered. Not so in the back seat. Its occupant had the window down and was already cracking away with the .22 H&R.

Having made the deer dance to the music of the .22, the deer were scattering all over the hill. One jumped into the road and started up it in some obvious distress from the .22. The Indian began to give chase but grandad still didn't have his gun operating for some reason. It was then that grandad's genius for improvisation came to the fore.

Having a small piece of rope with him, he quickly fashioned a loop at the end. As the Indian pulled alongside the deer, a young forked horn, grandad was able to get the noose of the rope around his horns. Yanking the deer against the side of the Indian's new Hudson, the deer, understandably, began to tap-dance, beating a smartly executed, staccato tattoo with his small, very sharp hooves against the side of the car. The Indian, adding new lyrics to his music, understandably, expressed some concern about the obvious damage being done by the deer beating the tar out of the side of his new car with its horns and hooves. I have to admit it was considerable noisy and exciting.

Grandad, in some pique at the Indian's lack of sense of humor and good sportsmanship, drew his hunting knife, reached out the window and cut the critter's throat so as to end the spirited exchange between the hapless source of our Bambi Burgers and the hide of the Hudson. A profuse amount of blood erupted and sprayed all about and into the car, satisfactorily baptizing the front seat occupants and, incidentally, the Indian's new upholstery. He slammed on the brakes. New lyrics were added. With feeling.

Bailing out of the car, we surveyed the gore and damage. I marveled that the hapless creature could have done so much alteration of the sheet metal and paint with his small hooves and horns. But, alas, such was the case. The Indian was adding a hunting dance to his music, obviously one of the native customs to show his gratitude to the Great Spirit for a successful hunt; though his tone of voice might have been easily misinterpreted by someone not well tutored in the lore of his tribe. In fact, to the unschooled in such ritual, his language and dance might even be misunderstood as anger about the damage to his, used to be, new Hudson. Fortunately, grandad and I knew better and were duly appreciative of the Indian's performance in propitiation of the hunting gods.

The carcass was loaded and transported back to the claim without further incident and the venison was excellent. All's well that ends well. Oddly, the Indian did not volunteer his car for future excursions after meat for our lodges. The ways of our Native American neighbors are somewhat strange to us at times.

***

My old school chum, Russell, came over with his tractor, cleared the weeds, and provided a channel so I won't flood out when the rains come. California is entering its sixth year of draught. So far, 1992 is proving to be the worst year on record for disasters- Flooding, Riots, Earthquakes, Draught and Bankruptcy. Imagine the State paying its bills with I.O.Us!

Yet, Russ and I, exemplifying the true Can Do Americanism that still thrives in some of us good ol' boys, loaded the cabin and moved it ourselves to my new location in Bodfish; proving we are still not too old to cut the mustard. In this spot, I can still watch as the fading twilight turns the trees and hills into soft, then sharp, silhouettes in the clear air and I begin looking for our earliest and most easily discernible constellation Ursa Major, Big Dipper, to appear overhead.

My first night in the place, I was sitting and reading by kerosene lamp when a mouse strolled in the door as if he owned the place. In my surprise I exclaimed: "Get out of here!" He got. Some of these little varmints, like government, once they get their snouts in the trough, eat and destroy more than they are worth. Too bad it's so much trouble to get a hunting license for them (the bureaucrats, not the mouse).

Firing up the water heater was interesting. The place had been abandoned for about a year and when I lit off the heater, assorted spiders and two lizards came bailing out of the contraption. I squashed the spiders, black widows, and caught the lizards for relocation to a more suitable environment.

That evening, the largest cricket I have seen in some time came in to keep me company while I was reading. Him, I left alone. I enjoy cricket music and they don't eat much. Had a heck of a time with the stove; the resident black widows gave me a run for the money but I finally managed to discomfit them, but awakened the next morning to find one had kept company with me in the corner of the bedroom- Squashed the uppity bugger proper.

A curious thing: The Planning Department tells me that if I saw the cabin in half, I can keep both halves on the property without a permit or prohibitively expensive foundations. Seems there is a ten by twelve roof area limit on auxiliary structures. The cabin, with the attached screen porch, is ten by twenty. So I'll wind up with two ten by tens instead of a ten by twenty. Ah, the infinite wisdom of the government.

I have taken a break from the writing to visit the folks out at the old mining claim in Boulder Gulch and do my walkabout. I like to visit the old pines and granite boulders and commune with Grandma, Tody, Grandad, and Ronnie. I like to think these departed loved ones hear and see me. I ache for their love and counsel when I don't know what to do or what I should be doing. Whether it's true or not, I find comfort in the thought that they are with me in a way that transcends our limited physical reality.

I walk up the hill behind where the main cabin used to be. Ronnie and I, on one of his infrequent visits with our mother, slid down this slope on barrel-staves, makeshift skis, one winter when we had a nice snowfall. The old cabin had served as a cookshack until Grandad, with some help from me, had added on to it. In the summer, we would move the old wood cook stove out of doors, and cooking and eating took place under the pines.

Great-grandma (always grandma to Mom, Ronnie and me) took up residence in the other cabin. How I miss sitting in her lap while she would read to Ronnie and me.

I stand under the tall, old pine where I shot the hawk. I was feeding the chickens and rabbits when I spied the Red-tail land on the very top of the tree. The .22 Remington singleshot was, as usual, close at hand. I always kept a gun close in case of Indian uprisings, bear and lion attacks and the usual calamities which were sure to occur to a pioneer woodsman in the wilderness (Thanks, James Fenimore Cooper).

Unfortunately, the only round I had with me was a short already chambered in the gun. Now I know, looking back, that the Red-tail was probably not a threat (unlike owls and the wild donkeys) to our livestock. But it was a real enough threat at the time to me as a child and, carefully shouldering the .22, I took aim and fired. The hawk came tumbling down through the branches.

Running up the hill, I saw the hawk. He was standing on his legs, lop-sidedly, bracing himself with his right wing on the ground much as one might use a crutch, and breathing heavily. His bright, intelligent eyes pierced me. It was soon obvious that, due to the low velocity round and his natural bulletproof vest of feathers, that the small bullet had only knocked the breath out of him and knocked him off his perch. The fall had probably done him more hurt than the small slug.

I entertained the thought of doing him in with the butt of the rifle, but for two reasons did not. One: I might damage the gun and, two: I simply could not bring myself to do violence to such a noble bird when he was so obviously at such a great disadvantage. I won't flatter myself as to which of the two objects of reticence were most objectionable. I'd like to hold to the latter, and nobler, motive.

For some reason, I struck up a conversation with the Red-tail while he huffed and puffed, gathering his strength and getting his wind back. Now those of you not familiar with the ways of a boy in the woods might have cause to wonder about having a conversation with a hawk (or any other critter) that is lacking in the social grace of making small talk. But, for me, it seemed perfectly natural that I would be discussing the nature of his present discomfiture and explaining what had happened.

The Red-tail did not seem particularly impressed with my explanation; in fact, he seemed rather in a hurry to terminate the discussion with little regard to the polite niceties of civil conversation. Looking back on the incident though, I'm reasonably sure, had the hawk been able to voice his opinion of the affair, he would have added greatly to my, then, woefully, deficient knowledge of Maledicta and invective.

Teetering back and forth, he brought his dragging wing back up into normal position and, taking an experimental hop, began to hop, hop, hop, down the hill, his wings taking a couple of practice flaps. After a few yards of this exercise, he gathered speed enough to make a low-level take-off. Wings now fully distended, he glided downhill slowly a couple of feet off the ground. Then, with a few, slow flaps of his wings, he began to gain altitude. Finally, he was high enough to soar over the opposite hill from me and out of sight.

As I stroll the hills among the rocks and trees, the old, familiar sites bring on both the aching melancholy and the precious memories of precious loved-ones. My readers of some years have heard most of the stories and I won't repeat them. I know you understand the state of mind and heart that keeps drawing me back to this site and a few others of like preciousness. These are the pilgrimages that help me to maintain a perspective of the best of the child in me, that nourishes the poet and keeps butterflies and trout streams relevant; yea, essential, lending their part to the gentleness of strength to confront evil and to love sacrificially. How else, I often wonder, to love God and one's neighbor as oneself?

I usually sit outside and look at the stars when I'm at my place in Lake Isabella. Last night I watched as, within 20 minutes, six satellites passed overhead, three on a Southerly course and three on a Northerly. Signs in the sky I wonder?

A Great Horned Owl flew into the top of the large pine next to my chair. It was a full moon last night and, hearing the slow flap of his wings, I was able to clearly see his approach and landing. He perched for a while, his marvelously keen, efficiently light-gathering eyes searching for his prey. Soon, he launched and with measured flaps of his large wings, took up position in the top of a neighboring pine. After a few minutes, he spread his wings and swooped down from his perch toward the clearing beyond the tree and out of my sight.

As I have said, one of my favorite things to do in the area is visiting the folks out at the old mining claim. I just returned from such a visit to get away from the dreariness of day to day living. I sit with my cup of coffee and a cigarette and let my mind wander and wonder amid the familiar rocks, trees and hills. Grandma and Great-grandma died in their sleep in one of the old cabins, long gone to make way for the present campground. They died peacefully in bed without the antiseptic paraphernalia of exotic machines, tubes and hoses with which we now prolong life in the dubious notion that bankrupting, heroic measures are needed simply because they are available.

I wonder once more at the thought of Hallowed Ground. Perhaps it is the Choctaw Cherokee blood, I'm told, that courses through my veins, but if there is such a thing as Hallowed Ground, this is it for me; the site of most cherished, childhood memories and where such precious, loved and loving dear ones lived and departed. I wonder, also, about David and his longing for the water of Bethlehem. He must have felt the same way I feel when I'm at this spot. The bittersweet melancholy and loneliness that often envelopes me in these surroundings is ameliorated and assuaged somewhat by reminding myself that few have such memories to sustain them.

Also, the very freedom to come and go as I choose is something for which I am most grateful and something with which very few people are blessed. And while far from rich in material things, like my kindred soul brother Thoreau I will opt for such freedom in lieu of the unnecessary and cumbersome riches and baggage of those that think mere things are what will make them happy and secure. It is people, not things, which make for happiness, and, tragically, grief and misery as well, unfortunately. But the soul of a nation and that of the individual is in the joy and suffering that is God within us, is the express image of Him, and opens our hearts to both.

As I sit on a granite boulder beneath an old pine where, as a child, I once had placed boards in the branches for a aerie from which to think, read and survey my wilderness playground in the solitude and imagination of that best part within any child, I'm sensible of the fact that we are too seldom conscious of the things and people, the circumstances which will manufacture memories. How much kinder would we be to others if we only knew how forcefully such things will come, later, in our night visions as haunting, tormenting specters or beloved friends. Tragically, the choice is not always with us, but too often with those whose self-love has betrayed the trust of the friend.

The day is getting late and I must leave- Too bad. It seems something is out of joint when I am a visitor to what was home. Somehow, there is something wrong with this. Hearing the noise overhead, I watch a Stealth Bomber and its chase plane making a low level pass, about 1,500 feet AGL I judge, the fascinating form of the bat-like bomber seeming alien and threatening and, strangely out of place. Oh well, back to where I presently hang my hat; it isn't home, but what is this side of heaven.

***

It was a long hike from the trout stream, Bull Run Creek, back to where the car was parked. The children were quite young but, due to the circumstances, where I went, they went. It was dark and growing late and Karrie seemed to be having trouble keeping up. I became aggravated with her and asked if she wanted me to carry her. To my surprise, she said yes. This was not like my tough little girl. Even at her age, she could put most older boys to shame in her abilities, and especially, when hiking. And, I can proudly say, all my children have proved to be tough in the things that really count. But, at the time, I passed it off as her being in a mood; even my little angel could have her moods.

We finally reached the car and, driving back toward Lancaster, Karrie was extremely quiet. She was never a talker, being, like me, one to keep her own counsel and having difficulty expressing her true feelings. But it soon became apparent that she was actually not feeling well. On arriving at the house, I put her to bed and took her temperature. She had a high fever. I nursed her best I could and, fortunately, the fever broke and she began to sleep restfully. By morning she seemed to be all right. My little girl has great stamina and recuperative powers.

I missed one of the most precious opportunities a father could ask for. Karrie virtually never asked for anything. The greed factor is entirely missing in her heart and mind. I'll never forget taking her Christmas shopping and having to threaten her to even tell me of anything she would like. I should have carried my little girl that night. I won't get another chance like that one to show how much I love her. When my own sins and failures bear hard upon me, God brings such things to mind to remind me that as long as I do have such love, I'm not an entirely hopeless cause.

My point, to finally get to it, is that in spite of the hurt and grief of loving others, I wouldn't trade for the cold-bloodedness of uncaring, unfeeling selfishness I have been forced to witness in some others.

CHAPTER EIGHT

It might not have been a dark and stormy night, but it was sure black as the Ace of Spades.

A fellow and I had not known each other very long when we took that trip to the outback of the Black Hills area of the El Paso Mountains Northeast of Mojave. We were in my shiny, new, 1968 VW. I had bought the vehicle to deceive the CHP. Sure enough, I never got a speeding ticket in the bug so the concept proved sound.

We were loaded for bear (actually we were after Jackrabbits but were prepared for anything from a native uprising to attacking Roosians). We had, between us, my Colt Single Action Army in .357, a 12ga shotgun, a Ruger .22 semi-auto, a Ruger Single Six in .357, a .45 auto, and a .22 Remington pump. We also had enough ammo to justify the hardware.

It is a well-known fact among people that know me that the wives of my friends are not friendly to me for long. I'll explain.

Now, as I said, this fellow and I had not known each other long when we made this Safari. Therefore, his wife did not suspect that this might be the last time she would see her husband alive (or, at the least, back home within a reasonable span of time, say, sometime within the year).

It was full dark by the time we took the Randsburg road out of Mojave to the Mesquite Canyon turnoff near Garlock and pointed the VW's nose North on the dirt road into the boonies.

I knew the area well, having traveled it many times, but it was new to my partner. An owl landed in the middle of the road, staring into our headlights. We stopped and stared at each other until the critter decided to take off. We continued winding our way deeper into the outback. Up jumped a Jack and the war was on. We bailed out and cut loose with the artillery, dust, dirt and rocks showering about the hapless varmint. He escaped the hail of bullets and assorted shrapnel, a wiser bunny, acquainted now with the baser instincts of perverse humans.

We had driven for some time, ever deeper into the Big Lonesome and had a good time rapping off rounds. It must have been close to 10:00 p.m. when we crested a steep hill, the headlights piercing out into the blackness. With no moon and far off the beaten track, the night was as dark as any I have ever been in. I knew, approximately, where we were and which direction we were heading. But in the darkness, with many dirt tracks leading all over the place, I wasn't absolutely certain of our exact position.

Fortunately, it was a warm, summer night. As this fellow and I looked out into the inky darkness, we decided to risk going down the hill. It didn't look too steep at that point. So, climbing back into the Bug, we started down. We had only gone a short distance when the incline increased dramatically. But, since we couldn't back up, there was no choice but to go forward. We finally bottomed out on a small, flat area and the road ended, the headlights piercing out into utterly black emptiness. We were stuck where, upon inspection of the place, a construction crew that had built the high-tension utility towers had graded the road for access.

The little plateau where we were stranded ended at a cliff that, we discovered later, went straight down for about 300 feet. Being men of astute and sound minds, we sure weren't going to drive over a cliff. And, lacking four-wheel drive, we couldn't drive back up the road. What to do?

We walked back up the road to the place where we had stopped before our descent. Looking about, we came across a large piece of plywood. Turning it over we discovered it was a sign saying: Utility Road! Four-wheel Vehicles Only! Great! What idiot had knocked the sign down resulting in the stranding of a couple more idiots? Oh well.

Returning to the Bug, giving voice to the requisite deprecations and vilification's the situation warranted, we proceeded to gather brush and lit off a bodacious bonfire to light up the place and, hopefully, attract someone's attention to our predicament. To really appreciate our marooned status, one has to be familiar with the territory. To reach this garden spot of America, one has to take the Randsburg-Garlock Road. This eventually takes you to the Randsburg/Johannesburg metropolises. The combined population might have been around 200 or so. This highway is not exactly well traveled.

From our perch about halfway up the mountainside, we saw one set of headlights pass on the highway off in the distance in about an hour's time. We fired off a few rounds hoping someone might hear but not the fire, the shooting, nor our deeply felt and well-sounded curses and imprecations against the fates brought any response.

Since it was about midnight by this time, we made the rational decision to walk out to the highway. We could barely see well enough to scale down the cliff face with a few scrapes and bruises but we made it. Stout heart and all that. Not wanting to leave all the artillery, we took it with us and looked like a Cuban Expeditionary Force; bandoleer-laced Banditos.

Finally, reaching the road without breaking arms or legs, we started down that long, lonesome highway toward Johannesburg. About an hour into the hike, we came across someone's sense of humor. A hand-painted sign written in the middle of the road in white paint said: "HI!" We unlimbered the weapons and proceeded to properly ventilate the sign, blowing it and suitable chunks of asphalt away as an expression of our appreciation for the humorist's work.

As an aside, one might wonder about the shooting habits of this fellow and me. Yes, one might wonder. Suffice it to say we were never too concerned about ricochets as long as we could see for a mile and in a desolate area. I have been hit by ricochets twice; (been shot at twice as well) neither did any damage to my person. One is worth mention as it was quite strange.

I had been out in the Quartz Hill area hunting Mojave Greens. It was late as I got in my old Chevy truck and headed for the barn. As the hunting god would have it, there in the middle of the dirt road slithered one of the quarries. How obliging of the reptile. I had, at that time, a Single Action Army in .45 Long Colt caliber. Big slug.

Stopping the vehicle, I climbed out and unlimbered the Colt. The snake had gone into a convenient strike coil and I threw down on the varmint. BOOM! went the Colt; SMACK! went something against my chest. The venomous slitherer was doing a nicely executed headless twitch and at my feet was the flattened slug. The dirt road was so well compacted the bullet had actually done its job on the snake and bounced back against my chest.

But, anyhow, back to this fellow's and my trek. Further along, we saw a camper parked off the road. We shouted but there was no response. We weren't surprised since who wants to acknowledge a couple of strangers in the boonies who are out on a stroll after midnight? Going up to the camper and knocking at the door seemed unwise. Suppose it was inhabited by a paranoiac with a built-in 12 gauge? Discretion seemed to indicate that we keep on our way.

It was after 1:00 a.m. when we saw headlights in the far distance coming our way. Traffic! But, if we were to attempt to hail anyone down at this hour and in this desolate area, it might be best if only one of us appeared, and that without looking like highwaymen bristling firearms. Talk about sound judgment. No slouches, this fellow and me, in that department.

The approaching headlights gave rise to the scheme that this fellow would stand in the middle of the road and attempt to hail the vehicle while I waited in the bushes at the side of the road with all the artillery. If the vehicle did stop, my partner would explain our plight to the driver and try to get a ride to Johannesburg. There was the possibility, of course, that the driver might just as easily run my partner over; hence it was I that chose to hide in the bushes. Now don't think for a moment that the choice was a result of my buddy being stupider than I was; we tossed a coin and he lost.

Well, as luck would have it the vehicle turned out to be a pickup/camper and the driver was a man with his son who were on their way to do some quail hunting. My buddy was able to convince the guy that we were straight gun enthusiasts and the fellow was sympathetic to our plight. So, I was able to come out of the bushes and the fellow allowed us to stow our gear in the camper and we set out for Johannesburg.

Arriving in town, we retrieved our weapons only to be greeted by the local gendarmes. One was a crusty old coot and the other a young fellow. It happened that, observing the array of weapons at our disposal, these two officers had their curiosity piqued. As the older one demanded the weapons, he pointed to the sidewalk in front of the local cuttin' 'n' shootin' establishment where we chanced to disembark. It was liberally sprinkled with fresh bloodstains where, we were told, an earlier incident had taken place. It seems that some kind of altercation had resulted in one of the parties puncturing the hide of another due to a righteous disagreement about who bought the last round at the bar.

Talk about serendipity! It was just our luck according to the other events of the night that a couple of yahoos had made the local constables a tad wary of strangers bristling guns. The old coot was for hauling us off to the local hoosegow, but the younger, glory be! convinced him it would be better, after satisfying himself of our bona fides, to take us to Randsburg and let us call someone to come and rescue us. The old fellow was still not convinced that we were after jackrabbits with .45s and .357s but finally relented. My guess was he didn't want to be bothered with any more paperwork.

And, so, after satisfying themselves that the weapons were all unloaded (my buddy and I holding our breath as the old fellow performed the operation. We could just see him adding more glory to the legends of Johannesburg and splatters to the sidewalk in the process), we stowed the weapons in the trunk of the young deputy's unit and off we went to Randsburg. On the way, the young fellow was even decent enough to offer to put us up for the night, but as we explained there were a couple of women who, by now, were probably counting the insurance money if we didn't get in touch with them as soon as possible. It was now about 2:00 a.m.

Arriving in Randsburg, the deputy took us to the local Denny's and went in to explain the situation to the manager. This would take some explaining, as we had to bring all the weapons in with us. Our appearance didn't foster much confidence. Both needing a shave and dressed for desert hiking and, in all, looking like a couple of real desperadoes, we were, in a word, threatening! The deputy came back and said all had been arranged so, carrying our gunbelts and assorted weaponry into the restaurant, we aroused no little interest in the dinner guests present, who were fortunately very few at that late hour. We had no trouble getting a table to ourselves and, laying out the guns, belts and ammo on and under the table, we ordered coffee, the manager waiting on us as the waitresses seemed otherwise occupied. Too bad. I have always considered it my incumbent duty to liven up folk's, otherwise, dull days. Finally, there was nothing for it but to proceed to call the womenfolk.

It was now about three in the morning, but oddly enough they were still awake. After the normal exchange of pleasantries usual under the circumstances, it was decided to call an old friend of mine, a truck driver, to come and get us. Reaching him, he readily agreed to come and fetch us. I knew he would make good time. I had ridden with him before.

Sure enough, he was there in about two and one half-hours. Drunk. Oh, well. I should have thought about that before I called him. It was an interesting ride back to L.A. My truck driver friend's old Caddy convertible really burned up the highway. I bet my buddy's and my fingerprints are permanent fixtures in the upholstery.

The next day (same day, really) I got hold of triple AAA in Ridgecrest and the tow man knew the site of the VW. Seemed another vehicle had taken the same track a couple of weeks previously and they had had to build some road to get the car out. Cost him six hundred dollars. Fortunately, since the work was already done and I belonged to the Auto Club, it would be a freebie. Good old AAA.

My buddy and I went on to even more enjoyable trips to the outback, but his wife developed a certain nervousness thereafter about our association. I suggested an increase in insurance coverage but this did not seem to mollify her. Ah, women; there is just no understanding them at times. There was the time at Hamburger Mill Site and the episode with the, previously, unexploded parachute flare and the time we gave the dry lakes a wide berth but I will leave those stories for another time.

My son and daughter, Michael and Karen, shared in many of their dad's proclivities for adventure. Part of the reason, sadly, was that their mother didn't want them around. So, when I went somewhere, they went with me. As they grew older, the adventures became more adventuresome. They will have their own stories to tell their children. I hope they do it with charity toward their father.

This buddy and I would often go out to Kramer's Junction and hit the dirt roads until we got many miles off the highway. Out around Hamburger Mill Site and the Cuddeback and Harper Dry Lake area, we would begin to encounter our quarry: Jackrabbits.

Using single actions with fast draw rigs, we would fire about 100 rounds per rabbit. The fun was in the shooting, not the killing. And, it was as good an excuse as any to get out of the city.

Since we re-loaded our own ammo, I cast the bullets, the shooting was cheap. We could afford to be profligate in bouncing rounds off rocks.

Reloading can be a lot of fun. When I first started as a boy, I'll never forget seating my first primer with my Lyman tong tool. I was loading for the .270 and was as nervous as the proverbial cat in a room full of rocking chairs. But .270 ammo was expensive and, with true grit, I mastered the skill in order to be able to afford to shoot. I've never regretted the learning.

But my buddy missed throwing a charge once and nearly cost me a day's shooting. We were out at Cuddeback and a large, old jack bounced out of the brush. Pulling my Colt, I tripped the hammer only to have the round go *pumph* instead of *bang*! Staring at the gun, I was amazed to see the bullet sticking halfway out of the end of the barrel. Only the primer had fired and with sufficient power (about 600 pounds pressure) to force the bullet that far.

Far from our truck and with me cursing my buddy roundly, we started the long walk back. Suddenly, right there in that trackless, vast dessert there was a pair of rusty pliers right in the sand in front of me. Talk about serendipity! Using the rusty pliers, I was able to pull the slug from the muzzle and we were back in business.

Because of our crusade against verminous ground squirrels and jackrabbits, this fellow and I began to kid about a 500-pound rabbit looking for us to get even. I never realized that my little girl, Karrie, actually believed there was a monster rabbit after her old dad until she recently told me of it. You sure have to be careful around little ones. They have vivid imaginations. Even worse, they cannot discriminate when listening to grownups talk about 500 pound rabbits and the one that got away. And we all know about the *veracity* of fishermen.

I got even with this fellow the night I shot out his truck window. Well, shot out may be too strong. Actually I put a BB hole in it. I happened to be driving that night and among the weapons we had brought with us was a CO2 powered pellet gun. Just for fun.

Now the rule was that the windows were to be open so as to fling a round at the bunnies without the trouble of stopping the vehicle. But this poor fellow was cold and had rolled his window up. Sure enough, a rabbit bounced up on his side and with electric speed I flang a shot at him with the pellet pistol. But my buddy's window was closed.

It got real exciting for a moment as the BB zinged around the cab of the truck. Amazingly it didn't hit either of us. But there was a neat little hole in the center of the window and a thin crack straight up and down from it.

There was some discussion following this trick: "Why was your window up! Why did you try to shoot me! If I'd really wanted to shoot you, I'd have used the .357 you dummy!" And many other good-natured, comradely remarks. But he got even.

It was our custom to reload for the driver. One day, (I was driving and using the Colt as usual) a jackrabbit jumped up and I began to shoot. Bang! Click. Bang! Click. Bang! Click.

Now one of the reasons that this fellow and I are such good friends is the fact that we share the same twisted sense of humor. He had only loaded every other chamber in the Colt. Great fun; for him. Now you shooters out there understand the fun of shooting at bounding jackrabbits is seeing the clouds of dirt, rock and dust being blown around the poor things, educating them to the perversity of human nature and hastening them on their way, feeling the good, honest buck of a fine weapon in your hand, not the occasional and accidental killing of the poor things. But only a low-down skunk would do such a thing as cheating your bosom buddy to half a load. It also galled me that he thought of it first.

Remember the skit of Bill Cosby saving a snowball for revenge? Of course my buddy could no longer trust me to reload for him now. This was one drawback of his little joke. But, like Cosby, I waited.

It was nearly two years later. We had gone to Kelso Valley. My buddy had forgotten- I hadn't. I can wait a long time to get even and I never forget. He usually used a Ruger (just what you would expect of someone who would do such a dastardly thing to a friend. Anyone knows that only a Colt Single Action Army is suitable for the real purist). But this time he had brought a .22 auto and, thinking all was forgiven, was letting me reload as he was driving. Sure enough, a rabbit bounced up on his side and Bang! Click! Being an auto loader, one shot was all he got. Served him right. Justice is sweet. So is revenge.

What he was so appreciative of was my steadfastness, patience and ability to wait him out. I'm sure he knew there would come a time and was glad to get it over. But you can't help loving someone that shoots out a sliding glass door with a .45 Colt Auto- One of this fellow's neater tricks as he was demonstrating gun safety to a neighbor while living in Carson. His wife was not amused. But surely God gets a chuckle out of our antics. He has to have a great sense of humor.

There used to be a lot of game out in the dessert areas until the invasion of the bikers. They not only tore up the dessert, but, since many of them were riff raff, they tore down old, mining shacks and vandalized structures that had been standing since the 49er days. Beginning to find dessert tortoise shells with bullet holes in them evidenced one of the saddest commentaries on the change the new breed brought. It takes a special kind of person to shoot a tortoise.

Walking was the primary way to chase jackrabbits (though my buddy often threatened to shoot me in the leg to slow me down) and you get to know and appreciate the country. Somehow the noise of a two-stroke seemed to profane this beautiful, vast area.

I encountered my first Mojave Green out in that area. For several years I had trekked this country without ever encountering a snake. I was walking a ridge while my buddy and another friend of ours were in a gully down below. As I was about to set my left boot down, a movement caught my eye. There, where I was about to plant my foot was a rattlesnake! And it was green!

It had twitched itself into a coil to strike. I stood there, dumbfounded, with my left foot still in the air over the thing. Not only had I never seen a snake in the area for all this time, but also the first one I encounter is a rattlesnake! And the critter is green!

With my foot still in the air, I pulled my hogleg and proceeded to punch a hole right between its headlights. The varmint hardly twitched and remained in his striking coil. Only then did I realize I still had my foot in the air.

Backing off carefully, I called for the fellows to come up and take a look at the strange critter. Now neither of them had ever heard of a green rattlesnake either. After examining the thing, the fellows proceeded to ventilate him properly.

Some time later, I read an article about this snake called a *Mojave Green*. I discovered it is the most deadly snake on the North American Continent. According to a herpetologist at UCLA, its venom is twice as deadly as a King Cobra's. No one is working on an antivenin because death occurs too rapidly.

We were more cautious thereafter, particularly at night, in wandering the area. While teaching at Quartz Hill high school, I often took some of my pupils out to the hills behind the school where we discovered a large population of these things and laid waste to them.

My buddy will recall the time I tried to dig one out of a burrow with a short stick and nearly got nailed. To this day I don't know what prompted me to do such a stupid thing. But it recalls an incident involving a field trip and one of the science teachers, Ed White, from Quartz Hill.

Ed was out in the dessert with the class and was warning them about snakes. A particular point he made will never be forgotten. To demonstrate what never to do, he reached under a bush and was promptly bitten by one of the resident reptiles. The class, of course, was suitably impressed at the lengths the teacher was willing to go to teach them the hazards of reaching into bushes when snakes might be lurking there. It gave new meaning to the phrase *teacher dedication*.

Ed spent a couple of weeks in the hospital recuperating. Fortunately the little rattler was only a Sidewinder, not a Mojave, and had only one fang to boot. A few of the baser sort among the faculty asked Ed to repeat the demonstration on a number of occasions but he steadfastly declined.

But my buddy and I were always doing strange things together. I'll never forget the time we flew up to the Kernville airport for the fun of it.

I first started flying out of Torrance Airport in 1957. I started in an old J-3 Cub with an armstrong starter. That was real flying. For those of us with a passion for the wide (and sometimes wild) Blue Yonder, the truism that "There are old pilots and there are bold pilots, but there are no old, bold pilots" was quickly established in the Cub.

While living in Lancaster, I bought into an Alon that was a real kiddy car to fly. Easy. I had also acquired a venerable old Stinson Voyager. Not so easy. A heavy, but solid, old tail-dragger.

My old buddy often accompanied me, and one day we decided to take the Alon and fly up to Kernville. It was a bright sun shiny day but a little breezy. When we arrived over the lake, the wind was really whistling up the canyon where the strip was laid out. As I came along the downwind, we must have been doing 180 knots groundspeed. Turning base to final, we were much too high.

Kissing off that approach, I tried again. The tricky part was the fact that the canyon narrows quickly on the approach and you really have to crank the bird around in a hurry if the wind is blowing hard. But, once more, we came in too high. Not only were we being hurled down the canyon on approach, we were being kept high on final.

Since we had done a lot of sight seeing over Kelso Valley and the Piutes on the way, fuel was running low and I did not want to take the risk of kissing it off and going over to Inyokern, my alternate. Besides, the FAA, in its infinite wisdom, has made it against the law to run out of gas in an airplane. It was sweaty palms and white-knuckle time. I told my buddy "We're going to have to get this thing down this time!"

Having failed to make the landing on the first two approaches, I had at least realized that I would have to come up low, ignoring the field pattern altitude, and wrench the bird hard over on base. Actually, a base leg as such was out of the question; what I really had to do was make a gut-wrenching U-turn.

It seemed that I was having to point the nose of the craft right at the ground on final because of the excessively high wind. But it was the only way to lose altitude fast enough to hit the end of the strip. With the yoke far forward and the nose seeming to point straight down (and me not having practiced my proficiency in underground flying lately) the runway was instantly there, and sweat-drenched and white-faced, were on the ground, which once we came to a stop, we proceeded to get out and kiss.

But the fun was not over. With airplanes, not only does what go up must come down, what is down, must go up again. We still had the takeoff to look forward to. A few cups of coffee later, we were fortified to face the inevitable. The wind had not abated, only gotten worse. But a man's gotta do what a man's gotta do!

The strip was laid out in such a way that you took off toward the lake. With the wind howling toward us, we were thrown up quickly, no finessing. Now if you have ever piloted a small aircraft, you know how the various types of geography create what is called *ground effect*. You also know that as you pass over bare ground and hit a body of water (the lake) it can sometimes have a dramatic impact on the air conditions.

Sure enough, the fun was not over. As we passed over the edge of the lake and I began my turn, a huge fist (turbulence) hit the underside of the left wing so suddenly and violently that I struck the side of the canopy with my head hard enough to nearly knock me out. Fortunately, it didn't.

Little airplanes are fun, but I well remember Pappy Boyington's definition of flying: "Hours and hours of dull monotony sprinkled with moments of stark terror!" But, as with tobacco, shooting, fishing, prospecting and exploring wilderness areas, I have had a life-long love affair with airplanes and flying.

There are few experiences to equal the freedom of flight in a small aircraft. The Alon was a lot of fun, chasing clouds and clipping the tops of Joshua trees chasing Jackrabbits and bikers. The Stinson, by comparison, was a lot of work to fly. You really had to fly it point to point. The last time I flew it was really exciting to my two passengers and me.

I had completed the annual on the old bird and invited two of my old pupils from Quartz Hill to join me on its maiden flight. One fellow had never been up in a small plane before and had the natural reserve and nervousness that comes with the territory. However, the other had flown several times with me and knew I could be trusted not to introduce anyone to any unexpected thrills.

The takeoff was uneventful but as we got to altitude, I noticed the oil pressure had fallen to 20 pounds. Not wishing to take any unnecessary chances I told the boys that I was going back. It was a beautiful day and the landing went smooth as silk. Touchdown was perfect, but as the rear wheel hit the runway the bird developed a mind of its own suddenly and violently veering off the runway to the left in an abrupt ground loop.

Fortunately, the old Stinson being a very stable old bird we remained level and didn't even lower a wing. In a huge cloud of dust we came to a quick stop. Cutting the engine amid one fellow's war whoops and the other shouting "Never again!" we got out of the bird and discovered that the right spring of the tailwheel had broken, throwing the plane into a violent, left turn. It's too bad this one fellow's first ride had to be so exciting. I think he contents himself with building and flying models now.

Those were fun days. Life has become so very serious that if I didn't have the memories of these things I wonder how I would cope with it all. It does make me very sensitive to the problems of young people who no longer have the opportunities I have had, much less a gold mine (complete with trout stream) to escape to. As I mull over the life I have had, the good and the bad, I realize that I have been richly blessed in many ways that young people have been cheated of.

I've had my own time as a biker, and sure enough if you ride them long enough, they will get you. I survived my biggie with a left hand and leg wired together. Tragically, Diana, my eldest daughter was killed on one of the things. My eldest son, Daniel, still drives a big Harley. Oh well, Dad hasn't set the best example in caution. Unhappily, Karen and Michael, my youngest two, seem determined to take their chances as well.

It's the people that make life worthwhile. But our associations with others should be in a context of goodwill and friendliness. I've been blessed with having friends as crazy as myself, who can take a joke and can give as well as they take. I feel our relationship with God should be at least as good.

I miss taking my children and other young people fishing and shooting. I loved being with my children and other young people because they still believed anything was possible.

CHAPTER NINE

There are two disciplinarians in a high school: The coach and the shop teacher. No matter how many administrators are assigned the task, everyone knows they are just figureheads. The real power to get pupils, particularly the troublemakers and those referred to by other teachers and administrators as the "rejects," to perform and stay in school belongs to the sports and practical skills teachers.

Unlike the poor classroom teacher, the coach and the shop teacher can make life miserable for a recalcitrant pupil. This is particularly true if the pupil has an active interest in learning about cars, machinery, a sports scholarship, etc.

The shop teacher has to be a firm disciplinarian in order to keep the kids from killing or injuring themselves or others. Consequently, he can always cite safety as a reason for bouncing a kid out of class. And if you are dealing with 150 active teen-agers a day around hazardous equipment, caution is the name of the game.

However, I can think of no other classes I enjoyed teaching more than my shop classes. The administration invariably, having little idea of what working for a living was all about, or how to run a lathe or repair an engine, usually left shop teachers alone. They did have to intrude themselves occasionally in order to "evaluate" the teacher.

Shop teachers always get a chuckle, when not wanting to punch some administrator, out of these so-called *evaluations*. It's not unlike asking a politician to evaluate the way a mechanic fixes his car. They haven't the haziest notion of what is involved with teaching kids how to work with both hands and minds in the shops.

Consequently, while classroom teachers usually view administrators at large as nuisances, it is shop teachers that view them as some unmentionable substance, a richly earned reputation from my own dealing with a number of these *Little Caesars*.

I suppose this came about from the fact that school administrators in general are paranoid, and particularly about subjects (i.e., earning an honest living with their hands) of which they have no real knowledge. But they will be most bombastic about how much they know about how you are to teach a skilled trade. It reminds me of those unmarried marriage counselors and the child psychologist who has no children.

While doing that part of the research for my Ph. D. involving surveying teachers the most vitriolic remarks came from shop teachers concerning administrators. I have saved all the originals and may include them in some future publication. I'm sure they will be most enlightening to the general public.

Most concur that administrators take advanced courses for their administrative credentials in Bureaucratic Meddling; I must admit that those I had to serve under had graduate degrees in this area. Having no real knowledge of the skills being taught, these demagogues have to resort to threats of poor evaluations in order to keep the shop teacher in his place. Admittedly, shop teachers in general have a poor attitude when it comes to dealing with the administrative power structure.

I'm reminded of the time when a VP called the woodshop instructor to harangue him about some supposed misstep in dealing with a pupil. The instructor listened attentively for a few minutes then abruptly cut in and said loudly "(expletive deleted) you!" and banged the phone down.

For a while afterward the poor VP went around telling everyone "He can't say that to me, I'm an administrator!" He had few sympathizers. I knew of many that envied the woodshop teacher's ability to express so eloquently their own feelings toward this particular self-important VP.

But, so much needs to be said on this subject that I am forced to leave it to the future book I have threatened to write on education and its fools. I will say, in parting, that the handful of good administrators I have known have, invariably, come from some other background than the Ivory Tower.

The schools, in general, have suffered the result of a growing technology just as people have. Throwing computers at kids doesn't help unless the discipline, relevancy and morality are there as well. I used to tell parents that things were not as bad as they thought in the schools; they were worse! Unfortunately, most didn't believe me. But it was one of the reasons for my ministry in starting private schools.

I will never forget an incident while I was substituting at a High School some years ago. I seldom ever worked as a substitute, but circumstances led me to take this assignment at this time.

Working with teenagers has always been a delight to me. This particular class was a group of seniors. I usually try to engage young people in exercises that require them to think for themselves. The particular discussion we were having at this time led me to tell them: "Any real education you receive will not be because of this school, whatever real education you get here will be because of your own efforts." To my utter amazement, the entire class arose and began to applaud. They told me that I was the only teacher who had ever voiced their own feelings about the educational establishment. I was never invited back to sub in that school again.

It is well said that nothing is more common than people with talent, genius, and education, to be failures. It is, as Calvin Coolidge said: "Persistence and determination alone that are omnipotent!" However, persistence and determination are only possible when the goal is well defined and seen as worth the effort. Most people suffer the consequences of a lack of goal setting, of not knowing what they really want. Further, people, in general, are ignorant of what is possible, either through lack of education or experience.

Ignorance is a real killer. That is why I am such a strong advocate of education. But I mean real education. That is, the dispelling of ignorance. This is why illiteracy is so hurtful. You must be able to read, and read widely, to make any sense out of today's world and take advantage of any opportunities. We live in the information age, and lack of knowledge of information, and information resources, largely written, are the death-knell of any enterprise.

Jesus said we have not because we ask not, or, we ask amiss. Clearly a lack of information is working here. While we may ask amiss purely because of selfish motives, the most sincere individual may fail because of ignorance. Certainly God has a right to demand that we have clearly defined reasons for our requests. And if not, how can He, reasonably, comply?

A teacher brought me a quantity of silverware once while I was teaching metal shop. This was at the time silver was appreciating rapidly due to, we later found out, the machinations of the Hunt brothers. He asked that I melt it down for him and pour it in the form of ingots. This was simple enough. We had the proper equipment and teaching foundry work was a part of my curriculum. Using a clean, graphite crucible, I soon had the material poured for him and left the cast iron pig tray to cool. There was approximately two pounds of silver.

Now I am a firm believer in teaching able students to accept responsibility and had several that were my shop foremen. These young people showed exceptional ability and interest in metal work and were a great help to me. It was the job of my foremen to make tool and equipment checks at the end of each class. They also helped with the beginners. At the start of each class period, they would also make tool and equipment checks to make sure their class was not responsible for anything amiss. Due to this system, I seldom had any problems with missing items (unless I had to share a lab with another teacher; a real boondoggle).

One of the responsibilities of this one young foreman was the foundry section. He had to make sure the furnace was charged, sand and molds were in order, *etc.* Mistaking the tray of silver ingots for aluminum he dutifully dumped them into the crucible together with a quantity of aluminum. The fact that the silver was in a different tray and quite small and heavy compared to the aluminum didn't register with him.

When the teacher came to claim his silver, we went over to the foundry area and it was gone. I asked my foreman: "Did you see a small tray of silver ingots here by the furnace?" The look on his face was a marvel in human emotions, going quickly from surprise to horror. Haltingly, we got the sordid facts and stood looking at the crucible of molten metal in the furnace. There was no choice but to pour the stuff, which we proceeded to do.

The silver and aluminum had formed an amalgam, impossible to separate with the equipment on hand. The teacher was not happy. My foreman was devastated at his world-class boo-boo. But, as I explained to him, it had to be accepted as a lesson in paying attention to detail. If something is out of synch, such as a small tray of ingots when only the large trays are used for aluminum, you had better stop and think before you act. While the teacher was a contributor to this lesson, I think he would rather have had his silver.

***

A college roomie used to join me on my excursions to the outback. I remember the time when he had his new TR 3. It was a real fun car to drive, and not having a real death wish he insisted on my doing the honors of opening her up when the 3,000-mile mark showed up on the odometer.

We had just left Mojave and, heading toward Boron, I soon had the car pegged out over 100 mph. We had just passed a MG when it felt like the transmission was falling out of the car. Looking in the rear mirror, I saw a large cloud of blue smoke blow out and envelop the MG.

The engine had lost power and I steered the car over to the edge of the highway. The MG sailed by, the driver making an obscene gesture, and we got out to see what happened. Upon lifting the bonnet, it looked like a bomb had gone off in the engine compartment. There were holes in the engine block, dents in the sheet metal and oil all over. Thumbing a ride back to Mojave, we arranged for a local garage to pick up the car and we caught a Greyhound back to L.A.

The mechanic who worked on the car said the engine had swallowed a valve. He asked what speed we were traveling since he had never seen an engine so self-destruct before. There were even pieces of shrapnel in the carburetor intakes. The mechanic said it was only the third engine he had ever heard of TR having to replace entirely. But we had a lot of fun with it after my roomie got it back.

This story reminds me of another of my Quartz Hill pupils. While a youngster, he bought a Volkswagen Bug. Deciding to overhaul the engine, he set to work with a vengeance. Finishing the job, he cranked it up only to discover oil pouring out of the engine. As it turned out, he had forgotten a minor part, the bottle cap at the end of the camshaft. Now anyone who has knowledge of VW's knows that in order to fix this oversight, you have to once more tear the entire engine down again.

So, once more, he pulled the engine, tore it down and put it all back together again. It ran fine. For a short while. But it overheated and burned out. He had left a shop towel in the fan housing, and without proper cooling Bug engines very quickly give up the ghost. Another complete rebuild was in order. Now you cannot fault this young fellow for being a tad exasperated by this time. But, stout fellow, he didn't give up. One has to admire him for this if not for his mechanical aptitude and attention to detail.

Third time is the charm, right? Wrong! The engine ran well enough finally, when you could get it started. He worked feverishly to correct this problem. He had graduated from high school by now and was enrolled in the local J.C., Tumbleweed Tech (Antelope Valley Community College). Thinking that he had finally cured the starting malady of the VW, he ran out to take it to school one morning and it wouldn't start. Something snapped in his poor feverish mind.

There was a railing at the top of the steps of his house. He proceeded to climb on top of the railing and jumped off onto the top of the poor, old, hapless Beetle. He then proceeded to dance heavily all over the thing, pummeling it into helpless submission (and considerable, large dents).

He then, having shown his pique to the now thoroughly thrashed bug, went in the house and called a friend who helped him tow it to a corner in town, placed a for sale sign in it and called it quits on VWs. Not the first or last when it comes to a multitude of VW owners. I found them to be good little cars as long as you maintained them and didn't do things like leaving shop towels in the fan housing.

I acquired a vehicle from this young fellow some years later that showed his knack for kicking the tar out of them. I noticed peculiar dents in the car and, sure enough, he had showed it who was boss.

***

I just got back from a trip to my silver mine with one of my old pupils. A beautiful trout stream runs through the claim, and in spite of drought the stream was running nicely and we caught trout. I cooked them on the blade of my machete and ate them right beside the stream. Now how can you beat that for quality living! The country is so rough that it keeps the riff raff out and only other noble souls (fishermen) frequent the spot.

To repeat the story, the first time I ever visited the place in 1948 was at the invitation of an old man (probably my age now). He was the stereotypical prospector, grizzled, gray beard, gnarled hands, stooped back, faded Levi's, flannel shirt, slouch hat, etc. He happened by our cabin one day and was invited to lunch. While eating, he learned of my passion for fishing and he described where he was living and how to get there. He said there was a great trout stream with waterfalls and deep pools and plenty of large trout begging to be caught.

The old fellow lived in an old tin shack on the claim by the stream. He made enough panning the creek to supply his few needs and came down to town (Kernville) only when absolutely necessary. He recognized in me a kindred spirit and the first chance I got I took the rough map he had drawn for me and, with tackle in hand, went calling.

The stream was everything he said it was. A few other tales might have been embellished though. He showed me a dent in the shack at the side of the doorway that he said he made chunking a rock at a bear. According to him, the mine was last worked about 1928. It was a Lode claim, silver, and every winter the stream would flood it out. There were some old model T and A engines, and an old straight eight that they had used to try to keep the shaft (a stope) pumped out. He said they quit when they couldn't keep up with the water.

I filed on the claim, naming it the *Laura Jean*, some years later. Only then did I discover that the old boys that had worked the mine had never bothered with this nicety. They simply took the silver and didn't bother notifying Uncle Sam of their enterprise.

As a high school teacher, I have taken many of my pupils back to this pristine, wilderness site and given them the chance to share the wondrous joy of an unspoiled, mountain stream and the wildlife. So many magic hours with young people, my own children especially, in this truly magnificent setting.

It has seemed a sacred trust to maintain this spot. Its very ruggedness has, thus far, kept it so. Only the hardiest can make the hike in and these are, invariably, kindred souls. It is in such settings that we clean out our minds and souls and get our priorities right. There is no other counsel or medicine its equal. But that might be my Choctaw Cherokee blood on grandad's side speaking- Strong feelings for the land and critters there.

A friend has just come by to visit. As we often do, we got into a good philosophical discussion about religious things and I was attempting to explain my disgust with preachers in general. During our conversation he provided me with a perfect example of my statement that preachers (much like school teachers and university professors) major in abstractions, not things that are of any real value to our lives in this down and dirty real world.

Well, I had used the word *absolute* and he seized on that saying that God was the universal absolute. Now I know, good hearted as he is, he thought he had defended the honor of God and said something of real value that made perfect sense. But what that something was, there are no words in our vocabulary to explain.

In science, the concept of workability is the hallmark. That and replication are the essence of all science. If it works and can be repeated, explained, it's good science. Preachers are poor scientists of their trade. It is a shame that more preachers and politicians haven't quit stuffing the stove with pinecones. Once you remove all the emotional attachment and prejudice of the average preacher's verbiage, you have little left that has any practical benefit in the workaday world most of us have to contend with. Just take away his pet phrases and buzzwords and few are left with anything to say. Small wonder Sam Clemens said: "He was as happy as if church had just let out!"

Those pinecones burn hot and fast but they have no lasting value, unlike a good honest piece of oak. Now the pinecones are great for starting the fire, but you need the oak for the long haul. How's that for good old boy homiletics?

Jesus said he that overcomes, perseveres, will inherit the kingdom. The faint-hearted need not apply. He also said that we would be given the power to do so if we mean business. But there are many pretenders to the faith, without any real repentance from dead works, who, when the going gets rough or this world seems to offer a better deal or whose egos get in the way fall away. By their works we know them.

What reality of God answers to our grief, when we desperately need answers? I believe there is a very human aspect to God, which stands to reason. If He had wanted robots He would have created them. Instead, He made men in His image, creatures that could love and hate, work and fail, create and appreciate beauty, imagine and dream.

The humanity of the prophets and disciples is evident throughout the entire Bible. In Galatians 5:12 Paul wishes the Judaizers would emasculate themselves. In 4:9 Paul is indecisive about whether we know God or He us. In Ephesians 4:18 we are told that ignorance of divine things is due to hardening of our hearts; in 6:12 there are forces of evil in the heavenly realm. Colossians 1:19 there is a reconciliation of things in heaven to be accomplished. Indecision and human weakness are all there; no plaster saints.

Conviction of wrongdoing brings surrender and repentance, which brings obedience. That is the way of The Gospel. The conclusion of the Sermon on the Mount ends with the warning to count the cost and build accordingly. No one can do this without cold, hard facts in hand. If we are left guessing, God has played a cruel joke on us. However, if we are able to know it is worth everything to find out and pursue the very best that God has for us. And it should be exciting work, not guesswork.

It is one of my most infuriating traits (to my detractors in religion and education) that I insist that God is both reasonable and practical. I even believe He expects us to be these things as well. I believe in teaching young people the value of learning, of setting goals and persisting in accomplishing them, of persevering in tasks undertaken.

If Heaven is anything less than having joy in jobs that are worthwhile, of learning things of value, of being able to build, create, fellowship with those like-minded, of having fun, then it would be a cheat. But if it is all these things and more, religious leaders are having no success in showing it.

Heaven must offer both peace and excitement; it must be a place with a trout stream, mountains, and an abundance of wild life and unlimited opportunity to grow in mind and spirit. So I believe Heaven to be, particularly in the wilderness, in the stars at night and in the hopes, dreams and aspirations of young people who haven't learned what is impossible.

It is certainly a commonplace befitting our human condition lacking position in the higher classes make a virtue of the lower. It has somewhat to do with my own, professedly tongue-in-cheek, appellation of an *Okie Intellectual*. But it serves me well in getting the goats, if not the attention otherwise, of my self-assumed betters.

Reminds me of my brother; he didn't write much because he was proud but couldn't spell his way through a book of cigarette papers. It is a grievous loss because he could have helped so much in putting some things of interest to his own children in print and helping me in much of my own writing. It is sad to me that our great-grandmother, grandparents and mom didn't write down many of the stories they shared with us as children. I determined, years ago, that I wasn't going to let that happen, for better or for worse, to my own children. So it is that many of the incidents I describe in my own life are for their benefit. Sadly, there are some things, like what really counts in life, that are only appreciated with age and wisdom.

If I, to any degree, heed the wisdom of those that have served as the poets, the makers that encourage both the doing and the dream, I will have served well. I hope I write for posterity, not only my own children but all children. The vicissitudes of life too often prevailing over the desired ends and ambitions, it still remains to workers like myself to do all we can to help children dream dreams and live in hope.

The seeming disparity between an Andrew Johnson and Abraham Lincoln is easily resolved in the reading of histories. It is for that reason I encourage you to read Bowers' account "The Tragic Era." It takes the historian of the soul and appreciation of the poet to do justice to history. For this reason, our most ancient historians were, literally, poets. The mythic of some of the histories had more to them than a simple embellishment of facts. The exaggeration of truth is not always with the intent of passing a lie. It is not always for the purpose of making the teller more important than he really is. The Indian acting out the hunt serves to provide not just the bald facts, but also a story that will be remembered.

Sadly, many truths become legend and are distorted to the point of prejudice; and those that are ignorant of the facts, whether willingly so or not, begin to build their own "facts" on such distortions. Convinced in their own minds of a truth which has no basis in anything but presumption (like the theory of Darwinism), the followers of noble lies and fairy tales designed to promote their own peculiar prejudices often carry them to the extreme of persecuting those that refuse to believe a lie. God's "strong delusion that they will believe a lie... because the love of the truth is not in them" will be of such a character; the ministers of this grand lie will, as usual, come as angels of light.

My distinct advantage, as someone with nothing to lose or an empire to protect, is being able to deal with Truth. Over the years, because of my education and writing, I have come to know many wealthy and powerful men. The great majority of these, while agreeing with much that I write about, would never be able to put their own thoughts into print as I do. For that reason these men, many good men, would never put in writing what they share with me in confidence. I understand this and have never betrayed their confidences. But there was a time not long ago when honorable men were able to freely express their minds; when political candidates were not one dimensional players in a shlock drama in spite of, at times, making speeches to the sound of cocking pistols in their audiences.

One thing leads to another and I can't resist sharing another episode with another college roomie.

Cooking is not usually something young, single men use on their resumes; it's certainly never been high on my list of priorities, just a necessary chore to be gotten out of the way as an alternative to starving. This roomie was of the same persuasion. In short, we don't mind the eating, it's the cooking and cleaning that becomes an onerous task.

Well, the menu one night was beans and cornbread. It was this roomie who mixed the cornbread and we waited for the stove to do its job; and we waited, and waited. The stuff just didn't seem to want to bake properly. Waiting long past the appointed time when it should have been done, we removed it from the oven. It hadn't risen and what we faced was a pan full of a substance, which would have done good service as a Frisbee or discus.

The material seemed to be vulcanized like rubber and had the same pliable, plastic consistency of same.

Now he and I were intelligent young men. It didn't take us long to realize that he had used baking soda rather than baking powder in his recipe. Oh well, we ate the beans and forewent the cornbread. But there was no denying the fact that, as men, we would have done well to have had the proper guidance of the little woman in our lives. Women seem to take such tasks more seriously than men, and under their direction, the kitchen doesn't usually become a research laboratory.

It's a tragedy in our society that women sell out so cheaply. With nothing going for them but their sex, once youth is gone they have nothing left with which to trade in our culture. Buying into the Devil's game of adultery with no sense of family, commitment and fidelity, with divorce so simple to obtain poor, foolish women lacking a sense of self-worth fail to comprehend the end of such foolishness. Statistically, a single woman over 40 can forget about marriage. For those that find a man willing to take the chance, the prenuptial agreement makes it a sum-come-nothing game. Spreading themselves around in their youth, they discover, too late, that men aren't interested in used and wrinkled merchandise when it comes to legal entanglements.

Harsh and cruel as this truth is, it is still women who have brought this upon themselves. Their willful and often ignorant actions against fidelity and commitment have brought this to pass. I will never excuse the men who use this foolishness of women to excuse their own failure as leaders, who use this foolishness of women to fulfill their own lust, but it is still the woman's responsibility to accept the truth that she simply cannot save her cake and eat it too. As with men, it is still the right way or shipwreck and destruction. The historical imperative of virtue is not heartening: "One man among a thousand have I found, but never a woman!"

Women, not recognizing that men are not the enemy in failing to give in to their ridiculous claims to equality, invariably mistaking this for equal value, should pay more attention to the fact that they, not us, make the decisions that lead to their being undervalued in our culture. It is women who sell out to Playboy and Penthouse, the strip joints and jumping into one bed after another and so on. Tragically, I don't see any man of stature in the religious or political leadership that women can trust who would provide the motive for doing other. It has never been a question of equal rights, but one of equal value.

Walt Kelly portrayed in cartoon format the mouse that wanted to be an elephant. Coming upon a fairy godmother, he was granted his wish. He should have noticed something amiss when the godmother was found living in an alley as a street person. Sure enough, the mouse soon found being an elephant not all it was cracked up to be. Tearfully and fearfully, he was able to get the godmother to change him back into a mouse. So it is with women that itch for a something that will make them better than they think of themselves. Even finding a man that will allow them to rule doesn't relieve the itch. Sadly, often tragically, it often takes being an elephant for a while to appreciate being a mouse.

Admittedly, my relationships with women have too often been that of armed neutrality. I have had some unusual pets. I once had a skunk and, at another time, a porcupine. Both had some endearing characteristics, but required a large degree of accommodation to their natures and were difficult to live with. Not impossible; difficult. Some more easily daunted souls would say it isn't worth the effort. I disagree, though not so much that I ever tried to cuddle the porcupine or aggravate the skunk.

CHAPTER TEN

Weedpatch and Little Oklahoma are not the same places of my childhood where I would sometimes catch lizards. I still like the little fellows but a surprising thing has happened; here in the Kern River Valley over the past years I have witnessed an evolutionary change in the critters- they run faster than they used to! I know this is true because I can't catch them as well as I could when I was a kid; probably something to do with climate change a hole in the ozone layer or air pollution.

My mother and maternal grandparents provided a broad and varied background that enabled me to make do and appreciate the value of most things; could find pleasure in such circumstances as living in Las Vegas or Little Oklahoma. In my imagination I can enjoy such magic as to be the envy of the most skilled sorcerer or conjuror, but also able to appreciate the practical skills of shaping and forming of metal by lathe and mill, to turn walnut and ash into something of both beauty and practical value, to wire or plumb a house, to get an engine humming sweetly and teach these things to others. These are things that help to fulfill a man; that tells him life has meaning and is worthwhile, these together with things like family and friends are some of the whispered promises of immortality that among many other things causes me to believe in a hereafter.

As to family, a mother teaching the little one to do dishes, sweep the floor or do laundry might not speak as loudly for the present, but when that little one learns she is contributing something of value to the family it has eternal potential. When that boy is taught to take on the obligation for disposing of the trash, cutting the lawn or washing the car, he is learning lessons for living a productive life.

But in defense of our children listening to the noise they call music today, I know the music we were listening to in the fifties, much of it from the thirties and forties as well, was based on a culture and society that still lived in hope that things would only get better and better; jobs were plentiful, America was the preeminent world power, we were a nation on the go and a phone call or cup of coffee was a nickel.

In contrast to the songs of love, hope and a better future of my time, our children turn to the mind-numbing noise they call "music" glorifying suicide, violence, sex and drugs as an escape from having to hope in the face of hopelessness. Such noise is a mechanism for tuning out the mind and giving in to the animalistic senses that have no responsibility or accountability; an anti-establishment protest against being robbed and cheated of hope. A generation that has lost hope in eternal verities of love and goodness, the triumph of good over evil often opts for the glorification of evil as it gains the ascendance. At least it promises change and excitement and, therefore, some believe it must be better than the status quo, which they believe dooms them in any event.

However, even in Camelot there are inescapable realities. Dragons need slaying and damsels need rescue. The young knight must know his enemy and keep his sword sharp. A betraying Guinevere or Lancelot should never cause the loss of a crown and the Grail must be sought no matter the cost. Arthur must be true though all others play him false.

It would seem to be obvious that a man must be able to have hope of providing for a wife and children in order for love and romance to survive, to enable that girl to commit herself to a husband and children. The basis of this is a home of their own no matter how humble; remove this hope and you have the generation and the society we presently have; a generation that knows it has been betrayed and is ripe for rebellion and revolution, anarchy, or as seems the present path total enslavement to a government without conscience hypocritically portraying itself as "caring for the poor" and "working class Americans."

Even though Jacob's Staff has been traded for books, it is still the responsibility of the poet-historian to keep the legends alive and grave his marks. Truth will always sort through the myth of legends and make what is vital real. In the most clouded of memories, sharp spikes of light much as with Thoreau's flakes of light dart here and there, illuminating what is of real value in the keeping and the sharing with others, and we can never guess what is taking root in the minds of our children that will become their own epics.

In the twilight of life, we begin to sort through, even unconsciously, the things that make it all worthwhile, the faces and places, even demons that come often unbidden to mind. I would make more of fiction were that needed. But reality has been more than enough to pauperize any attempt to clothe it with more than an occasional lapse of memory, which in its kindness, covers many hurts.

We are all builders and makers regardless of the type of architecture. Even tents in the wilderness had to have their ribbons of color. The nomad needs something to draw his eye and tell him he is a man. Few things attract a man, as Thoreau made so plain, as his honest toil resulting in a structure, no matter how humble, which evidences his ability to do with his mind, back and hands. And, if the effort is directed toward the welfare of his family what a worker he is, putting even Thoreau to shame. We are inveterate builders, but even the cave will show signs of something more than utilitarian shelter. We will hang our pictures and bric-a-brac to declare our personness. The most humble of abodes will show some indication that building is more than providing a roof over our heads. This is the reason for my making so much of removing the onerous bureaucracy that precludes a man doing for himself. You must turn from the seemingly, meaningless disarray of twisted threads and knots of the back of the carpet and look at the grand design of its true face. In far too many cases government would have us leave off any attempt to make our own carpets by insisting there be no disarray of twisted threads and knots whatsoever, which would not be so onerous to me if government itself were not only a disarray of twisted threads and knots without the redeeming quality of any grand design when you turn its carpet over.

In one of my wilderness forays, I came across an old mining shack of rough lumber. The bare wood walls of the interior were covered over with the comics (funny papers to us oldsters) of a long defunct newspaper. Now any part of the newspapers would have served as well against drafts, but the comics? They were the needed color.

We are suffering the noisome pangs of politicians, once more, telling us what they are going to do for (more properly to) us. They will talk of building for the future. My grandad built a better privy than what these scoundrels are likely to produce and it smelled better than the stench of these charlatans.

Somewhere along the way, we got too busy for the things that really count. The work, books and beauty, the people are there but they want for attendance. As rich as the endowment may be, it profits nothing to those that will not take heed and invest it properly in those things of lasting value like family and friends.

"You have forsaken your first love... I would that you were either hot or cold but because you are lukewarm, I will spew you out of my mouth!" What a word of warning that should be to all! However, it falls on deaf ears of those who are more concerned for the cares and riches of the false than a reality where love conquers all. God's love goes begging as the professionals either prostitute it as religion or mysticize it to some ethereal realm out of existence.

There are few companions in my life like Thoreau despite his ego. Like he, I would fain have planted ... sincerity, truth, simplicity, faith, innocence, and the like rather than beans. There is time for planting beans and making pencils and they should not be in competition with those heart's longings for that which encourages the spirit and gives hope of better than meeting only physical needs or gaining the riches of this world.

Like Thoreau claimed to do, I sow in hope. While much of what I write has been called inflammatory I do not write in order to promote anarchy. I am not an incendiary but do hope to ignite hearts to a better calling than the evil system that does promote lawlessness and greed. And if, as Henry suggested doing, I provide some of the friction to an evil machine so much the better. In some cases, the system is of such a complexity that the simplest solution may well be to take an ax to such a Gordian Knot. Unhappily the Knot has its guardians who, unless they be subdued first, will inveigh with all their might against all who oppose them. It will take a good many ax-men to win such a battle.

The very complexity of the evil system of government leads directly to the attempt at simple solutions. This is an historical imperative and most often leads to slavery or revolution. It is an historical imperative for the very reason that too many men's hearts seldom seek the welfare of others but are motivated by the desire to live without honest toil; by the desire to steal, lie, cheat and engage in every form of immorality freely and without restraint. The worst of such men become politicians.

It was early recognized that Law was an absolute necessity to restrain evil and punish the evildoer. Though this would seem to be self-evident, it is still required for each generation to teach the next. Our failure to educate our young people to the facts of our national history and the great men and women who sacrificed so much to give us the greatest and freest nation the world has ever seen has led to a generation that neither knows Joseph nor the God of Joseph and appears to be headed in the direction of lawlessness, especially as they witness the politicians, the rich and powerful ignore the laws with impunity.

One of my favorite things to do in this area is visiting the folks out at the old mining claim. I just returned from such a visit to get away from the dreariness of so much bad news abounding all about. I sit with my cup of coffee and a cigarette and let my mind wander and wonder amid the familiar rocks, trees and hills. Grandma and Great-grandma died in their sleep in one of the old cabins, long gone to make way for the present campground. They died peacefully in bed without the antiseptic paraphernalia of exotic machines, tubes and hoses with which we now prolong life in the dubious notion that bankrupting, heroic measures are needed simply because they are available.

I wonder once more at the thought of Hallowed Ground. Perhaps it is the Choctaw Cherokee blood that courses through my veins, but if there is such a thing as Hallowed Ground, this is it for me; the site of many cherished, childhood memories and where such precious, loved and loving dear ones lived and departed. I wonder, also, about David and his longing for the water of Bethlehem. He must have felt the same way I feel when I'm at this so very special place. The bittersweet melancholy and loneliness that often envelopes me in these surroundings is ameliorated and assuaged somewhat by reminding myself that few have such memories to sustain them.

Also, the very freedom to come and go as I choose is something for which I am most grateful and something with which very few people are blessed. And while far from rich in material things I will opt for such freedom in lieu of the unnecessary and cumbersome riches and baggage of those that think mere things are what will make them happy and secure. It is people, not things, which make for happiness, and, tragically, grief and misery as well unfortunately. But the soul of a nation and that of the individual is in the joy and suffering that is God within us, is the express image of Him, and opens our hearts to both.

As I sit on a granite boulder beneath an old pine where, as a child, I once had placed boards in the branches for a aerie from which to think, read and survey my wilderness playground in the solitude and imagination of that best part within any child, I'm sensible of the fact that we are too seldom conscious of the things and people, the circumstances which will manufacture memories. How much kinder would we be to others if we only knew how forcefully such things will come, later, in our night visions as haunting, tormenting specters or beloved friends. Tragically, the choice is not always with us, but too often with those whose self-love has betrayed the trust of the friend.

The day is getting late and I must leave- Too bad. It seems something is out of joint when I am a visitor to what was once home. Somehow, there is something wrong with this. Hearing the noise overhead, I watch a Stealth Bomber and its chase plane making a low level pass, about 1,500 feet AGL I judge, the fascinating form of the bat-like bomber seeming alien and threatening and, strangely out of place. Oh well, back to where I presently hang my hat; it isn't home but I remind myself as I do so often that this world is not my home, I'm only passing through.

***

Like the ending of Fitzgerald's masterpiece "The Great Gatsby" I often find myself fighting against the current of the times, trying to go back and recapture the past. And like Fitzgerald himself, I have not grown so old and disillusioned that I wouldn't still like to believe in love. Even at the time of Harper Lee's Pulitzer-winning "To Kill A Mockingbird" there was a key element in the era in which her story was cast reminiscent of the time of Gatsby, the element of stability in America.

It takes the stability of the past to make sure progress toward a future. But such stability is based on the foundation of family. For those that have had such stability, the times in which we now live do not hold the same certainty of the future with which so many of my generation were blessed.

Apart from academic literary and social criticism, both Fitzgerald and Lee did manage to capture important elements of what made America work that held promise of a future. But after the Great War the Market crashed and brought a cataclysmic end to the euphoria of the twenties, prohibition ushered in organized crime and the ugly specter of racism in the thirties continued to rear its ugly head and another world war remained to be fought.

Sinclair Lewis would portray the hypocrisy of religion in "Elmer Gantry" and John Steinbeck would limn the condition of the poor from the Dust Bowl in "The Grapes of Wrath." Yes, America had problems; problems of frightful dimensions in the not distant past and there were those like Woody Guthrie trying as these others to raise the social consciousness of Americans. But the emphasis remained on home and family, on those values that had made America a great nation in spite of its several failings, failings made so apparent by the works of Fitzgerald, Lewis, Steinbeck, Lee and so many others. But despite such failings, these great writers also expertly and with great sensitivity, described those attributes that made America great.

Alexander Pope wrote: "Vice is a monster of such frightful mien, as to be hated needs but to be seen." Then Pope adds his caveat that once vice gains a foothold and becomes too familiar it is embraced. Contemporary America certainly evidences the truth of this. Those things considered vices in the twenties and thirties are now embraced and the vices of the past are touted as quaint anachronisms born of naiveté.

Among those "quaint anachronisms" was the shame of welfare as a way of life, divorce, unwed mothers and illegitimate births. But once these vices gained a foothold and society began embracing these things and started down the path of making them acceptable, they have made monumental contributions to the loss of the stability of the home, the foundation of any society and the loss of which leads to the loss for hope of a future.

Yes, I admit to fighting the current of time, of the longing for a time I still remember when there were such things as family values and lying, cheating, stealing, sexual perversion were considered shameful and disgraceful. In spite of the ugliness of much in the America I recall as a child, the need for the stability of the home was not in question. It took such stability for what were considered virtues to be taught and have any relevance.

Now, vice of every description having been seen too oft and having become too familiar with its face, as Pope warned, is embraced. And although many might accuse me of a nostalgic longing for the simple verities of the past, can any legitimately tell me that children are now born into a better world than the one of the past for which I long?

Lacking leaders in this nation that are free of scandal themselves there are none that dare confront the scandal of others in order to restore trust and integrity to our elected offices. And no amount of "Dear Abby" or attempting to use God for political gain, or even with the best of intentions, will suffice to cure the problem of our departure from the past emphasis on stable and virtuous homes.

My great-grandmother would often warn my brother and me of the path to perdition beginning with a boy taking a pencil that did not belong to him. We were fortunate to have such a great-grandmother; we were fortunate to be raised in such a way as to know embarrassment if caught in a lie, to be able to blush at off-color stories. We were fortunate to have been taught that lying, stealing, cheating were wrong and shameful things… this in spite of our living in the dirt-poor area of Little Oklahoma in Southeast Bakersfield and being surrounded by characters so well described by Steinbeck.

Would any of you say that my great-grandmother intended, or did, harm to my brother or me by trying to instill a sense of shame in us for doing things like lying or stealing? But it took a woman of her own personal integrity to make the story of that boy and the pencil real in our lives. How many children today have such an influence in their lives? Where is the influence of someone like my great-grandmother evidenced in the homes of America today or in the lives of our leaders?

About five years ago a deputy sheriff pulled into my yard during the winter. He had a little girl about two years old in his car. She was dirty and barefoot, but smiling, a real little sweetheart. Her little toes were working energetically so I knew her little feet had to be cold. A small dog had been with her so the deputy had it also. He wanted to know if I recognized her. I didn't.

After he left, I couldn't help thanking God it had been a cop rather than some monster posing as a human that had found her. And while I don't envy the deputy having to go through all the red tape that comes with finding a child wandering alone on the highway, the mind reels with the tragedy that might have been averted!

I once chanced on a toddler, still in diapers, standing out on a road in a housing tract. I was able to locate the mother with the help of some neighbors. She was passed out with a boyfriend, both naked, the booze and drugs in full evidence.

It was a few years ago that some children came knocking and screaming at my door to call 911. A little boy had put his arm through a window and was bleeding profusely. His little sisters were with him and I was the closest neighbor. They didn't have a phone and the parents were nowhere around.

What is generally not known, since we can be grateful that most parents do keep an eye on their kids, is that if you make a 911 call under these circumstances the whole panoply of government services come into play. The ambulance, fire truck, and police come together. A call automatically goes into Child Protective Services.

Well, the result of all this was that the parents were located, the little boy received proper medical treatment, and the parents became fully involved with the police department and CPS (having worked in CPS I know the routine by heart).

It could have been far worse: One New Year's Eve some time ago was marked in Bakersfield by two little boys being burned to death while left alone as their mother partied at a local bar. Being separated the father learned about this later; an all too typical scenario of such tragedies involving children.

Leaving small children alone in any circumstances is extremely risky. I was quite young and with my mother and a stepfather in Cleveland when I was very nearly scalded to death from boiling water. I never learned where my mother and stepfather had been when it happened.

The recent flap over a single woman giving birth to eight babies and having six other children already does have some talking about how taxpayers are being ripped off to support such irresponsible behavior, but making forced contraception a requirement for welfare causes quite a stir as you can well imagine. However, a story in The Modesto Bee on January 2, 2001 really says it all. A young welfare couple Michael and Veronica Maul have five children all under the age of five. He is 24 and she is 20. He has a criminal record and they are complaining that society is not doing enough to support them financially.

The story generated considerable response in Letters to the Editor. But they can be summed up very neatly by one that expressed the sentiment of the many others: "Michael and Veronica Maul have a lot of nerve asking society to house and feed them and their five children… I am sick and tired of having the government, federal, state, and local, taking 40 percent of my income just to take care of these people who do not take the responsibility of providing for their own children. When is this insanity going to stop?"

The word "insanity" is the correct word. It is insane to reward illegitimate births through welfare, to reward those that refuse to get an education and rut like barnyard animals with no thought for the resulting children who have no prospects for a future but to load the criminal justice system and further increase the number of those on welfare.

But what politician or pundit dares state the facts in this regard? Enforced birth control! Horrors! Hitlerian! To which I reply: No, not Hitlerian, but common sense in the face of the present insanity of a system of welfare that has gone infernally awry! The legalized extortion by Caesar that takes from responsible people and gives to those like the Mauls must stop! And requiring contraception for welfare eligibility is the only way that will work.

I am continually in the debt of those that confront so many issues that plague America. And there is no need for me to attempt writing about issues these others cover so expertly thanks to a free press. But an issue like welfare reform that includes forced contraception, that's a different matter and no politician or pundit will take this one on. But none can sensibly and logically deny that to write about welfare reform and not include this is nothing but verbal flatulence. Reproductive Rights? No. Personal responsibility and accountability are the issue, without which we cannot survive as a nation. A legitimate concern for children on the part of individuals and society must be evidenced before they are born, not afterward.

Here in "Mexifornia" it is obvious so many illegal aliens and anchor babies are an enormous drain of taxpayer money and adversely impacting social services, schools, and medical facilities; but no one at the state or federal level will do anything about this. But if Mexico's drug wars begin to escalate in the streets of my native state in places like Rodeo Drive, Beverly Hills, and Malibu and some politicians and judges are shot or kidnapped perhaps something will be done. History is replete with examples of the "unthinkable" happening and it would be naïve to reject any possibilities when it comes to reacting to circumstances of such great magnitude that demand Draconian actions.

However, there is nothing being proposed by President Obama or those in Congress that would do anything to change the course of the path America is being taken when those "unthinkable" measures like troops not only on our borders but patrolling our cities and concentration camps begin to appear are the only options left for the survival of our nation. Or will the President and Congress continue to fiddle over what is being called the "vanishing $1.4 trillion" while America burns? In the meantime I'll continue to live in my memories of an America I once knew, and refresh those memories in writing of the Norman Rockwell America I knew that still believed in God and honored him even in our schools, the America that produced people like my great-grandmother and saved the world from the Axis Powers.

***

My good friend Byron, the Episcopal Priest, came by yesterday and we were having the usual interesting discussion about religion, politics, and world affairs when I asked him how it was that Christians are quite content to have God and Jesus, but would rather the Devil would just go away as an embarrassing tenet of their beliefs? It is almost as though to even mention the Devil as being a part of Christian theology is an embarrassment to some Christians despite the fact that the Evil One has such a prominent place in the Bible. I told Byron I have concluded many professing Christians have succumbed to the kind of latter day "modernism" that equates those that believe there is a Devil with the aluminum foil hat folks, you know, folks like me.

Still, I can't accept the way things are going in America without believing these have some diabolical and malevolent orchestration of events that in my opinion are dooming our nation. For example who was minding the "peanut butter store" and who was paying any attention to predatory lending practices even putting illegal aliens into houses that even if they were citizens could not possibly afford that precipitated the mortgage meltdown crisis and the following enormous bailouts without any accountability?

And despite the acclaim of so many adoring fans who would be so naïve as to believe Obama was going to "clean up Washington" and make things different? Well, those that voted for him. But it doesn't take much mental acumen to figure out mopping a dirt floor only produces mud, provided you could even find someone dumb enough to do the mopping. Congress has long been a "dirt floor" and all attempts to mop it have only produced mud.

And while Obama isn't dumb, but only appears to be mentally deficient with his stuttering verbal pauses, when not cleaving to a carefully prepared script, trying to answer honest questions, as few of those that inadvertently slip in, in my opinion he is a sinister emissary of Satan and has a sinister agenda devised by his master and intends to enslave America by plunging our nation so deeply into debt that ordinary citizens cannot help but become the slaves of government by the inexorable erosion of responsible citizens being extorted to pay for the irresponsible all the while continuing to reward the greed and avarice of the few profiting from the misery of the many.

For those that have difficulty with my Biblical view of the situation, it remains a fact that the GOP certainly could have offered someone better than the dead man walking McCain, so just how did that actually come about? And how did someone with Obama's shadowy past and utter lack of qualification and evil associations come to be the choice of the Democrats? I use the phrase "evil associations" because I believe those supporting Obama's rise to power to be in league with the Evil One as well.

But America has been on the path of self-destruction long before Obama came on the scene, though he may preside over our demise and plunge into a slave nation, the irony of which I find in America having begun by profiting from the evils of slavery that became the source of much evil in America such as Lincoln's War, the attempt at national suicide from which America was never to recover, established a Triune Federal Dictatorship and promoted welfare for millions as a way of life.

We are not hearing much from Obama and associates about securing our borders and expelling illegal aliens. Are the jobs Obama is talking about going to go to them as well? I have to wonder. Just how seriously is the problem of drugs and illegal aliens pouring into America going to be taken by this new president and his administration? Is Congress now going to pay any real attention to the problem? Or will the Devil have it all his way by successfully promoting Obama's plan to enslave America through unfathomable debt exacerbated by our open borders and continuing to extort legitimate citizens to pay the bill for millions of illegal aliens that benefit only the wealthy in league with the Devil?

A Demonic *One World Order* is straight out of the Bible, so I don't wonder at Obama's intention to facilitate this happening; part of the program being promising prosperity, peace and safety only becoming possible when America becomes part of globalization rather than trying to remain an independent nation. In the process of this happening I expect to see more legislation restricting what freedoms we have left, attacks on gun ownership, freedom of the press and speech, lawlessness increasing as the barbarians of the cities fight for their part of the action. And the more such lawlessness increases, the more the Devil and his crowd will use such a thing to enact laws to "protect" law abiding citizens.

Desperate circumstances demand desperate measures to counter them. During WWII we became such a desperate nation but were able to overcome because we were united as Americans, we were in the fight together against the villainy of the Axis Powers. We are no longer such a united nation of those real Norman Rockwell Americans; we are fragmented and divisive but are faced with extremely desperate circumstances. Devil or not, I'm intensely interested in watching what measures are going to be taken and how things are going to play out as, I am sure, you are as well.

***

One of the reasons I subscribe to the theory we are alone in the universe, that ours is a privileged planet in a unique solar system is that each of us as unique individuals are alone. And it is that peculiar singularity that catches my attention and draws me into a deep and profound meditation of life and death, how each of these is such a profound mystery beyond anything our science has been able to define or explain. But since we are each as individuals captive to a body that carries about this lone and unique to the individual fire of life that no one else can see burning, cannot possibly see things as the individual does through the fire of their own minds this is sufficient for me to believe we are equally alone in the universe. We are social beings, we crave society, but at no time does another find access to that personal fire burning within each individual that so often leaves some feeling alone in a crowd. The universe does appear a crowd, but only to our physical senses.

However, the far greater part of the universe is not available to our physical senses anymore than you can "see" my mind and imagination at work within me, and what we see of each other's bodies is not what we consist of; our bodies are not what we "are." And too many times does an attempt to share this that we really are falls into the hands of one that may betray; making us cautious about sharing some of the deeper thoughts and feelings of what we really are. Even a writer like me finds the occasional red flag of warning before putting some of my innermost thoughts on display; but this is only prudent of most people.

Obviously if we are not alone and intelligent life exists elsewhere that would provide intellectual fire beyond imagination and I applaud the science like SETI directed toward the search. But to be alone in the universe as an intelligent species; that would be fire beyond any intellectual comprehension and one reason the majority in the intellectual fraternity are loath to admit of such a thing even as a possibility.

But Michio Kaku whom I greatly admire advanced the possibility one reason we have not been contacted by other civilizations in the universe is they may have reached our nuclear capability and destroyed themselves, an acknowledged real threat to our own species. More of late it has been posited by some few scientists they may have built a Large Hadron Collider that went as infernally awry as some fear the one we have just might. But I speculate to the other side, that we are actually alone in the universe as an intelligent physical species, yet a species endowed by divinity in some few, endowed by the diabolical in some others, while the greater mass of our species never develop a soul that comes into full flower, the illustration of the profligacy of Nature casting a hundred or more seeds of which some will be sterile without the germ of life while the greater number with that germ of life will surely die that one alone might survive and come to fruition to carry on the cycle of life peculiar to its kind.

Since I believe in God and a spiritual realm unseen by human eyes but more real than our physical universe which scientists estimate is only 4% of the sum total, the greater part being unseen, unknown, and possibly unknowable there is a lot of room for God and Satan, angels, and demons, a spiritual universe in which physical matter as we know it is only a minor speck. Our own personal "universe" is what makes us spiritual beings, and each such person knows they are truly alone in that universe. "You can kill the body but you can't kill the soul" is a well known phrase, and one I believe is true. I believe life, the soul, returns to God the Creator of these. It will be how we cultivated our souls through our minds leading to actions of which we will be judged in the hereafter.

"Guard your heart with all diligence for out of it are the issues of life." Some do, the great majority do not. Whether we are in for a deep and devastating global depression and America succumbs to printing tons of fiat paper in lieu of value based currency is really of little moment to me. In respect to wisdom I have chosen to live simply and free of debt, as I believe wise people do. But it is in the keeping of the heart in the universe of the mind with its solitary inhabited planet that is uniquely you as a person where the real issues of import make themselves known and the decisions are made of eternal significance. I have the great advantage of not being accountable to any earthly monarch, but to my Father and God in heaven. And believing this, in the words of Scripture "what have I to fear that men can do to me." Men's hearts may begin to fail for fear of what seems to be approaching in the ways of the world; but I believe there is a better path, the royal path that credits being individually responsible and accountable before both God and men for our actions, yet a path if we are to take Jesus at his word few choose to take, which goes a long way toward explaining why evil men and evil times are in the ascendancy.

***

The Devil seeks worshippers and God seeks lovers. I have this problem with the word "worship" when it comes to my heavenly Father. The parent does not demand worship of a child, but out of love demands obedience for the sake of the child. And this is how I see my relationship with God. If we love God we will be obedient and do what is right; just as any child would that does not want to bring shame on their parents.

But while God is love, he will not be mocked. And the travail of America is a result of our nation mocking God. Despite the great number of churches and proclamations of belief by various well known personalities including politicians even a child is known by their works and just so with a nation. There are many forms of "worship" but only obedience to God shows whether he is loved. God does not need cathedrals or monuments, liturgies or chants he only needs us to love him, the reasonable expectation of any good and loving parent of their child. The expressions of love are manifold, but the true lovers know the difference between the real and the feigned whatever is offered as the tokens of love. But between parents and children the key element of children obeying their parents is the one essential of love.

Satan thought he could prove Job a hypocrite; but he failed because Job sincerely loved God as proved by his obedience despite his much suffering. If America is being tried by Satan as he was permitted by God of Job I doubt our nation is going to fare as well as Job in the end because hypocrisy abounds, and I doubt there is going to be any repentance and wearing of sackcloth and ashes by our leaders.

America has been known as a good nation, and some believe a blessed nation with freedom and liberty the envy of the world that found favor with God. There is no discounting the good that America has done for other nations even saving the world from the Axis Powers, but our Achilles heel was slavery and a war fought with England over profits as much as any desire to be an independent nation. Lincoln's War, an attempt at national suicide was one from which America never recovered, and the festering cancer of slavery for profits has been there even throughout the Norman Rockwell America I knew and loved and no amount of "civil rights" will cure the cancer. On the contrary, the more laws based on racial distinctions the more the cancer has spread to the point where political correctness alone has made the courts eunuchs and handed Satan a tool for causing anger, resentments, and dividing Americans.

Trade curses all it handles and the love of money is the root of every kind of evil. While many would point out America was founded a Christian nation based on a belief in God with the Bible as its national textbook the problem remained that we were not a nation founded on love of God, but what was construed as the "worship" of God. But it was a corrupt form of worship that not only allowed slavery but eventually led to "The business of America is business," which is why we face the present danger of economic collapse since the business of America led to luxuries and further alienating the "haves" from the "have-nots" rather than any form of self-reliance and true independence. We became a nation of spoiled children that had no love of our heavenly Father, but rather forsook him in exchange for a life of ease and entitlement.

For years I have studied and turned many a thought around in my mind seeking an answer to why America should be going down the path that is so evident today, a path toward destruction that seems absolutely lunatic in so many ways. But then I recalled that God is neither slack nor slow in his judgment as men see it, but is longsuffering and not willing that any should perish and takes no pleasure in the death of the wicked.

Satan rewards some of his worshippers with riches, but God rewards his children with his love. And no child of God would shame him by seeking wealth and power over others to their own ends. We are led of scoundrels because an evil system of government evolved from the greed and lust for power and riches, and as people turned away from God the more success Satan had in placing his worshippers and servants in the seats of government based on wealth rather than godly character and virtue.

I'm a believer in Biblical prophecy, and as such I believe America is that Great City Babylon of Revelation. America has always had a form of worship while denying the power thereof, a form of worship that in too many ways and at too many times attempted to substitute for love of God. Even now there are what are called "Megachurches" contrary to the principles Jesus taught that the real prophets of God do not wear soft clothing and live in kings' palaces, that the children of God are to be recognized by their love for one another and not the size of the church or the preacher's doing well for himself as a gospel-peddler. Many such churches should have their leaders repenting in sackcloth and ashes right along with their kindred politicians.

As times become ever more dangerous for America we look for decisive leadership we can trust to save our nation. But confusion and chaos abounds rather than any sense of order. The Scripture declares God is not the author of confusion, but of order. It is evident to me Satan is the author of the confusion throughout the ranks of our leadership and sweeping across America. What's to be done? On an individual basis just make sure where your own heart is; the rest is in God's hands.

***

We know the truth of eloquence at the podium being only rhetoric in the study. Perhaps Emerson's remark struck a chord with Theodore Roosevelt; it would have lent itself well to "Speak softly and carry a big stick," a quote in a letter to Henry L. Sprague by Theodore Roosevelt that later developed as his foreign policy as president.

I believe many of us are sick of hearing glittering generalities attempting to pass as specifics by mere oration, but are seen to be only rhetoric in the study. Personally, I would prefer the "speak softly/big stick" approach to solving our problems rather than rhetoric.

But I have to wonder when Moses was offered the biggest stick of all to use against Pharaoh he demurred because of his lack of eloquence? From the narrative of the burning bush episode Moses confronts God's telling him to go speak to Pharaoh because of his being a poor speaker so how was he expected to speak before Pharaoh? God reminds Moses he created his tongue and mouth and would be with his mouth and teach him what to say. But when he continued to argue the point, the anger of the Lord was kindled against Moses so God tells him his brother Aaron has no trouble speaking so he will be his mouthpiece.

Well, it has always seemed to me "I AM" should have known beforehand he was going to have this problem with Moses so why become angry with him? And if God didn't know, that poses some real problems that Biblical commentators have struggled with at voluminous length surrounding the idea of God being omnipotent, omniscient, and omnipresent. But as I have mentioned several times God is perfect by his own definition of perfection, not by the definition of men. There are just too many instances in the Bible where God has seemed not to know something, and even misjudged the character of some of his chosen ones to maintain some humanly flawed concept of God's "perfection" by the standards of men.

What need of messenger angels if God did not need them? What need of prayer that is directed toward changing God's mind about something if God's mind cannot be changed? What kind of relationship would it be if God could actually read your mind, what kind of conversation would you have with anyone who could do that? I have no doubt God knows our hearts and can certainly identify his own children, but in so many ways do I think differently about God than others, that there is a very human element to the Creator that made man in his own image.

We read God was sorry he had created man and determined to wipe him out by a great flood. But he found Noah to be righteous and saved him and his family only to have the cycle of violence and perversion throughout the earth repeated almost immediately beginning with Noah's son Ham.

Kids say the darndest things, but they also ask some very intelligent questions. God gave us a questioning mind, and I don't think he wanted robots but children able to ask questions of him, intelligent questions worthy of his children, and many an intelligent question arises about God from reading the Bible; not with a religious prejudice already predisposed to never question what is accepted orthodoxy of some particular belief system but intelligent questions any parent would value from their child.

Obviously a child can ask a question the answer to which they are too young or inexperienced to understand. At that point the parent can only muddle through the best they can, and in some cases the Bible does some "muddling through" best it can; so many volumes by Bible exegetes attempting to explain the visions of Ezekiel, Daniel, the Apostle John and others for example. There is the matter of faith to consider of course, and sometimes the parent just has to tell the child to trust them rather than attempt to answer a question. There are many things in the Bible where God requires we simply have to have faith and trust him, that there is an answer to our question but we are not capable of understanding it. God's Creation alone poses questions to which we have no answers, and we still have not solved the two great mysteries of Life and Death.

In these dangerous and most uncertain of times my faith in God is all I have of any real value, a faith that defies the many charlatans attempting to pass themselves off as "prophets" or someone with an inside track with the

Lord to which only they are privy. I don't hold with any religion that professes it alone has the ear of God, or requires any secrecy among its "believers."

Great variety exists among families, and the family of God is no exception. My love and trust of friends is not contingent on their agreeing with me in every particular, and this includes those whose beliefs concerning God differ from my own. As it is, my questions do not seem to bother God and I'll continue with my questions, attempting to sort out the answers best I can. After all, over a long lifetime I've become quite an expert at "muddling through best I can."

***

The Temple that Solomon built was not required of God; it was built because God realized the need out of the weakness of people to have such a structure. While Jesus pointed out the Temple of his time was supposed to be a house of prayer, he did not evidence any grief in his statement that it would be destroyed.

Various impressive structures supposed to honor various deities tell us a great deal about the kinds of gods people believe in. But I confess the magnificent Christian palaces leave me a little uneasy about how such people view their personal relationship with God. After all, when David had his mind set to build a temple God instructed Nathan to tell the king how the Lord dwelt in a tent and needed no temple built by the hands of men. There was also the matter of David being a man of war with bloody hands to consider, but God did relent to allow Solomon to build a Temple. But I'm sure God knew the temple would be destroyed, just as did Jesus of the temple in his time. And it was the first martyr Stephen that incurred the wrath of the crowd to stone him who pointed out "Howbeit the most High dwelleth not in temples made with hands; as saith the prophet, Heaven is my throne, and earth is my footstool: what house will ye build me? saith the Lord: or what is the place of my rest? Hath not my hand made all these things?"

Reading Stephen's condemnation of false worship in which the temple was the centerpiece, the people were infuriated at his pointing out they actually worshiped the temple rather than God whom it was supposed to represent, a "temple" in which Jesus had chased out the money changers. Alas, too often have such "temples" been more a place of business than houses of prayer.

In the main impressive structures meant to glorify God fail of their main purpose, which is ostensibly to reflect the beliefs of the builders. I am a lover of great architecture, a lover of the great cathedrals, but only as they reflect the genius of the designers and builders of such magnificent structures knowing God does not need them, and may even find them embarrassing, especially when so many are mortgaged as though you could put God in debt for a "house."

If we look at the magnificent temples men have built for and to themselves many of which are banks, corporate headquarters, temples to the worship of Mammon such as those in D.C., I understand such temples. However, I also understand the need of a meeting place where a gathering of quite a number of believers needs accommodation. But such a meeting place should not be an embarrassment to God, as I believe many such are by their blatant opulence. As to megachurches and TV productions attempting to rival Hollywood as pleasing to God, I cringe in embarrassment for the Lord because I have both a heavenly Father and a friend in God.

***

Even some Christians find the mention of Satan somehow distasteful, a kind of boogeyman that is an embarrassment to those thinking themselves too "enlightened" to believe such an entity actually exists. After all, how is it that a creature older than dirt with monikers like Old Serpent, Dragon, Old Scratch, Beelzebub, Lord of the Flies, that goes around dressed in a red union suit with a pitchfork, has horns, a tail and cloven hooves instead of feet, a face like a goat and sulfurous breath that offers to show a girl his etchings in a toasty place underground furnished in brimstone and filled with snakes, toads, bats, owls, beetles, spiders and assorted goblins and gargoyles still gets the chicks? Well, to be exact Satan was none of this but on the contrary according to Scripture was a beautiful creature, which is why he may have been the progenitor of the First Eternal Triangle.

A reading of the so-called Lost Books of the Bible (they never were, but the name attracts the gullible), the pseudepigrapha, and the Apocrypha, quickly shows the reader why these are not in the canon of Scripture. Many are worthwhile in respect to their historical value, but they are not of the same quality of the canonical books. Much of the Talmud, even cabalistic literature, Jewish and Christian, provide insights to biblical study. The many translations and versions are valuable in such study as well. Jewish fables, as the Apostle Paul called them, and Jewish myths as per Titus are, for the most part, excluded from the canon and for good reason as noted. But the liberties taken by some scribes are still in evidence in places in the Received Text. Textual criticism is essential to separate these, as well as some Christian fables, from the actual manuscripts available. But the Jewish story of "Lilith" has a history, and while you can read it for yourself I have what I believe to be an interesting twist to the story, one I believe explains why the curse of God fell especially hard on Eve in the roles of sex and childbearing.

For years I have been telling church leaders there is a desperate need for a new theology. No matter how many beautiful stories you tell, how many beautiful theories you evolve, they crumble before stubborn facts that won't simply go away. One such fact that Bible Christians must confront is the Serpent in the Garden. This creature had the power of speech and walked erect. Christian theology has always had Satan using this creature in the temptation and deception of Eve as per II Corinthians 11:3. I think Adam was there also, not out mowing the lawn. In fact, Genesis 3:6 declares: ... She also gave some to her husband, who was with her...!

But he was probably waiting to see what happened to Eve before he took a bite. I conclude this from the fact that when confronted by God for his disobedience he took it like a man and blamed it on his wife. And God. The resentment of women toward men has a long and legitimate history.

God's curse on the serpent was that it would crawl on its belly and eat dust forever after. Obviously, it didn't crawl previously. Those that would try to tell us that Satan and the serpent were one and the same cannot reconcile such a thing with snakes as we know them. It is, therefore, much more to our advantage and for the sake of good scholarship and reason, to take the view that the serpent God cursed was not a snake as we know it, and was a creature much like Adam and Eve. This becomes vitally important theologically if the Christian view of Satan is a distorted one, and he is more like the accuser and adversary of Jewish theology.

It would naturally follow from the history of serpents in antiquity, the view of humankind that they represent cunning and evil, even the Dark Side of Beauty, that the story of the serpent in the Garden should be interpreted as allegorical to the curse of God; snakes being only representative of this creature. Revelation 12:9 and 20:2 refers to that ancient serpent called the devil or Satan that leads the whole world astray. But the Genesis narrative leads one to believe the serpent was a distinct creation of God separate from the Devil, especially so in the light of the fact that God would not include Satan, in either Christian or Jewish theology, among the wild animals of creation but was among those appearing with the sons of God in Job.

It isn't likely, either, that Satan entered the serpent and used it in some anthropomorphic (Satanic version) state. God's judgment of the serpent wouldn't make any sense in that event. An innocent animal damned because it was used of the Devil? But the Law of Moses required an animal used in Sodomy to be killed along with the person who used it. Why? The animal certainly wasn't guilty. So we cannot discount the possibility entirely; yet the injustice of it rankles. In any event the picture of Satan and the serpent cooperating in the downfall of Adam and Eve in some manner exists. And if the serpent was far more than traditional theology, Jewish or Christian, interprets it some fascinating possibilities suggest themselves.

In the Temptation of Christ, Satan is an evil angel, not a snake. His other appearances throughout Scripture are that of an evil angel. So, in the Garden the serpent is to be understood as a distinct creature from Satan. But the serpent is among the wild animals God created. Just how wild is wild since all these animals were subject to Adam and tame enough for them to pass before him in review for naming them and seeking a companion, a suitable helpmeet from among them? And surely Adam wasn't expected to find a suitable helpmeet from animals as we understand them to be.

Here, as in many other places in the Bible, there is cause for caution in taking some words at face value. Just as there is a hierarchy of angels like seraphim and cherubim, Michael the Archangel and Gabriel the Messenger Angel, and Raphael in the deuterocanonical book of Tobit, there is a hierarchy of the wild animals of Adam's time.

The serpent was the craftiest and most cunning of the lot we are told. And, probably, the most beautiful and human-like, possibly even homomorphic. And it would certainly seem from the account that Eve was familiar with this creature and she and Adam had probably been visited by it before. As a result, there is no surprise expressed by them at its appearance at the time of The Fall. Working strictly from the sparse narrative, I would guess that the serpent had already worked up a trusting relationship with Adam and Eve, laying the groundwork for cooperation with Satan's ultimate plan of causing our first parents and special creation of God to rebel.

Back to the early creations of which Satan may have been the creator: If we take the view that God was experimenting with various creatures before he created Adam, it would mean that God (Elohim) was making a lot of mistakes in such creations like the dinosaurs and pterodactyls. But from the narrative, I would think it far more likely that Satan created such creatures and his attempts were flawed by his growing disenchantment with being number two in the Celestial hierarchy. Perhaps this led to his mind becoming dark, malignant and malevolent, and such creatures showed this dark side of his increasing evilness. The early and long involvement of people with grotesque and hideous representations of gods, goddesses, spirits and demons like the gargoyles and goblins possibly have a basis in fact of such things. This dark picture includes things like evil spirits inhabiting animals and demon possession.

The story of the Garden I believe to be based on facts and may put things in perspective. God's beautiful creation of Adam and Eve was in contradiction to the creations of Satan thus incurring Satan's hatred. The Devil's creations were ugly. He isn't called a Snake, Dragon, and Beelzebub, Lord of the flies, for no reason. But God's creations were beautiful. So Satan decided to hurt God and destroy this beautiful creation made in God's own image, but how to go about this? He plotted carefully. And he had help; the serpent. However, Genesis 3:1 tells us that the serpent was a creation of God. In fact, it was more subtle, craftier and more cunning than any of the wild animals the Lord God had made; moreover it had the gift of speech! Paul in II Corinthians 11:3 says: ... Eve was deceived by the serpent's cunning....

We are dealing with a creature unlike any we know. But it had to have been among those creatures Adam named in seeking a companion. Bible commentators have strained at this trying to make the serpent a dumb beast without the power of speech among other things. But that cannot be reconciled with the actual narrative, especially not with the plain fact that Adam was trying to find a suitable helpmeet among other creatures.

Not only was the serpent more cunning and crafty than any of these other creatures, it is within the bounds of speculation that it might have thought itself worthy of being Adam's choice of a companion. Having not been chosen by Adam, God creating Eve instead, the serpent may well have had a genuine hatred of Eve as a usurper. Furthermore, I would think this serpent might even have been a homomorphic female! After all, Adam wasn't looking for a Steve; he was looking for an Eve even though the serpent did not make the cut.

Unrequited love? Possible. And hell hath no fury.... If this is the line of thought, it explains a lot. Women don't trust each other; they steal the husbands and boyfriends of other women. As a consequence, the serpent was an ideal candidate for Satan's approach to get its cooperation in causing The Fall. It may have gone something like this:

Satan to the serpent: "Hey, Serp, you beautiful thing, you know how God has something new he calls Adam and Eve. You've met them already as neighbors when you went over to tell Eve about the Tupperware party. You know he even made them a cushy place, a beautiful garden without gophers or mosquitoes where they are living the good life not even raising a sweat! Hades! We do all the dirty work and these bland goody goodies get all the perks! It isn't fair, I tell ya!

"Well, I think I know where God blew it my lovely. He told these creatures they could pig out on anything in the garden except for the fruit of one tree. All we have to do is get them to cross God and eat from that tree and we've got 'em."

"I admire your thinking Satan. I've already had a few talks with these creatures and I think the woman is the one I can get to. She is really a curious thing. Tell her she can't have something and she wants it, tell her she can't look into a box and she can't wait to open it. And she has her sex that she uses to keep Adam shaped up and get her way. And you know how stupid males of every kind are about that!"

"I think you're right Serp; she has already been complaining about Adam not asking God for a raise and not standing up to him and being a real man! She really got to him on that one, and if we play our cards right, he'll probably go along just to show her he isn't afraid of God!"

Now if the serpent was a female, she knew just how to get to a man. Get Eve to question Adam's manhood. Something like: "If you were any kind of a man, you'd stand up to God! Here, take a bite and prove you're a man!" God condemns Adam for listening to his wife. Therefore, she had to have said something. I offer this as a possibility.

But since Adam had turned her down, the serpent had to get Eve to do the dirty work (One thought I have had on this subject deserves mention. I doubt Satan would have found the serpent such a willing ally if she had known she was going to become a quadriplegic in the process. But that's the chance you take when you listen to the Devil).

I ask you to forgive me a flight of fancy and whimsy; story telling seems to be one of my stronger compulsions. But whatever mechanisms were at work in getting the serpent's cooperation in getting Adam and Eve to betray God, it was successful. But hasn't it ever crossed the minds of my brethren in theology that Satan and the serpent must have known God wasn't going to take this lying down, that there had to be consequences of this action that would fall on their heads as well as Adam and Eve's?

Satan and the serpent must have thought that causing Adam and Eve to incur the wrath and judgment of God would benefit them in some way. It is not reasonable to suppose they would take such a risk unless they saw some advantage to themselves in doing so. Revenge? Possible. Unrequited love? Possible. There are examples enough of such self-destructive behavior. But it may have also been possible that Satan believed himself powerful enough to withstand God, that he felt threatened by God's creation of Adam and Eve and God's plans for them, plans that would supplant Satan and his hierarchy of angels.

Forced out of the Garden, it isn't surprising that the earliest religions were focused on fertility. As per God's judgment, the earth would no longer yield her strength so easily, and the battle for food became a desperate one at times. Further, the pain and danger of childbirth put women at risk. The discovery in places like Sumer of so many figurines of pregnant women is proof of this preoccupation with fertility and goddesses like Ishtar came into vogue.

The prominence of fertility being a sign of God's approval is a repeated theme in Scripture. In Genesis, Eve thanks God for the birth of Cain. Of course, she didn't know he would be a murderer. In Genesis 30:23 when Rachel bears Joseph, she says: "God has taken away my disgrace!"

Now, about the enmity God pronounced between the Serpent's seed and Eve's. Just what is the distinction between the two seeds, the seed of the woman, humankind, and the seed of the serpent? Eve is called the mother of all living, but she could not have given birth to the seed of the serpent; that was a distinct seed from that of Man. The conflict between good and evil was to be a conflict between the seed of the woman, humankind, and the seed of the serpent called by Jesus in Scripture "The Children of the Devil." These are the liars, murderers, hypocrites, Judases, those that betray the love and trust of others like adulterers and molesters, take advantage, use and abuse, torture and maim for the fun of it, conscienceless, some are the monsters in human guise that prey on women and children especially.

A thought worthy some speculation is whether the serpent, if a female, could reproduce? We are not told that the serpent was cast out of the garden with Adam and Eve. But why would God allow it to remain? Engaging my proclivity for whimsy, I pose the following for consideration: Cunning, crafty, but beautiful! The description of the serpent would support this attribute as well. God made the serpent, and all that God made, we are told, was good; that is, pure and beautiful. The serpent included.

Another point that might support the thought that the serpent, beautiful and extremely intelligent (you know, this characteristic might have put Adam off, come to think of it?) would be all the more incensed at Adam's not choosing her; which brings me to a very interesting conjecture: Eve, a woman, pitted against another female of a different species. Men fantasize and write stories, make films about beautiful females from the planet Playtex. Who cares if they have pointy ears or some other differences which, as long as they don't subtract from the over-all beauty (might even enhance the libido in the process) and have all the other important parts of their superstructure and plumbing in order?

Now with the Inquirer and Globe as trustworthy sources of information (Men In Black) about alien life forms and their cohabitive conduct with earthlings.... But I digress; however, I wonder how many of you know Isaac Asimov wrote "A Guide to the Bible"?

So here we are. Adam and Eve forced out of the Garden and we have the origin of the Eternal Triangle (But with the Serpent, instead of Ingrid Bergman, playing the part of the Hypotenuse); an interesting scenario. Requests for the movie rights will be entertained. I suspect Adam, however, was somewhat miffed at the loss of his position in the Garden, and not too likely to take up with the serpent in spite of bestiality, sodomy, and polygamy having an ancient ancestry. This left the serpent at odds for a mate since she couldn't make it with Adam (unless one of those ancient predecessors of Homo sap was around to comfort her). So this beautiful creature may have waited around for a time until you know who appears on the scene: Cain!

I am assuming that at this time the curse of God against the serpent that she would crawl on her belly and eat dust was, in whatever figure, delayed, just as the death of Adam was going to take centuries. It is also possible that snakes, as we know them, were figurative of God's judgment and have a special connection to Satan and the serpent of the Garden. One thing is certain; snakes have always played an important part in religions throughout history; particularly in regard to fertility rites and as phallic symbols as well as symbols of evil, cunning, and deception. "Wise as serpents"; ever wonder why Jesus used this description, a commonly held perception though obviously a myth. Yet it is grounded in the reputation of that ancient story of the Garden.

Thus a possibility for two different species: the sons of God being Eve's offspring and the daughters of men with whom they intermingled being those of Cain. I offer another thought; suppose Satan, if he had creative power, made it with the serpent? In the NT, God by the Holy Spirit impregnates Mary. Did Satan, in an evil parody, impregnate the serpent? After all, she had a legitimate gripe with Satan: "Hey, you got me into this; now be a gentleman and do the right thing by me!" Her description as belonging to that class of wild animals God created comes to mind here. As with a woman scorned, Satan might have been made to see it her way rather than being subject to her wrath. Women (regardless of species, I suppose) can do that, you know. If so, she might have gone off apart from Adam and Eve and in that land of Nod, had a daughter waiting for Cain?

This might be credible if you take the children of the Devil having their ancestry traced to this source, the sons of God commingling with the daughters of men with Cain as the original man in the scenario. Something of this nature might explain why the oldest religions discovered emphasized the Queen of Heaven, the worship of a Goddess over the earth and mankind that depended on her to promote fertility.

A possible act of desecration of some very early churches is carvings of nude women indicative of this kind of Goddess worship. Discovery of stone phalli under church altars is proof of the continued beliefs of fertility worship in the Christian era. But this kind of fertility religion came into real conflict with the Masculine God of the Israelites. It was one of the factors in distinguishing the importance of ethical monotheism as opposed to the predominate pantheism of the surrounding nations like the Babylonian and Chaldean, especially in regard to the rebuke of human sacrifice and nature worship. Ethical monotheism created great conflict between a Goddess of fertility, the Serpent, Queen of Heaven, and God the Father, Male dominant!

As to intercourse with the Devil, this has an ancient tradition. "Rosemary's Baby" has its roots in such stories.

Lucifer, Greek Phosphorus, meaning Lightbearer, the morning star i.e. the planet Venus at dawn or Hebrew, shining one, has virtually no legend and is not mentioned in Scripture. Some misguided translator, in an attempt to connect the name with the apocalyptic literature intruded the name and it is found in the King James Bible, but correctly omitted in modern translations.

St. Jerome among the church fathers made an attempt, on this basis of the apocalyptic literature and Jesus' remark about Satan falling like lightening from heaven, to equate Lucifer with the Babylonian account in Revelation and Isaiah, chapter 14. Milton's Paradise Lost enhanced the propagation of this idea. Due to this concept, the name Lucifer was held to be the name of Satan before his fall from heaven. But it has no history earlier than that of Jerome.

However, a handwritten account called the Aradia or The Gospel of the Witches by an Italian witch, Maddelena, in 1886 at the request of Charles Leland of the Gypsy Lore Society states that Lucifer, as Sun God, had an incestuous affair with Diana, his sister, the Roman moon, earth and fertility goddess. They had a daughter, Aradia (or Herodias) who was to have come to earth and teach men and women the secrets of magic.

That such stories and legends may, in fact, have a basis such as the hypothesis of Satan and the serpent having a daughter, the possible wife of Cain, should be taken into account by theologians. The paradox of good and evil recognized by all major religions and philosophies must have a sensible root and basis of fact. A fact remains throughout history that people without conscience have always been around. This Bad Seed must have an explanation. Granted that genetic research holds some hope of answers will not mitigate the mystery of the origin of genes that leave an individual without conscience or the source of such a gene, or the lack of such a gene that predisposes to evil behavior.

The art in the famous cave at Lascaux in France is typical of the use of pictures to influence successful hunting. That we are talking about Homo sapiens-like creatures so many years ago is most remarkable. The fact of hominids of great antiquity capable of fashioning implements with which to hunt, etc. should give theologians pause, and those creatures that pre-date even these? If Homo sapiens has only been on the scene for 25,000 years, who, in the sense of Hominidae, or what, made these paintings?

A fascinating point is that Satan possibly had worshipers of Paleolithic times, man-like pre-Adamic creatures from great antiquity. The Scriptures put Satan at the head of those angels who kept not their first estate. Jude 6 and Revelation the twelfth chapter are interpreted to mean this. Those early

Cathars of the 1200s thought Satan, not God, created the earth. They had a little trouble with the church because of this among other things. I haven't even gone into the potential of alien visitors, apart from God, Satan, and angels to earth, of what cultures, civilizations may lie beneath the oceans, of the Atlantis's of the mind. With the progress of technology to explore these things, who can guess what may yet appear on such horizons of discovery?

Much of this is speculation, but with enough facts to arouse curiosity among those given to speculation about a universe most of which is unseen, unknown, and possibly unknowable. This gives those like me a great deal of latitude to speculate about the spiritual realm that may be more real and vast than we in our mortal state can possibly imagine.

***

Perhaps like me you listen to the prognosticators of a rosy financial scenario out of the Obama camp and get the feeling a whole lot of people are in for a shock of disillusionment. As far as I am concerned, Obama supporters are already whistling through the graveyard. Those like me believe he is a tool of Satan and no amount of whistling through the graveyard is going to keep the demons at bay. In my opinion, America is headed for economic collapse and I remain of the belief our nation is that Great City Babylon of Revelation.

Whether I am right or not, there is no escaping the fact our sorry excuse for "leadership" in America seems at best chasing their tails rather than paying any attention to the things like our open borders threatening us, inviting any and all of our enemies to enter and do us harm at their good pleasure. Insane!

As I see nothing of anything approaching economic stability or peace in the world, but on the contrary more barbarism as world conditions worsen and things like world famine possible I am naturally drawn ever closer to Paul's admonition in II Timothy 2:15: "Study to shew thyself approved unto God, a workman that needeth not to be ashamed, rightly dividing the word of truth."

If you have stayed with me this far, it might be well to take a little breather. So, before I get into the further discussion of my heterodox opinions concerning my thoughts about religion, I'd like to indulge in a little whimsy as is my wont.

One of my pronounced interests is science. This helps considerably in Bible study. But it also helps to maintain one's sense of humor in such things. If you lose that, you've lost it all. Considering what most of the churches taut as Bible Study and Teaching, you really do need to keep your sense of humor or you would wind up screaming most of the time. But God really has the number of many of these people. Amos: 5:21 and 23: *I hate, I despise your religious feasts; I cannot stand your assemblies... Away with the noise of your songs! I will not listen to the music of your harps.*

I love women. I love writing about them and the relationships between men and women. I wrote an essay entitled "Fathers and Daughters." This was the foundation for my book: "Birds With Broken Wings." This led to an examination of the historical problem of the relationship between men and women, one that led Sam Clemens to call men and women natural born enemies. Being unwilling to accept Sam's dismal assessment of the situation, largely because of what I learned as a man from my beautiful daughters, I began to write of what I call "The Missing Half of Humankind: Women!"

As an academic, I have been immersed in the studies of philosophy and theology. It finally penetrated my thick skull that women were conspicuous by their absence from such philosophies, philosophies that have determined the course of history and nations. The specifics of such attention by me as a man has led to the greatest challenge of my life, an attempt to find a solution to the historical problem of relationships, to discover the reasons that the philosophies of men have determinedly excluded women throughout the history of humankind. That this is an enormously complex problem is proved by the thousands of books, films, and innumerable talk shows directed at the problem. It is my considered opinion that it is treated far too simplistically.

One example: I asked a beautiful woman friend of mine to ask an organization of 150 women to whom she had access to put this question to the group: Since the number one complaint of women concerning men is that men don't listen to them, what, exactly, is it that women are trying to say that legitimizes their complaint? When my friend did as I had asked she was astounded at the resulting confusion and lack of being able to formalize and articulate an answer to this question.

But when it comes to discussions concerning religion the confusion is rampant; and few seem to follow Paul's admonition concerning the need to study to show yourself approved, but seem to believe they can leave their brains at the door when entering the sanctuary.

When Paul preached his sermon to the Greeks of Athens (Acts 17) he said he had found an altar of theirs with the inscription: *To An Unknown God.* Then he said: "Now, what you worship as something unknown I am going to proclaim to you." And Paul proceeds to do so.

When your religion requires you pay homage to unknown deities just in case you might miss one you don't know about, you're in trouble! Modern man is heir to a great number of superstitions and myths that still hold sway in the minds of untold millions of people worldwide. In this country we thrill to movies of the occult; we love our Dracula's and Frankenstein's, the

Mummy, Werewolf, witches and goblins and things that go bump in the night. Transylvania and the Carpathian Mountains, the Great Pyramids, Isis, Thot, etc. continue to capture the imagination of multiplied millions.

It's fairly common to find well-educated people of wealth and influence in the grip of Astrology, Freemasonry, and Rosicrucianism. The Ouija Board and scrying still have their adherents. Palm readers, Dream Analysts, and Sooth Sayers still ply their trades throughout the world. People still read Nostradamus and Cayce with belief and anticipation. I am not opposed to people given to these things, but am opposed to those that would take advantage of others by making claims of supernatural knowledge for profit. In point of fact, there are too many Christian pulpits filled by the same kind of charlatans.

The macabre, the weird, the supernatural, from the innocuous rabbit's foot to stringing up chickens and sacrifices of every kind, to magic potions and elixirs, blessed candles and medallions, the list goes on and on. All of which should tell us something. Paul tried to tell those Athenians: God is not in birds, animals, idols or buildings, but within us. Well, the Divine Spark may be there but a whole lot of people searched and still searches elsewhere, worshiping the creature instead of the Creator.

Since science does not answer to the need people have for God, cannot tell us what life is or explain what departs at death, since so many superstitions and myths still guide millions, it would seem there should eventually be an answer to what is being searched for. To the Christian, the answer is in Christ. But literally billions of people know little or nothing of Jesus Christ. I think it vitally important for Christians to examine their belief system in the light of the fair, sensible rationale that God is not going to send good people to hell because they never heard of Jesus.

We have to explore the evidence suggested by myths, and writings of books like the Bible. And in searching out answers to our questions about the nature of God in such writings and stories, many things come into conflict with the beliefs of many people.

As to the Bible, Adam and Eve think they can hide from God. Even Cain thinks he can get away with murder- So much for Biblical affirmation of the omnipresence of God. Later, even the prophet Jonah thinks he can run away and hide from God. As with the story of God having to come see for himself if things were as bad in Sodom and Gomorrah as he had been told, God asking Satan where he had been and what he had been doing in the book of Job, it is highly unlikely the ancients thought of God being everywhere at the same time.

Angels as messengers: What is the need of such beings if you already know what's happening? Jacob's vision of a stairway from earth to heaven with angels going up and down and God at the top of this stairway shows the perception of messengers from and to God.

The story in Daniel 10 of one who looked like a man coming to the aid of the prophet is a fascinating one. But how, I ask myself, could this creature have been delayed for 21 days by the Prince of Persia? Bible commentators construe this prince as Satan. The angel Michael comes to this creature's aid and it is only then he is able to come to Daniel.

There is mention of a "Book of Truth" from which this messenger to Daniel declares certain prophecies. In chapter 12 we have the passage concerning Michael and his angels that occurs in Revelation 12 where they overcome Satan and his angels. The angel Gabriel is described by Daniel as both a creature that looks like a man, 8:15, and as a man, 9:21. Gabriel is the announcing angel of Luke 1:19 and 26 who appears to Zachariah and Mary.

As a fallen angel, the book of Zachariah in the OT gives us a picture of Satan as the adversary and accuser of the brethren, a popular theme of Hebrew theology. In the OT we have a picture of the law being given to Moses by God. In the NT it is understood to be administered through angels, Galatians 3:19 and Hebrews 2:2.

Throughout the Bible and other literature of antiquity, angels, spirits, play a prominent role; one for which God has need of such creatures to do his bidding. But some, the elect, as the NT says, are to judge angels in the future. We are also told that some can actually entertain (be hospitable to) angels without knowing they are angels.

Thus the ministry of angels is made prominent in the literature of the Bible (as well as the myths and legends of other cultures), and these angels appear disguised on occasion. The angels of Satan are busy as well, Satan disguising himself as an angel of light and his servants masquerading as ministers of righteousness. II Corinthians 11:14.

Women, Paul says in I Corinthians 11:10 should not pray with their heads uncovered lest they be a scandal to their husbands and to angels. The covering of women's hair when they pray is a sign of the authority of men over them. The basis of Paul's admonition is that just as man is the image and glory of God, the woman is to be the honor and glory of the man. This is the basis for my believing something transpired between Eve and the serpent of the Garden that caused God's curse to fall especially hard on women.

Satan (or a like figure) and demonology are very prominent parts of religious beliefs. The Bible, being a coherent source of such traditions and beliefs, sheds a lot of light on questions concerning these things. But it also raises a lot of questions as well. Yet, with so little in the way of cognitive and reasonably accurate literature comparatively free of myth and legend of the biblical period of history, even secular scholars have need of frequent recourse to the Bible. It continues to stand alone as a respected and respectable source of veracity and integrity, and was at one time the textbook of America.

While most Christians shake their heads in agreement to the sage dictum of lighting candles rather than cursing the darkness, I've found great antagonism to the lighting of candles that shed unfavorable light on comfortable dogmas like "You just have to have faith and believe," no matter how ridiculous and contradictory such beliefs may be.

For example, we have a very different picture of the attributes of God from the OT account than that of the churches. Despite a "new covenant" it is this flawed perception of the nature of God that the churches hold that has led to so much chaos and uncertainty, schisms and divisions; and, in the past, burning heretics at the stake! The doctrine that God is omniscient, omnipresent, omnipotent, and perfect by a dictionary definition is the product of man's religiosity and not a claim of the Bible. It is at this point that all good Catholics and Baptists start collecting wood in preparation for lighting my fire.

Since I have no desire to become a candle to light their darkness, in other words, no martyr complex, I can only hope such people might take a long look at the evidence of their prejudices before striking the match. But there are a number of skeptics and scientists that ignorantly worship at the throne of Evolution who would be just as quick to do me in. Shame on all of them!

But the fact is that Neandertal suddenly, abruptly, disappears, and a few thousand years later, suddenly, abruptly, Homo sapiens appears. What sense is to be made of this enigma? The Bible being a credible history, more so than any competitors such as most of the myths and legends of other cultures gives some intriguing insights for those with enough honesty and determination to sort through it.

When we have exhausted the wisdom of men and the Pythias of Delphi, the Sibyls of Rome and Orphism, the searching's of Pythagoras, Plato, Zoroaster, the early Babylonian, Egyptian, Persian and Iranian cosmologies, we are still confronted with the paradox of good and evil, and ineffectual philosophies of dualism as attempted explanations.

The early attempts at codified law such as that of Hammurabi and, later, Moses and post-exilic redactors and scribes, reflect the most ancient consciousness of the need of law directed at morality and the stability of the family, the foundation of all cultures. But all attempts to codify *The Way of the Good*, which have been in general agreement by all cultures throughout history, have met with resistance by the lawless ones; those that continue to do evil in spite of all efforts by the Good.

Will a sensible cosmology be the ultimate answer? The essence of the Gospel whether anyone has ever heard of Jesus or not, to love God and love others as yourself, would seem to be a sensible answer. Yet, men will do evil; and the very existence of evil thwarts every attempt to make the Good prevail. Clearly, we do not yet have an answer to the paradox, and given worsening conditions worldwide will we simply run out of time before we can find an answer to this threatening dilemma? It is at this point I find a great deal of comfort and assurance in knowing the Bible's answer to the question rather than having to rely on any human inventions.

We read in Paul's epistle to the Romans that humankind suffered terribly by forsaking the true knowledge and worship of God and turning to idols and immorality; the result being the total obfuscation of the real nature of God and His relationship with people. This corruption of the truth of God is summed up in Romans 1:21-25: "For although they knew God, they neither glorified him as God nor gave thanks to him, but their thinking became futile and their foolish hearts were darkened. Although they claimed to be wise, they became fools and exchanged the glory of the immortal God for images made to look like mortal man and birds and animals and reptiles. Therefore God gave them over in the sinful desires of their hearts to sexual impurity for the degrading of their bodies with one another. They exchanged the truth of God for a lie, and worshiped and served created things rather than the Creator."

As a result of forsaking the truth and real knowledge of God, mythologies as well as the things enumerated in Romans evolved. In general, these stories attempted to explain God and the supernatural. Cultures began to become distinctive and their mythologies show their imprint. The Greek culture was replete with a pantheon of demigods, gods and goddesses. The Egyptians had a great inventory of such, as did the Romans. Such stories have a basis in truth, though often corrupted. The credit I accord them is the humanity ascribed to these deities. In spite of the corruption of the truth, there remained a common element throughout that no matter how exalted; these deities were susceptible to common, human frailties.

I do not attempt to make a god in my image. I believe God made us in His. But I do want to confront the hypocrisy of the churches in their making God inhuman; to confront them for the grievous errors and for the damage done by the churches and other religions like Judaism and Muslimism in making God inhuman; for example, the hypocrisy of things such as the Inquisition and the Salem Witch Trials. Can anyone believe God should take the blame for such things done in his name?

It is the faulty thinking in the philosophies of men that has made the character of God appear as something he is not. And I cannot help but believe that if men had included women and children in such philosophies, a lot of the harm done by them would have been avoided. It isn't a question of equal rights, but one of equal value.

Theologians, Jewish, Christian, and Moslem have resorted to all kinds of foolish mechanisms to protect God's honor. Reading some of this material in various commentaries one cannot help thinking: With friends like these, God doesn't need enemies! From portrayals as an inept and superstitious fool to a bloodthirsty despot, you find it all in the philosophies of men and their "scriptures" who, most of them self-deceived, have tried to uphold the honor of God all the while impugning him instead.

I am grateful for the fact that The Lord has a sense of humor. In point of fact, he must have the finest sense of humor of all. Despite the fact that he must be the best parent of any thereby seeming to spoil some of the fun while we are growing up, the typical attitude of children toward parents that prevent them doing something that might harm them, our heavenly Father does bear with a lot from his children. But if our own joy is to be in The Lord, we find not only the happiness that comes of obedience but able to exercise the sense of humor which is a gift of God as well.

***

While I realize that like Ezekiel I am preaching (prophesying) to a "valley of dry bones" the "confusion of tongues" of Genesis chapter eleven has hit America in a big way. To listen to the politicians and pundits is to hear this "babble," this confusion of tongues coming from Obama, Congress, the prognosticators of Wall Street, and how the looming economic disaster for America is being spoken of in many different "tongues." But to attempt to make any sense of what is being said is to hear nothing but a confusion of tongues and there is no certain trumpet sound to be heard from a leadership that would gather a divided and fragmented people together in unity to save our nation from economic collapse.

The many experts addressing our nation's woes have their texts, and I am quite familiar with them. The problem is that the experts and texts do not agree on a course of action and are often contradictory. I have chosen the Bible as my text in addressing the problems facing America, and while the same accusation may be leveled at me and my text it really does come down to a matter of choice and I have made mine. But it may be safely said that while I am a very well university educated man and quite familiar with the texts of these others, they are woefully ignorant of mine but they feel free to impugn it.

Now I could continue my sermon using only the safe secular terminology of the well educated man that I am as I have so many times thereby avoiding the embarrassment of not being taken seriously. But it is too late and we have run out of time as a nation for me to play it safe, to any longer tolerate the "wise of this world" that will have nothing to do with God and the Bible and have no answers for the things that are destroying our nation and calling out for God's judgment upon America. No matter the number of detours of my life, no matter how many times I have tried to outrun "The Hound of Heaven," it seems always my destiny to return to preaching what I believe I need to preach though it be only to a valley of dry bones. God will flesh out those bones if he chooses.

While it is true the Bible used to be America's textbook, it is equally true that the real prophets of God were never intended to live delicately, to wear soft clothing and live in kings' palaces. Jesus made this quite clear, and when the churches of America began to enrich themselves and made the Gospel a "profession" it didn't take Emerson to write "Ichabod" over their doors though he did so; the wealthy churches of America the pulpits supplied by false shepherds had already did this and continue to do so rather than follow the example of the prophet Samuel for whom I was named and dedicated to God as was he. The schools of the prophets became cathedrals of wealth preaching a false god and a false gospel.

As a Bible scholar I understood many years ago the typology of the Tower of Babel as America, the eschatological nation that would forsake God and attempt to exalt itself by building a "tower to reach heaven." Well, we reached the moon and have sent rockets far out into space, wonderful advances in science, technology, and medicine, but the typological Tower of Babel to be fulfilled by America was to be built to the worship of Mammon, and in the meantime the people of America increasingly forsook God while worshipping money and began to suffer a confusion of tongues among our leaders dooming any cooperation in saving our nation. In the process, America became indulgent and spoiled, given over to the love of money, of being entertained and glorifying violence, sex, and perversion while destroying children and families all the while turning ever further away from God in the hellish, satanic process.

While America has been unique and served a unique function in world affairs, while it has done much to help others the Devil and his profit motive and promise of riches was there at every turn, and while America has been envied its wealth and freedom it has become hated for the bullying hypocrisy of its leaders. But it is an infant nation historically and the Bible speaks of the end in global terms in which America has no place among the far more ancient nations of the End of the Age. God is going to bring judgment against America for its sins of slavery, adultery, perversion, self-indulgence, the rewarding of false prophets and whoring after the god Mammon, the election of Obama the Hamite being the fitting instrument of God's judgment including the enslaving of all Americans that cannot help but bring about total economic collapse, a burgeoning, bloating government that produces nothing feeding off a declining number of producers till the point is reached where it must resort to cannibalism by eating its own, which in a sense it has already begun to do and in the process becoming a "creature" rather than any longer being a nation of individuals. This is why I do not see America playing a role in the End Times prophecy of Revelation; I see America as *That Great City Babylon* in the following:

Revelation Chapter18: [1] And after these things I saw another angel come down from heaven, having great power; and the earth was lightened with his glory. [2] And he cried mightily with a strong voice, saying, Babylon the great is fallen, is fallen, and is become the habitation of devils, and the hold of every foul spirit, and a cage of every unclean and hateful bird. [3] For all nations have drunk of the wine of the wrath of her fornication, and the kings of the earth have committed fornication with her, and the merchants of the earth are waxed rich through the abundance of her delicacies. [4] And I heard another voice from heaven, saying, Come out of her, my people, that ye be not partakers of her sins, and that ye receive not of her plagues. [5] For her sins have reached unto heaven, and God hath remembered her iniquities. [6] Reward her even as she rewarded you, and double unto her double according to her works: in the cup which she hath filled fill to her double. [7] How much she hath glorified herself, and lived deliciously, so much torment and sorrow give her: for she saith in her heart, I sit a queen, and am no widow, and shall see no sorrow. [8] Therefore shall her plagues come in one day, death, and mourning, and famine; and she shall be utterly burned with fire: for strong is the Lord God who judgeth her. [9] And the kings of the earth, who have committed fornication and lived deliciously with her, shall bewail her, and lament for her, when they shall see the smoke of her burning, [10] Standing afar off for the fear of her torment, saying, Alas, alas, that great city Babylon, that mighty city! for in one hour is thy judgment come. [11] And the merchants of the earth shall weep and mourn over her; for no man buyeth their merchandise any more: [12] The merchandise of gold, and silver, and precious stones, and of pearls, and fine linen, and purple, and silk, and scarlet, and all thyine wood, and all manner vessels of ivory, and all manner vessels of most precious wood, and of brass, and iron, and marble, [13] And cinnamon, and odours, and ointments, and frankincense, and wine, and oil, and fine flour, and wheat, and beasts, and sheep, and horses, and chariots, and slaves, and souls of men. [14] And the fruits that thy soul lusted after are departed from thee, and all things which were dainty and goodly are departed from thee, and thou shalt find them no more at all. [15] The merchants of these things, which were made rich by her, shall stand afar off for the fear of her torment, weeping and wailing, [16] And saying, Alas, alas, that great city, that was clothed in fine linen, and purple, and scarlet, and decked with gold, and precious stones, and pearls! [17] For in one hour so great riches is come to nought. And every shipmaster, and all the company in ships, and sailors, and as many as trade by sea, stood afar off, [18] And cried when they saw the smoke of her burning, saying, What city is like unto this great city! [19] And they cast dust on their heads, and cried, weeping and wailing, saying, Alas, alas, that great city, wherein were made rich all that had ships in the sea by reason of her costliness! for in one hour is she made desolate. [20] Rejoice over her, thou heaven, and ye holy apostles and prophets; for God hath avenged you on her. [21] And a mighty angel took up a stone like a great millstone, and cast it into the sea, saying, Thus with violence shall that great city Babylon be thrown down, and shall be found no more at all. [22] And the voice of harpers, and musicians, and of pipers, and trumpeters, shall be heard no more at all in thee; and no craftsman, of whatsoever craft he be, shall be found any more in thee; and the sound of a millstone shall be heard no more at all in thee; [23] And the light of a candle shall shine no more at all in thee; and the voice of the bridegroom and of the bride shall be heard no more at all in thee: for thy merchants were the great men of the earth; for by thy sorceries were all nations deceived. [24] And in her was found the blood of prophets, and of saints, and of all that were slain upon the earth.

The real children of God here in our nation have nothing to fear of his judgment of America; they will continue to do what they have always done, and that is to do right no matter what others may do and to place their faith and trust in God knowing all things will pass away to be replaced by a new heaven and earth wherein dwelleth righteousness. While there is no happy ending for America and a world that is Satan's domain and will be destroyed, the children of God have every reason to rejoice in their faith and trust in a heavenly Father that all turns out well by his hand rather than that of the Devil and his servants.

***

Erich von Däniken made a real hit with "Chariots of the Gods," and while much of what he speculated about has been disputed, in some cases disproven, his basic ideas remain as valid as those of scientists whose own speculations about some things concerning the universe and unsolved mysteries right here on our own planet are extreme lacking empirical evidence.

Years ago I came to the conclusion the Great pyramids of Giza for example could not have been constructed by any of the theories advanced. It is good to see more people in the scientific community admitting they really don't know how some of the monolithic structures by the ancients were built or even when or why in many cases. There is growing agreement that the technology and tools required was beyond that fitting the time frames given to some of these structures, but why consign those believing in extraterrestrials as a possible explanation to being crackpots when some theories by scientists are no more viable?

Agreed one cannot keep their university credentials as scientists by giving any credit to the Bible as a possible source of information for the "unexplained," but it should be pointed out that the angels of the Bible are in fact extraterrestrials. However, trying to explain visitations by "gods" of the past and their work on earth would be impossible for the ancients involved and witnessing such things. The fact that the ancients had knowledge of things far beyond their native capabilities of their eras such as astronomy and metal working must have had an outside source of some kind is patently obvious to me. The discovery of iron could not have been "accidental" and no amount of physical labor with mallets and copper chisels, ropes and ramps could have produced the Great pyramids no matter how graphically portrayed by the History or Discovery Channels.

The lack of any written records by a race of gods or other extraterrestrials does make one wonder? Other than the glyphs and some other curiosities and artifacts we are left to our own devices in attempting to make any sense of these ancient wonders, the how and why of their construction? The constellations as they came to be known could not possibly have been determined by the naked eyes of the ancients so who was responsible for "star maps?"

Ours is a unique and privileged planet in a unique solar system with none other like it. In fact, in theory our planet and solar system shouldn't even exist so I take it to be a special creation of God. But it seems plausible to me the gods determined to make man in their image, the children of the gods, and a great deal of experimentation was going on long before this decision was made as with various other creatures throughout millions of years. But in a mere moment of time, Modern Man suddenly appears as a special creation capable of the things resulting in our present marvels of science and technology as all other hominids and like creatures disappear leaving only Homo sapiens to develop into a species capable of civilization and all that has resulted from it. That this special creation of Modern Man and all that has followed is no more farfetched than some scientific theories and only separated by accepting that an ultimate Creator was in charge of things rather than accidental, mindless, mechanistic forces.

I've written so much on this theme I don't want to belabor it here. My books are readily available online and through bookstores for those interested. But in light of current events and with so much uncertainty abounding about the future I thought it good to remind people "We are not alone." Whatever your beliefs may be, the Bible continues to be an excellent resource of study when it comes to what the ancients knew, though the obvious difficulties of attempting to explain some of these things by ancient writers are quite understandable. But taken together with the ancient myths and legends, the glyphs and artifacts, monolithic structures and so on a plausible scenario does present itself for which the Bible is the key textbook.

As children of God, we have a heavenly Father with a hierarchy of angels, sons of God watching over things, but there is still the problem of evil which the Bible attributes to Satan, a son of God and his followers gone bad accounting for some truly monstrous creations like the dinosaurs, venomous insects and snakes. Some intermingling of the sons of God and daughters of men resulting in a good deal of chaos in the distant past may be represented by the infamous action of Noah's son Ham and the builders of the Tower of Babel, even the monsters in human guise still preying on women and children. However, behind the stories are facts represented by the ancient monuments, knowledge and accomplishments which such ancient peoples were incapable of producing unaided by superior beings possessed of superior tools and technology.

Scientists feel free to discuss parallel universes, wormholes, string theory, etc., so why not "angels" capable of the things described in the Bible? One is science and the other religious. The difficulty is neither side is willing to admit of how closely allied the two really are. Science does not know what life is or its origin. Those of us who believe in God have no difficulty accepting God as the giver of life, but must be willing to accept the lack of empirical proof science requires though I believe Creation itself declares that God "IS!" I just don't believe it should be a source of dissension between the two. After all, there are good people in the scientific community who also believe in God.

With so many anomalies and unexplained mysteries I believe it is good to have an open mind to what is called the "supernatural" and not discount the possibilities. For those who do not get caught up in the fanaticism of various cults and are capable of being open minded and objective about the supernatural it is a fascinating area of speculation and I believe we have the God-given attribute of imagination in order to speculate about such things. It is only when such speculation turns into a tyrannical system of religion like Islam for example that it becomes satanic and dehumanizing, especially for women.

***

What with so much talk of desperate financial times and people being forced out of homes and tent cities forming it would do well for folks to consider their priorities and simplicity in living. "The best things in life are free" is a song with a pretty sentiment once the most basic of needs like food, clothing, and shelter are met. However, Americans "have gotten used to better" than what those of my generation recall of the past. But that "better" has too often been the result of unearned "entitlements" and has left many without the needed survival skills that may be required for their future. I wish this younger generation had the benefit of my experiences in what "simplicity in living" is really all about.

When first moving to the Kern River Valley in 1948 with my maternal grandparents to settle on a mining claim that is now Boulder Gulch Campground, I found this area every boy's dream for hunting and fishing. The unspoiled forest, the wild Kern River and Bull Run Creek where trout abounded, it is no wonder that over the years despite encroaching "civilization" it remains my choice for quality of living; and I can hardly fault those moving here for the abundance of clean air and water, among other things.

In looking back, I realize how very difficult life must have been for my great-grandmother and grandparents under such conditions. The old tarpaper shack we lived in, the outhouse and wood stove, coal oil lamps, a hand-dug well for water, the bitter cold of winter and summers over 100 degrees at times, but never a word of complaint from the folks. They were a rare breed of honest people who were used to hardship, worked hard and thanked God for the little they did have. But I also realize it was the love they had for each other and me that kept things going.

Having long ago left off the hunting and fishing, now preferring to watch the quail, dove, and those beautiful gray tree squirrels rather than viewing them as food supplying the family pot this has been a change in my life as I grew older; but the mountains, Bull Run Creek and so many other things remain as they were when I was a boy. The valley has all the amenities for modern living now, but I have retained from those earliest years without electricity or indoor plumbing an appreciation for simplicity in living, without any of the illusions, and the Valley still affords people the opportunity to live simply and enjoy Nature.

Before plastering his cottage at Walden in preparation for his first winter there, Henry Thoreau wrote of how pleasing to the eye the rough, unfinished wood, the bark and knots exposed. I know what he meant. Having done so much building myself, there is something about the bare, raw wood of the construction, working it, the scent of it that makes the covering of it with things like plaster, drywall, stucco seem a somewhat melancholy task.

As a boy, I experienced the same thing with those marvelous balsa and tissue model airplanes. Once all the intricate work of construction was done, I would gaze at the model, all the various delicate parts fully exposed, all properly constructed and the nearly gossamer web work of formers, stringers, longerones, ribs that brought those carefully cut, placed, glued, and sanded parts together into an airplane and it was a somewhat melancholy task, the covering of such beautiful, intricate work of my fingers and mind with the tissue, and then the painting, concealing such a work of art constructed from what at first appeared to be a jumble of miscellaneous and seeming unrelated pieces with no discernable use or purpose.

Some years ago I would learn of the high prices being commanded for "used boards." People would buy old barns and outbuildings in order to have the weathered boards, sometimes intricately grooved or holed by insects, such boards being pleasing to the eye and were used for other forms of decorative construction or by artists. My own little cottage in the country has such boards mentioned covering my screened front porch. I look up at the weathered, bare wood with the same pleasure Henry expressed, considering it a sin should these weathered boards, mottled and stained with the rains and snows of many winters, April and May showers and summer heat, ever be profaned by paint.

Admittedly, with increasing age I do find myself increasingly coarse in my manner of living, and this applies to this little cottage in the country as well, where spiders spin their webs unmolested, except for the occasional black widow or recluse, and I enjoy the company of forest birds and critters. As my manner of life coarsens in some ways, it seems I take greater pleasure in things like butterflies and my wild, country companions.

I have lived in virtual palaces, with concomitant large mortgages, houses that would grace Malibu or Beverly Hills for which I could not even pay the property taxes today, that have not been so pleasing to my eyes as this decaying little cottage that seems to be gently weathering old age, keeping pace with me. What small amount of paint there is on exterior boards like fascia is peeling, the roof requires patching once in a while, I haven't either swamp cooler or A/C for summer nor thermostatically controlled heating for winter and these things seem in keeping with my own mood and lack of concern for such things in declining years, during which time the things I used to believe of so much importance and consumed so very much of my time, effort and money, so much of my life seem very nearly trivial to me now.

No, my mind still does good service and I have not forgotten why such things were once important to me. Admittedly a writer lives in his or her mind, welcoming the solitude of their thoughts rather than society, though I do enjoy the occasional visitor, and generally wishes to simplify their lives for the sake of writing. It just seems that I could have chosen a better path long before I did the one I have been following these past few years, a life of simplicity without the acquisition of things, and has other priorities than the lives most account "successful."

I neither fault nor begrudge wealth to those who can responsibly use it beneficially though greed seems to be the driving force in the majority of cases. However, to acquire wealth for whatever motive requires a talent, and it is a talent, that I lack. Regarding philanthropy and works of charity, however, come to think of it Thoreau did mention his offer of help to the poor of Concord, provided they would live as simply as he did. The poor declined his offer.

Perhaps it is also a talent to live in genteel poverty without complaint, something I may have inherited from the folks by their example. I don't want much and as a result I find I don't need much. What "wealth" I now posses are the books I have written and the stories I'm able to share with others. But alas, so many such stories have fallen into the category of "Once upon a time in America…"

As a friend of God, Abraham expressed genuine concern for the Lord's decision to destroy Sodom and Gomorrah if the Lord found things as bad there as he had been told and tried to dissuade him from taking such action lest the innocent should perish right along with the guilty, saying to the Lord, "Shall not the judge of all the earth do right?"

Just try to imagine yourself standing before God and posing such a question. It would take a pretty strong friend, one genuinely concerned for the honor of God to do such a thing. But how could Abraham even think God might be making a mistake that would impugn his honor as the righteous judge of all the earth? Quite obviously Abraham had better knowledge of God, as we would expect of a real friend, than most today that purport to speak for God and he believed the Lord capable of error. But as a friend, he could honestly express his concern without fear that the Lord would become angry at Abraham even suggesting such a thing.

Still showing concern for the Lord's honor Abraham asks that if he should find only fifty righteous in the city, would he turn away and spare it from his wrath? The Lord agrees he would spare the city for the fifty. But Abraham continues to try and dissuade God until he gets the tally down to only ten righteous and the Lord agrees. Of course, Abraham was also concerned about his nephew Lot who was in Sodom. And that by itself is a curious story in the relationship between the Lord and Abraham and I have studied and written quite a bit about this.

Things go badly for Sodom and Gomorrah and God destroys the cities failing to find even ten righteous that would save them. But suppose the sodomites continue to grow in number and power here in America, so much so God determines it is time to rain down fire and brimstone on our nation? Where is the Abraham such a friend of God that would attempt to dissuade the Lord? Now, taking the term *sodomite* at its broadest meaning includes politicians who are perverts given to every kind of perversion and I would not attempt to dissuade God from destroying D. C. in particular since I would find it difficult to believe there are even ten righteous in that city, and I believe Emerson and Clemens would agree with me.

For many the story of the exchange between the Lord and Abraham is apocryphal and not to be taken seriously. But I believe it and I do take it seriously. One reason for my doing so is that it is affirmed in the New Testament, and for me makes the statement by Jesus that only a few are going to be saved out of this evil world system all the more true and believable. America has turned away from God and gone whoring after Mammon together with every vile form of perversion imaginable including perverts wanting to get "married." What a stench America must be becoming in the very nostrils of God! It is no wonder I see America as the Babylon of Revelation whose end like that of Sodom and Gomorrah the destruction so quickly and suddenly done as to "come in one hour!"

But it just may be easier for God to get the ear of Russia's Putin than the ears of any of our leaders here in America. Putin is trying to bring religion back to Russia while our leaders with the cooperation of the universities and ACLU are attempting to destroy our Christian heritage as a nation, and the servants of Satan including far too many in the churches are attempting to make God look ridiculous and real believer's second class citizens at best. But I continue to take the position that God will not be mocked and he will not always strive with men but will, probably soon, call an end to the work of Satan and his followers. Great, swelling words coming out of Washington will not save an America that has turned its back on God, especially when Satan's servants like Obama and those in Congress are doing all they can to direct attention away from those things like open borders and the really significant things that are destroying our nation.

Perhaps some will find it odd that Putin has seen the light and believes religion, especially Christianity tends toward a moral society. I remember a time in America (Once upon a time in America…) when the Bible was still America's preeminent textbook, still found in the schools of America and treated with respect. In today's America fools mock God and make a mock at sin with the help of gospel peddlers wearing soft clothing and living in kings' palaces, often shaming God by TV productions not unlike those of Hollywood.

We know the ancients that may have tried to describe visits by extraterrestrials (angels?) by stone monoliths, paintings, carvings and glyphs could not possibly understand the marvels of such beings, and probably did not understand just what they were asked to do by these beings. But the Bible being the written expression of such beings and the things done has the advantage of being a written account. Even at that, having no real knowledge of science and technology the written accounts are often difficult to understand, often worded by those better at framing events in accordance with the times, lyrically and reflecting myths of which they were knowledgeable and could at least in some manner relate.

Over the decades of my life I have found it far easier to believe what I read in the Bible than what I read in people, especially people who wield power over others and take advantage of others. Such people make no sense whatsoever. They lie, cheat, and steal with abandon believing this world is all they will ever know, that there is no God or judgment to come. But for the children of God, whatsoever things were written aforetime were written for our instruction that we might have hope.

We do not know the population of Sodom and Gomorrah when Abraham bargained with God to spare the cities for the sake of ten righteous, but if considered statistically perhaps it would compare with ten million in America. Try to put yourself in the place of Abraham attempting to get God to spare America for the sake of ten million righteous. Think America would fare better than those ancient and perverted cities? Personally I have my doubt, especially when I believe Jesus was correct about few being saved and I further believe so many are born without a soul to be saved to begin with.

***

A family shrine while common in many cultures is not all that uncommon here in America. My own consists of the photos on a shelf here next to my desk of loved ones gone on before me, all of whom I expect to join in heaven. In the evening I light a candle at this shrine and turn off the light and commune with these loved ones and also spend time in silent contemplation allowing my thoughts to roam free. Here in the country there is no distraction of traffic or noise of any kind, so it is a very quiet time as I reflect with these loved ones on the events of the day and other matters that come to mind. It's a peaceful way to end the day, and my communion, this "quiet time" continues as I get into bed for the night.

Of course, the Lord is always there as well since he is the one that gives me hope that what I'm doing is not superstitious nonsense but really meaningful. But I always wish I could speak to my loved ones in person once again, that they were still here with me. I don't doubt that they are with me, in a sense they have never really departed, and I think this is much more than just memories at work; I actually believe they still live and continue to be with me though in the altered state of spirits, which while unseen I believe to be of greater reality than what we can see because they no longer suffer the limitations we suffer in these physical bodies.

My physical limitations due to this vile body of clay caused me to set up this shrine quite some time ago; I can't see my loved ones except in these photos and my memories of them, but it pleases me to be able to set aside this special time each evening as quality "family time" and I believe it pleases them as well. But I have never been blessed with any kind of epiphany, there haven't been any audible responses from loved ones or the Lord, but I'm reminded of Jesus calling special attention to those who believe and have not seen. I've no doubt my belief in God whom I have not seen and yet believe he is real and communicates with me is in the same category as my believing the same thing of my departed loved ones. It has been my good fortune to have such loved ones, those who truly loved each other and me to look forward to seeing once again. Not everyone is so blessed.

We all need a place of retreat for our minds, especially in these dismal times with so much uncertainty and bad news abounding. When the wicked prosper and walk on every side, I have only to look at the honest and loving faces of these loved ones gone on before me to relieve me of any anxiety or fear, and I find the peace of mind I need in those loving faces of my dearest ones, and great joy in believing I will once more be reunited with them when I put off this temporary body and receive the eternal one my loved ones now enjoy, eternal bodies free of any physical ills or limitations.

Heaven for me is defined by these loved ones now gone on to be with the Lord. Not streets of gold or palaces, but a place of loving people such as those I know and love. I don't doubt God is not through with the creative process, but I believe he needed such people as my own loved ones to continue with his plans once this world has passed away, all of his children gathered to him and all things become new. The universe is a big place, and I don't doubt God has plans for us to help in his ongoing creation within the universe and perhaps even beyond.

While the things I have described are not unique in any way, all such things are unique to the individual. You doubtless have your way of perceiving God and an afterlife, you may have a shrine or light a candle; you may have beliefs widely divergent from mine. But whatever your beliefs may be, there is the need to have some means of peace of mind, some means of retreat from the things of the world in order to have any hope of knowing what the real values and priorities of this life ought to be.

***

Quite naturally one does not expect to hear the flutter of angels' wings in the halls of Congress; but flutter of bat wings? Well, those do come to mind since having "bats in the belfry, he's batty, have you gone bats" have long denoted someone not of sound mind and this pretty well describes my own opinion of Obama and those of Congress. Have these all gone batty; are *We the People* at the mercy of a bunch of lunatics? Quite possibly we are. I know how extreme such a thought is, but what is going on defies any rational explanation, goes beyond even the rampant greed and corruption we associate with politicians; it is in a word *batty*, though to avoid slang *bizarre* would be quite accurate. Our government has actually become quite bizarre! And for most, that's a pretty scary thought especially if you associate politicians with vampire bats.

A favorite and classic SciFi film "Forbidden Planet" has it "monsters of the Id" were to blame for destroying the entire population of the planet overnight. As scholars puzzle over many ancient mysteries like the pyramids and other monolithic structures of the distant past, one has to wonder why so many pictures, stone carvings and figures are so grotesquely diabolical? Were such things the result of monsters existing in the minds of those that did such works? And if so, where did the idea of such monsters originate? Just what was at work that caused such horrors as human sacrifice to gods? Jesus declared there were indeed children of God and children of the Devil. In my opinion, the diabolical ancient pictures and artifacts have a basis in real entities.

As a believer in God, I take the Biblical view that the world is Satan's domain and orchestrates our government and will continue to do so until God declares an end to the Devil's system of evil, a web of evil intrigue that spreads throughout the world. I'm satisfied with this explanation for the bizarre behavior of those in our government that seem intent on destroying America; but then those that want power and authority over others for personal benefit, politicians being of this class, are not of a healthy mind Devil or not.

Those monsters of the Id certainly come to the fore when it comes to the brutal savagery we see too often against women and children, in the monstrous atrocities committed by religious fanatics and others in various parts of the world. And what but monsters would actually enjoy the wars that have killed so many untold millions?

Yes, I believe there are both angels and demons. But the ancient artifacts seem to favor depictions of demons. The casting out of demons and unclean spirits was a part of the ministry of Jesus and carried on by the Apostles. There are, I believe, spirits both clean and unclean. It does strike me as odd the ancients seemed more preoccupied with grotesque representations of such spirits and gods than those beautiful. If you were asked to draw a picture of an angel or a demon which would you prefer, which would come easier for you to draw? I suppose most people would say they would prefer to draw a picture of an angel, but they might be lying. How about viewing a nice film of angels with a happy ending or some demoniacal, blood-splattering slasher film? How about video games? Which do people prefer; angels or demons and destruction? Is it a matter of "boring" when it comes to angels or is it something far more than this, perhaps those monsters of the Id demanding satisfaction?

I have to suppose ancient races of people had similar choices but for the most part came down on the side of horrors. Were they simply more superstitious than we "moderns" or perhaps more knowledgeable? It seems the same evils were present for ancient people as they are for us, but they tried to put a face to these evils. Ah, along with increasing civilization comes something called "sophistication." I have to suppose Satan and his demons are capable of changing with the times and know how to be sophisticated when necessary otherwise the universities of America would not be Public Enemy Number One!

Over a very long period of time with increasing civilization and life for some became less brutal beauty began to be represented more frequently, but the diabolically grotesque continued to hold sway. Hollywood has certainly focused on the grotesque in far too many instances. Change does occur and the innocent films like "Gidget," the great Broadway musicals gave way to the grotesque, to blood and gore. Not that these were not represented by films from the very beginning, but they were not predominate. However, behind all the monstrosities from the beginning of the most ancient times has been Satan; the master choreographer of horror, savagery and brutality.

In too many cases it doesn't take that much to strip the veneer of civilized behavior and a return to savagery for survival. But the children of God have no such "veneer" to be stripped of and regardless the circumstances will behave accordingly. In the very worst of circumstances this may be the bellwether for the statement of Jesus that very few are going to be saved out of this evil world system, that few enter the straight gate to the path of eternal life.

Here and now, it is far more likely we are going to continue hearing the flutter of batwings than the wings of angels out of D. C. What is lacking is the kind of editorial cartoons showing close-ups of the bats, putting a grotesque face to evil like the ancients did. Have you ever seen the face of a bat close up? You won't confuse it with the face of an angel of God. Oh, but bats are real you might say and angels… well, maybe yes, maybe no. Yes, the bats are real enough; but for me the angels are real as well. As for this last presidential campaign, the players, the winners and losers, the words *batty* and *bizarre* still fit and I doubt anyone has a better explanation than I have offered by way of Satan orchestrating events like the chaos in our government until God calls a halt to it. But the manner in which God will do so, well, whatever your personal beliefs may be I would prefer to be on the side of the angels rather than the bats when this happens.

***

Time may be relative, but death is not; "dead is dead" Young Frankenstein said. Now, while he changed his mind that was a film. But I believe Henry Thoreau had a better idea in saying the plant only dies down to the root, ready to spring back to life when the conditions make it possible for it to "resurrect" once more. And so I believe in resurrection to life everlasting for the children of God.

Still, the quest for an answer to what "Life" really is goes on among scientists and we will continue to be titillated by "Crossing Over" in spite of the many charlatans, and as long as humankind is possessed of self-awareness, imagination, and curiosity, whatever the source of these, we will continue the quest. I look forward to the "surprises" along the way.

In the meantime, I maintain the hope that I will only die down to the root and spring forth again in the hereafter to join loved ones and friends that have gone on before me, no matter where they have "gone on." It will be heaven enough for me to rejoin these loved ones and friends wherever they are. It's all about the kind of hope that love inspires. Those without such hope cannot possibly find much of value to comfort them in this life.

But it certainly would be no kind of heaven if the monsters that prey upon women and children were to make it, and I hold to the biblical belief that Jesus declared there are those born of the Spirit of God and there are those that are not, that there are children of the Devil just as there are children of God.

However, Jesus declared his kingdom was not of this world; but even some professing Christians that should know this act as though they did not. As the song has it, "This world is not my home, I'm only passing through." A real faith and belief in God, the proof of hope and love in a person's life will always manifest itself by the way a person chooses to live in this world.

***

This is one I owe those that believe in God and also believe Satan is attacking America and believers like a roaring lion seeking whom he may devour. The story begins with my three weeks in intensive care because of pneumonia last November and not expected to live. But I did live, though shortly before I was to be released my doctor asked me a chilling question "What do you know about Hospice?" I replied "That's where people go to die."

My doctor is one of the kindest and most caring persons you could ever hope to meet; more than my physician she is a friend, and as a lover of

190

literature has always received with genuine gratitude an autographed copy of every book I publish. She also knows I live alone, that my condition was such that would require help enabling me to continue the work of writing even as my physical health deteriorated. But to continue living alone in my own home and continue the work would require a hospital bed and oxygen generator which hospice would provide for me. And so it was that these were delivered with the help of my friend Mike Turner who oversaw the operation to make sure these were properly installed before my release from the hospital.

At that, the first days and nights at home alone were really brutal for me. After three weeks in a hospital bed I was very weak and barely able to perform the most essential tasks. My friend Mike and others like Byron would come by and help as they could, I had a marvelous lady to do the shopping and things like going to the post office and drugstore.

There were no illusions about my having become a "short timer" now; you don't qualify for hospice unless your time is short; but I was grateful for the people like my doctor and other friends like Mike and Byron, pen pals like Alicen, Tony, and so many others that encouraged me to keep on keeping on and helped make it possible for me to do so. I had unseen friends as well, the angels God had assigned to watch over me as he has done throughout my whole life just as he has given me friends like Mike, Byron and others who have always been there for me when I have needed their help.

Eventually I began to gain the strength to resume writing, determined to finish the work I believed God had assigned me. There were many books to be finished and published, an odyssey of the many twists and turns of my personal relationship with God throughout my life that involved religion, philosophy, science, the mysteries here on our own planet and in the universe, the chicanery of politicians and other evildoers like the monsters of Satan in human guise that prey on women and children, I sometimes varied between belief and heterodoxy, between gratitude and railing anger at God as in the case of the untimely and tragic deaths of my daughters, my angels Diana and Karen.

A month ago, I had an attack that required my friend Mike calling the paramedics. I don't even remember being taken to the hospital, but when I was admitted for the pneumonia last November I had signed a "Do not resuscitate" document and wore a green DNR bracelet during the three weeks I was there. Mike would tell me later that the doctor in this latest incident asked me whether I wanted to be aspirated and I replied "Yes." I do not remember any of this, and had the doctor the time to check the paperwork he would have noted that "DNR" document and allowed me to pass away. God's direct intervention? I believe so. As some would later tell me, the work God had assigned me was yet unfinished.

But once more it would take the angels, some in human form to enable me to come back to my place alone and carry on with the writing. This last incident, they wanted to place me in a nursing home for "evaluation," but I knew such a thing would result in a potential incarceration from which I might well not be released and I refused. But my refusal was only made possible by the determination those in charge recognized in me and some believers who shared the conviction that God had work for me to finish that could only be done if I were able to function right here in my own place. These people, angels, really went to bat for me, even at the risk of their own jobs to make it possible for me to continue to write and publish here at my own place.

With all that has been happening with our President and Congress making many of us wonder if it is our normal allergies that are causing us problems but rather the effect of politicians. I suspect the latter, that We the People have become allergic to government, causing some of us to break out in hives and other ailments.

However, while Satan is attempting to destroy America and is attacking believers as never before God does battle for his children and will have the last word. My personal testimony to God's work in my life is to encourage God's people; that no matter what the Evil One does, no matter what happens to America all turns out well in the end for God's people, and those of us who are blessed with the hope the love of God and the love of others inspire will eventually be reunited with our loved ones and friends gone on before us who are already safe with our Heavenly Father. This is the peace of God that we, the people of God have and the world can never offer. And there are the angels, some unseen and some in human form that do battle for us as well. This is my personal testimony on behalf of God for those who may need to be encouraged, and I am blessed to be among those who are the living proof of God's love and faithfulness.

About the Author

Samuel D. G. Heath, Ph. D.
Americans for Constitutional Protection of Children

Books in print by the author:
BIRDS WITH BROKEN WINGS
DONNIE AND JEAN, an angel's story
TO KILL A MOCKINGBIRD, a critique on behalf of children
HEY, GOD! What went wrong and when are You going to fix it?
THE AMERICAN POET WEEDPATCH GAZETTE for 2008
THE AMERICAN POET WEEDPATCH GAZETTE for 2007
THE AMERICAN POET WEEDPATCH GAZETTE for 2006
THE AMERICAN POET WEEDPATCH GAZETTE for 2005
THE AMERICAN POET WEEDPATCH GAZETTE for 2004
THE AMERICAN POET WEEDPATCH GAZETTE for 2003
THE AMERICAN POET WEEDPATCH GAZETTE for 2002
THE AMERICAN POET WEEDPATCH GAZETTE for 2001
THE AMERICAN POET WEEDPATCH GAZETTE for 2000
THE AMERICAN POET WEEDPATCH GAZETTE for 1999
THE AMERICAN POET WEEDPATCH GAZETTE for 1998
THE AMERICAN POET WEEDPATCH GAZETTE for 1997
THE AMERICAN POET WEEDPATCH GAZETTE for 1995-1996
THE AMERICAN POET WEEDPATCH GAZETTE for 1993/1994
THE AMERICAN POET WEEDPATCH GAZETTE for 1992
THE AMERICAN POET WEEDPATCH GAZETTE for 1990-1991

Presently out of print:
IT SHOULDN'T HURT TO BE A CHILD!
WOMEN, BACHELORS, IGUANA RANCHING, AND RELIGION
THE MISSING HALF OF HUMANKIND: WOMEN!
THE MISSING HALF OF PHILOSOPHY: WOMEN!
CONFESSIONS AND REFLECTIONS OF AN OKIE INTELLECTUAL
or Where the heck is Weedpatch?
MORE CONFESSIONS AND REFLECTIONS OF AN OKIE
INTELLECTUAL

Dr. Heath was born in Weedpatch, California. He has worked as a manual laborer, mechanic, machinist, peace officer, engineer, pastor, builder and developer, educator, social services practitioner (CPS), professional musician and singer. He is also a private pilot and a columnist.

Awarded American Legion Scholarship and is an award winning author.

He has two surviving children: Daniel and Michael. His daughters Diana and Karen have passed away.

Academic Degrees:
Ph.D.U.S.I.U., San Diego, CA.
M.A. Chapman University, Orange, CA.
M.S.(Eqv.) U.C. extension classes at U.C.L.A. Los Angeles, CA.
B.V.E. C.S. University, Long Beach, CA.
A.A. Cerritos College, Cerritos, CA.

Other Colleges and Universities attended:
Santa Monica Technical College, Biola University and C.S. University, Northridge.

Dr. Heath holds life credentials in the following areas:
Psychology, Professional Education, Library Science, English, German, History, Administration (K-12), Administration and Supervision of Vocational Education and Vocational Education-Trade and Industry.

In addition to his work in public education, Dr. Heath started three private schools, K-12, two in California and one in Colorado. His teaching and administrative experience covers every grade level and graduate school.

Your writing is very important. You are having an impact on lives! Never lose your precious gift of humor. V. T.

After reading your book, HEY, GOD!, I will only say this...you are so far into flagrant heresy that it is highly unlikely that you are saved...you are in the position of a self-excommunicated man...that you are on the road to hell.
I would not waste even this much time on you except for my personal debt to you for having presented the gospel to me. That would be the great irony: the man who led me to Christ roasts in the lake of fire forever...you are a perpetually lawless man whose wives treated you just as you have treated the Church... be not surprised at your present lonely condition. It will get worse. Much, much worse. In hell, it will be forever... here is my counsel... recant publicly and send out a newsletter telling your readers that you have done so.
(Comment by Gary North, friend of the author since high school, son-in-law of Rousas J. Rushdoony and founder of INSTITUTE FOR CHRISTIAN ECONOMICS and leader and publisher for CHRISTIAN RECONSTRUCTION).

You raise a number of issues in your material ... The Church has languished at times under leaders whose theology was more historically systematic than Biblical ... (But) The questions you raise serve as very dangerous doctrines.
John MacArthur, a contemporary of the author at Biola/Talbot and pastor of Grace Community Church in Sun Valley.

You have my eternal gratitude for relieving me from the tyranny of religion. D. R.

Before reading your wonderful writings, I had given up hope. Now I believe and anticipate that just maybe things can change for the better. J. D.

I started reading your book, The Lord and the Weedpatcher, and found I couldn't put it down. Uproariously funny, I laughed the whole way through. Thank you so much for lighting up my life! M.G.

Doctor Heath, every man with daughters owes you a debt of gratitude! I have had all three of my girls read your Birds book. D. W.

I am truly moved by your art! While reading your writing I found a true treasure: Clarity! I felt as if I was truly on fire with the inspiration you invoked! L. B.

You really love women! Thank you for the most precious gift of all, the gift of love. Keep on being you! D. B.

Your writing complements coffee-cup-and-music. I've gotten a sense of your values, as well as a provocativeness that suggests a man both distinguished and truly sensual. Do keep up such vibrant work! E. R.

Some men are merely handsome. You are a beautiful man! One of these days some wise, discerning, smart woman is going to snag you. Make sure she is truly worthy of you. Desirable men like you (very rare indeed) who write so sensitively, compellingly and beautifully are sitting ducks for every designing woman! M. G.

Now, poet, musician, teacher, philosopher, friend, counselor and whatever else you have done in your life, I am finally realizing all the things you say people don't understand about a poet. They see, feel, write and talk differently than the rest of the world. Their glasses seem to be rose colored at times and other times they are blue. There seems to be no black or white in the things they see only soft pastel hues. Others see things as darker colors, but these are not the romantic poets you speak of. C. M.

You are the only man I have ever met who truly understands women! B. J.

Dr. Heath,

You are one of the best writers I've had the privilege to run across. You have been specially gifted for putting your thoughts, ideas, and inspirations to paper (or keyboard), no matter the topic.

Even when in dire straits, your words are strong and true. I look forward to reading many more of your unique writings.

Plate 1 - Mt. Vernon Kindergarten - 1940

Plate 2 - Faith Tabernacle & Faith Grocery Store -
1941 The corner of Cottonwood and Padre

Plate 3   John Bradden Caldwell - Bakersfield - 1937

Plate 4 - The Grandparents' Ice House

Plate 5 - Grandad, Dee Dee & Me - Mohawk Gas

Plate 6 - Grandma (Tody), Dee Dee & Me

Plate 7 - Dee Dee & Me in front of
Faith Grocery Mohawk Gas Pump Easter - 1940

Plate 8 - Dee Dee on The Pony In front of Faith Grocery - 1939
I refused to mount the beast in spite of all the threats
to my well-being. Still don't like the hayburners

Plate 9 - Me and Dee Dee

Plate 10 - Soldiers

Plate 11 - Sailors

Plate 12 - St. Joseph's Military Academy in Florida

Plate 13 - Great Grandma (Mary W. Hammond) Dee Dee & Me

Plate 14 - Grandad & Grandma in front of the house.

Plate 15 - John Bradden Caldwell Special Deputy for Kern County

Plate 16 - Grandma (Tody) & Me Grandad & Dee Dee

Plate 17 - Great-Grandma, the love
of our lives, reading to Johnny

Plate 18 - Mother - India Joyce Caldwell

Plate 19 - Fish from the Kern River

Plate 20 - The Fisherman

Plate 21 - Grandad in full regalia

Plate 22 - Main cabin on the claim

Plate 23 - The "Cookshack." O'Dell Johnson in
the doorway. The claim was called the "Big George."

Plate 24 - Chicken coop and privy on
the Claim (Now called Boulder Gulch Campground).

Plate 25 -The -Main- cabin at Boulder Gulch.
Old -Stude- in front. Note ice box & wash basin.
At least we had the Zenith Battery radio.

Plate 26 - Curly Nelson & Grandad after a day of
fishing in the Kern. That's watermelon in Curly's hands.

Plate 27 – Ronnie and me with
two deceased ground squirrels.

Plate 28 – Tody sweeps porch.

Plate 29 - View of cabin and old "Stude"

Plate 30 - Tody and grandad

Plate 31 - Old Kernville Elementary, Jr. High Graduation - 1950

Plate 32 - We were all younger in 1954 I think
this is my 'first' wedding picture. Ronnie at the right.

Plate 33 - Young, divorced and a Cadillac
convertible. The Southbay of 1958 Redondo Beach.

Plate 34 - Me with a couple of my students
at Bull Run Creek (My silver mine).

Plate 35 - After a 'hard day' fishing. All the comforts of home.

Plate 36 - Karrie and Michael Early construction (doghouse)

Plate 37 - Karrie started early on horses

Plate 38 - Ronnie, Susie, Jennifer and David

Plate 39 - Ken, Mom, Jennifer and David

Plate 40 - Danny, Diana and Me - 1960 – 2

Plate 41 - Danny and Diana